The Urban Book Series

Igor Vojnovic, Department of Geography, Michigan State University, East Lansing, MI, USA

Claudia van der Laag, Oslo, Norway

Qunshan Zhao, School of Social and Political Sciences, University of Glasgow, Glasgow, UK

The Urban Book Series is a resource for urban studies and geography research worldwide. It provides a unique and innovative resource for the latest developments in the field, nurturing a comprehensive and encompassing publication venue for urban studies, urban geography, planning and regional development.

The series publishes peer-reviewed volumes related to urbanization, sustainability, urban environments, sustainable urbanism, governance, globalization, urban and sustainable development, spatial and area studies, urban management, transport systems, urban infrastructure, urban dynamics, green cities and urban landscapes. It also invites research which documents urbanization processes and urban dynamics on a national, regional and local level, welcoming case studies, as well as comparative and applied research.

The series will appeal to urbanists, geographers, planners, engineers, architects, policy makers, and to all of those interested in a wide-ranging overview of contemporary urban studies and innovations in the field. It accepts monographs, edited volumes and textbooks.

Indexed by Scopus.

Shaoxu Wang · Kai Gu

Spatial Justice and Planning

Reshaping Social Housing Communities
in a Changing Society

 Springer

Shaoxu Wang 🆔
School of Architecture and Planning
University of Auckland
Auckland, New Zealand

Kai Gu 🆔
School of Architecture and Planning
University of Auckland
Auckland, New Zealand

ISSN 2365-757X   ISSN 2365-7588 (electronic)
The Urban Book Series
ISBN 978-3-031-38069-3   ISBN 978-3-031-38070-9 (eBook)
https://doi.org/10.1007/978-3-031-38070-9

This Springer imprint is published by the registered company Springer Nature Switzerland AG
The registered company address is: Gewerbestrasse 11, 6330 Cham, Switzerland

Preface

Spatial justice is concerned with the critical spatial study of social justice. It has attracted increasing attention in the past 20 years or so, especially from geography, planning, and urban design. Despite recognition of its potential for advancing urban justice theory and practice, spatial justice faces major challenges. In particular, the intellectual content of spatial justice requires greater clarity, the operational aspects of spatial justice in empirical studies remain contested, and ambiguity about the practical bases of spatial justice has undermined its wider application in planning practice. The challenges stem in part from the nature of the field and its relationship to various disciplines and areas of practice. In connection with planning for social housing redevelopment in Aotearoa New Zealand, this book is a contribution to meeting these challenges.

Social housing provision and redevelopment that aim to improve the situation of disadvantaged communities are major planning activities. Such urban projects are complex processes that involve the dynamic interaction between planning, built forms, and local residents. Planners have endeavoured to promote equity and social well-being with considerations of diversity and participation. However, there are discrepancies between preformulated justice norms and development outcomes in particular contexts, and disconnections between place- and people-based planning for community regeneration. These potentially contribute to further social inequality and physical segregation.

This book explores the substantive nature of spatial justice and its significance for planning research and practice. The idea of spatial justice encompasses the institutions, policies, and practices involved in formulating the organisation of space, thus shaping human interactions that define (un)just geographies. Concerned with both process and outcome, it has the potential to promote justice as a result to be achieved and a means for achieving desired results in planning. Although spatial justice provides a powerful conception for rethinking (in)justice, the following questions regarding spatial justice and its use in planning still need to be answered: What is involved in spatial justice research for planning? In what way and to what extent can analyses of spatial processes and outcomes be integrated to better promote planning for justice? A new conceptual framework is needed to enhance the practicality of the use of spatial justice in planning.

Social housing-led community regeneration provides fertile ground for exploring the theory and practice of spatial justice for planning. Following the principle of equality of opportunity, social housing policies and (re)development plans tend to be oriented towards social equity in many cities around the world. In particular, compact, mixed tenure, and sustainable urban developments are regarded as the just built environment, as they enable equal accessibility for all. But there are contradictions between the imagined spatiality of justice and individuals' socialised sensory space. Taking action to protect community character and human rights has been used by social housing tenants to resist changes in many cities. These actions have achieved positive results in the process of community regeneration. But the primary focus on development outcomes neglects residents' experiences of empowerment. In many cases, enhancing access to planning processes is yet to be fully realised.

Spatial justice presents an integrative and unifying theory concerning place, policies, people, and their interplay. In conjunction with Edward W. Soja's work, a new analytical framework comprising a geographical morphological study, housing policy and plan analysis, and embodied research is established to investigate the spatiality of (in)justice and the (in)justice of spatiality. Similar to many new-world countries, social housing in New Zealand cities since the 1980s has been influenced by neoliberal policies centred on processes of privatisation, marketisation, and commodification. This book documents and explains, from the perspective of spatial justice, the processes of social and physical reconfiguration in public housing areas in Aotearoa New Zealand. In conjunction with spatial justice studies in other parts of the world, this book not only makes a timely contribution to the search for solutions to the acute planning problems in social housing provision and renewal in Aotearoa New Zealand, but also strengthens the theoretical foundation for promoting justice in a changing society generally.

A number of colleagues at the University of Auckland provided constructive criticism in the process of our research. Mohsen Mohammadzadeh, Patricia Austin, Elizabeth Aitken-Rose, Lena Henry, and Karamia Muller have our gratitude for their support and thoughtful comments. We would like to extend our sincere appreciation to people from organisations in Glen Innes, in particular the Ruapotaka Marae, Tāmaki Regeneration Company, Glen Innes Library, Glen Innes Village, Tamaki Community Development Trust, Tāmaki Housing Group, and Rākau Tautoko: Building Engagement and Empowerment. John Holyoake, Afoa Tevita Malolo, Joanna Brain, Tracey Wakefield, Paul De Rungs, and Tara Moala have been most generous in providing us with local knowledge and community information. Thanks to all the interview participants for their interest in this project and for sharing their thoughts and life experience. We express our deep thanks to many friends in Auckland: Yin Xu, Xindong An, Tanya Mead, David Haines, and Matt Riley, who have contributed a great deal to the development of research ideas.

We are also very grateful to Professor Jason Hackworth of the University of Toronto, Professor Jason Kovacs of the University of Seoul, Professor Jason Gilliland of Western University, and Professor Sigríður Kristjánsdóttir of the Agricultural University of Iceland, who provided valuable comments on our research and shared their knowledge of planning and urban redevelopment in North America and other parts of the world.

While the diversity of research in spatial justice has helped advance the understanding of the complexity of the concept, confusion and controversy have also arisen over the various theoretical formulations put forward by researchers from different philosophical and epistemological backgrounds. Spatial justice is only one component of the vision of a good city. Nevertheless, it provides principles and operational values for more inclusive urban development. Our enquiry into spatial justice, which crosses geography, planning, and urban design, is a step forward in exploring its possibilities and realising its full potential.

Auckland, New Zealand, July 2023   Shaoxu Wang
                                                                        Kai Gu

Contents

About the Authors

Dr Shaoxu Wang was a Researcher at the School of Architecture and Planning, University of Auckland before she began working at Auckland Council. She has an educational background in geography and planning. Focusing on social and spatial inequalities, marginalised groups and social policy analysis, her research bridges sociology, human geography and planning.

Dr Kai Gu is an Associate Professor at the School of Architecture and Planning, University of Auckland. Supported by the British Economic and Social Research Council, the Canadian International Development Agency and the Natural Science Foundation of China, most of his research publications are on urban morphology and planning. His recent research projects explore the spatial composition of urban landscapes and socio-economic processes in the production of (in)justice.

List of Figures

List of Tables

Chapter 1
Introduction

Abstract Justice has long been a consideration both within and outside urban planning. Edward W. Soja's idea of spatial justice, supported by critical spatial consciousness, seeks to build a new understanding of justice. But ambiguity about the theoretical and practical bases of spatial justice has undermined its wider application in research and practice. Drawing on a geographical morphological study, housing policy analysis, and embodiment research, a new conceptual framework is established. Its use is illustrated in an investigation of planning for social housing redevelopment in the context of Aotearoa New Zealand. The intention is to bring into sharper relief the potentially powerful, yet often obscured spatial characteristics of social housing communities and the characteristics of those communities in space that are essential to promoting spatial justice in planning.

Keywords Spatial justice · Planning · Social housing redevelopment · New Zealand

1.1 Research Context

Cities are changing at an unprecedented pace virtually worldwide. This is evident in the extent of new developments and regeneration of established urban areas. At the same time, interest in urban research, both among researchers and professionals, has grown rapidly and diversified. Research topics concerned with urban regeneration and renewal range from partnerships between government and the private sector, city marketing, privatisation, displacement, mixed tenure and inclusion, to social and spatial justice. Justice is a frequently occurring theme—as an outcome produced by urban regeneration and as a mechanism embedded in the process of urban regeneration. Studies of justice issues within urban regeneration largely focus on either outcome-oriented justice, by building evaluation frameworks with measurable indicators, or process-oriented justice, through exploring the participation of local residents in the decision-making process and the empowerment of disadvantaged people (Jonkman 2019; Shen et al. 2015; Thurber and Fraser 2016).

© The Author(s), under exclusive license to Springer Nature Switzerland AG 2023
S. Wang and K. Gu, *Spatial Justice and Planning*, The Urban Book Series,
https://doi.org/10.1007/978-3-031-38070-9_1

There has been an ongoing debate around outcome- and process-oriented justice. Distributive justice (Rawls 1971) is an outcome-oriented approach invoked to answer the question—is this a just outcome? For example, combining distributive justice and geographical difference, Harvey (1973) argues that social justice is 'a just distribution justly arrived at' (p. 99). However, even when justice is the criterion for evaluating planning outcomes, as the object rather than the subject of planning, the specification of the substance of and requirements for justice remains outside the planning process (Lake 2016).

The aim of process-related justice is to have diverse urban voices involved in the process of decision-making. It has contributed to the communicative turn in planning theory, which emphasises the planner's role in mediating among stakeholders (Fainstein 2000) and the process and relationships between the social agents of change that produce and reproduce distributive patterns (Cardoso and Breda-Vázquez 2007; Young 1990). In relation to the decision-making process, process-oriented justice is evident in collaborative planning (Healey 1997), advocacy planning (Davidoff 1965), equity planning (Forester and Krumholz 1990), and extended treatments of planning ethics (Campbell and Marshall 2006; Howe 1994; Marcuse 1976; Wachs 1985).

The growth of justice research and practice has led to the realisation that neither outcome- nor process-related justice alone is sufficient to achieve justice in planning (Fainstein 2000; Lake 2016). Combining outcome- and process-oriented justice, the notion of spatial justice, as deliberated by Soja (1996, 2000, 2009, 2010a, b), is concerned with the way institutions, policies, and practices combine in formulating the organisation of space. It is about how this dynamic process shapes human interactions, rather than whether or not a certain phenomenon or event is just (Soja 2010a, b). Examining this intensive process reveals whether these organisations and policies produce or reproduce domination and oppression, which are unjust (Dikeç 2001).

Spatial justice relies heavily on a critical spatial perspective incorporating the rebalanced ontological trialectics of sociality (social/societal)–historicity (temporal/historical)–spatiality (spatial/geographical). Prior to Soja, Lefebvre (1974), Foucault (1975), and Harvey (1973) asserted that space is an irreducible, essential quality of humanness and social being. However, according to Soja (2010a), spatiality had previously been relatively neglected. By emphasising the spatiality of human life and formation of spatially conscious politics, Soja (2010a) argues that space and time, along with their more concrete and socially constructed extensions, geography and history, are the most fundamental and encompassing qualities of the physical and social worlds in which we live. Underlying this premise is the conviction that approaches to and principles of justice are time and space specific (Dikeç 2001). Such a conceptualisation suggests that form and process are inseparable and should be considered together. Therefore, social and spatial relations and geographical setting are equally important to any analysis.

Soja's trialectics of spatiality provides an epistemological basis for the understanding of space and is the starting point of spatial justice. In his book *Thirdspace*, Soja (1996) combines Henri Lefebvre's description of the three 'moments' of social space—perceived space, conceived space, and lived space, with postmodernism to develop his interpretation of the three elements making up the trialectics of spatiality, and the relationships between them. Firstspace refers to materialised, socially produced and physical objects; Secondspace refers to the conceptualised space and mental space of experts, such as planners, urbanists, and architects; and Thirdspace can be understood as users' space and is full of their experiences and subjectivity. According to Soja (1996), space should be understood as fluid and hybrid, with interplay and negotiation between the ideas, actors, and power of these three dimensions.

Spatial thinking opens up new possibilities for reconsidering justice issues in relation to the process and outcome of the production of space, the underlying power and ideology of spatial operations, and the blend of interplay and negotiation between the different actors embodying different spatial knowledge and experience from Firstspace, Secondspace, and Thirdspace. This new understanding of space extends beyond the existing focus on the distribution of resources or policy- and plan-making processes, to a more dynamic spatial perspective of justice. Built on the rebalanced ontological triad, the idea that spatial justice is therefore equal to, rather than a substitute or alternative for social justice, has had a significant influence on recent justice studies, especially in planning (Hafeznia and Hajat 2016; Israel and Frenkel 2017; Marcuse 2009; Stanley 2009).

Although spatial justice provides a powerful conceptual rethinking of (in)justice, there are still questions to be clarified. Soja's ideas of the ontological trialectics of human existence, trialectics of spatiality, and dialectics of spatial justice and social justice provide a framework for conducting justice analyses. However, his notions of spatiality and spatial justice have been criticised as overly abstract and not practical compared with other perspectives of justice. Hitherto, limited effort has been made to empirically substantiate the idea of spatial justice in terms of how and to what extent it can be applied in empirical studies and integrated into practice for established planning systems. Through exploring the three moments of spatiality (perceived-conceived-lived) and how they interact with each other, this research aims to develop a new framework and apply it to planning for social housing redevelopment.

As a necessity of life, housing is acknowledged as a human right and the role of government is to ensure housing needs are met (Leckie 1989). A house is a space for people to eat, sleep, and live, offering protection and privacy relatively free from restrictions or interference from others (Bratt et al. 2013; Waldron 1991). Social (state or public) housing policy is a means and outcome of government intentions and intervention in housing provision for people on low incomes; its formation, reforms, and redevelopment have long been an important economic and political agenda world-wide. Housing issues, especially social housing provision and redevelopment, hold an important position within a broad set of urban planning practice (Campbell 1996; Doyal and Gough 1991; Fainstein 2010; Sen 2009; Soja 2010a).

Social housing is always a controversial topic in Western society, especially at the building and regeneration stages (Reeves 2006; Vale 2013). Paul Reeves (2006) defines housing regeneration as 'the demolition of existing housing stock, in part or in whole, on an area basis, and its replacement with new dwellings along with the refurbishment of existing ones' (p. 202). Major changes in social housing projects are expected to rekindle lost vitality and offset economic decline, social and economic change, and physical and environmental dereliction.

Social housing redevelopment is a complex process involving changes in built forms, planning policy, and local residents (Bloom et al. 2015). Not surprisingly, housing justice, 'the socially and environmentally fair and just distribution of housing benefits in a society' (Gurstein and Young 2013, p. 4), is an important topic in both justice research and housing studies (Goetz 2013; Gooding 2016; Kenn 1995). The question of justice has a crucial relationship with the spaces in and over which policies are enacted and their outcomes conceptualised. It is argued that social housing renewal warrants spatial justice in which processes and outcomes are dialectically dependent on and reproductive of space (Ferrari 2012).

1.2 Research Objectives

Much has been written about the concepts and principles of spatial justice, both within and outside the discipline of urban planning. Spatial justice and its rationality take on different meanings across space and time and people, and its definition and usage have changed over time. Even though spatial justice is a significant and necessary component of the vision of the good city, it is often questioned and frequently traduced in the name of efficiency or the public interest, thus constituting a suitable subject for analysis. Spatial justice is more aspirational than operational, and clearly formulated methods for spatial justice research and effective planning implementation are required to realise its full potential.

This book seeks answers to the following questions: (1) In light of the epistemological value of spatial justice, to what extent and in what way can spatial justice theory be translated into planning research and practice? (2) In the context of the delivery of medium-density and mixed-tenure housing, how can spatially just processes and outcomes be promoted in social housing redevelopment? And (3) What New Zealand experiences and lessons can contribute to international research on spatial justice and planning practice in social housing redevelopment?

From the perspective of spatial justice and in line with the developed conceptual framework, the objectives of this book are threefold: (1) Advancing the development of spatial justice through articulating how such a conception can help to integrate the analysis of outcomes and processes in planning for social housing redevelopment; (2) characterising the spatiality of (in)justice and the (in)justice of spatiality through tracking the physical changes and outcomes of community regeneration, identifying how ideologies and social, economic, and political motivations have shaped the space, and exploring local residents' lived perceptions and experiences as impacted by community regeneration; and (3) making a timely contribution to the search for solutions to the acute planning problems in social housing redevelopment in New Zealand and adding a New Zealand dimension to international efforts to promote justice in urban redevelopment and other changes.

1.3 Towards a More Integrated Framework for Analysis

There are interplay and negotiation between the Firstspace, Secondspace, and Thirdspace comprising the three dimensions of spatial justice. They are not exclusive, but rather three interrelated perspectives for understanding a certain place. Soja (1996) discusses the epistemology of each perspective. Implying a Firstspace–Secondspace duality, he argues that these first two perspectives dominate mainstream spatial thinking and analysis with their respective focus on the 'analytical deciphering' of physical objects in perceived space and explaining the underlying assumptions of conceived space. Seeking to deconstruct this duality, Soja (1996) proposes his Thirdspace epistemology, where '…everything comes together… subjectivity and objectivity, the abstract and the concrete, the real and the imagined, the knowable and the unimaginable, the repetitive and the differential, structure and agency, mind and body, consciousness and the unconscious, the disciplined and the transdisciplinary, everyday life and unending history' (p. 57).

Here, Soja is trying to avoid predominant dualities such as physical space and mental space, subjectivity and objectivity, the abstract and the concrete, and the real and the imagined. However, the issue of how to interpret the fluid and hybrid Thirdspace in the context of certain phenomena has not yet been fully addressed. This research seeks to enrich and extend the understanding of the trialectics of spatiality by exploring the interwoven relationship between these three spaces.

To explore new possibilities for better understanding the three spatial dimensions and formulate a more integrated framework that accounts for their interplay and interweaving, this research investigates each moment of the spatial trialectics, and how it embodies and shapes the other two moments. In this endeavour, conceptual and practical enquiries into different moments of spatiality and empirically based responses seek to produce a holistic understanding of spatial justice.

First, from the standpoint of physical Firstspace and the physical-temporal dimension of justice, three layers of spatial knowledge are explored by seeking answers to three questions: (1) How are spatial characteristics produced socially and historically? (2) How does physical space contribute to the formulation and shifting of policies and plans? and (3) What are the impacts on space users? Aligning with Soja's (2010a) emphasis on physical space, geographical morphological analysis (Conzen 1960) helps to articulate the spatial characteristics of the city. Evolutionary (Talen 2002) and configurational (Vaughan et al. 2005) approaches to the spatial composition of urban structures are concerned with the relationship between spatial forms and socioeconomic processes in the production of (in)justice. Working from the existing three-dimensional physical fabric of the city and two-dimensional maps and ground plans, geographical morphological analysis helps to characterise urban manifestations and decipher the inherent information they contain about the social agents of change responsible for urban (re)development. The use of historico-geographical mapping and geo-spatial techniques reveals the spatial differentiations of both physical and social urban landscapes.

From the standpoint of conceived Secondspace, the research questions guiding the investigation are: (1) What are the ideologies and values underlying urban policy and planning? (2) How do these ideologies and values define the characteristics of physical space and community? and (3) How do policy and planning influence residents' daily lives? To explore the ideologies and values at play in Secondspace (conceived space), housing policy and plans will be analysed from a political-economic perspective. In the Marxist tradition, Secondspace is 'dominating space' representing power and ideology that exercises social control over knowledge (Lees 2004; Soja 1996). As such, the political-economic analysis concentrates on the ways in which policies and plans define an area and the underlying ideologies and values at play.

To build spatial knowledge of Thirdspace as users' space, the study seeks to answer the following research questions: (1) What are residents' embodied experiences of the physical and social community environment? (2) How do residents negotiate the changes in physical space, and policies and plans? and (3) How do social housing residents interact with commercial housing residents in the process of social housing redevelopment? Soja (2010a) places emphasis on the importance of socialised lived space to social justice. This research therefore explores Thirdspace (lived space) from the perspective of embodiment (Fenster 2013). Drawing on postmodernist thinking, embodiment studies focus on the experience and resistance embodied by individuals and their influence on urban spatial changes. As a natural site, the body is not only a concrete, material, animate organisation of flesh and bone, but also an existence marked by specific cultural, historical, and geographical circumventions. As such, the body is the intermediary connecting an individual's inner feelings and sensations with the outside world (Nast and Pile 1998). Embodied practice plays a role in experiencing the outside built environment, expressing inside affect, emotion and identity, and reshaping urban space through the vivid cultural, historical, and political characteristics of individuals. This theory has the potential to connect planning and the individuals attached to specific urban spaces to achieve spatial justice in the complex process of community renewal activities (Sandercock 2004).

1.4   Methods

The programme of work comprises a geographical morphological study, planning policy analysis, and a social survey exploring residents' embodied and lived experiences.

First, using a combination of fieldwork, historical and more recent plans, and documentary and archival records, systematic form complexes and sequences of urban tissue types are recorded for the study area. Plan units are delimited following the techniques of morphological analysis (Conzen 1988). Although these procedures have been used successfully in different cultural regions, this is their first application for the purpose of spatial justice research. The resulting morphological analytical maps provide a visual and geographical representation of community characteristics, with the distribution and pattern of the plan and social housing units on the ground today revealing geographical differentiations in the community.

Secondly, a critical discourse analysis is undertaken from a political-economic perspective to understand how current urban planning defines and codifies social and spatial justice. Discourse analysis is an interdisciplinary approach that regards language as a form of social practice (Fairclough et al. 1997). It has become an important approach in urban studies to interpret the urban policy implementation process, and thus reveal the discourse underlying this process and ways in which key actors exercise power (Hastings 2000; Jacobs 2006; Tett and Wolfe 1991).

Thirdly, embodiment research offers a unique spatial perspective in which bodies are places where discourse and power relations are simultaneously mapped, embodied, and resisted, and where identities are performed and constructed (Bonner-Thompson and Hopkins 2017; Harvey 1998). Residents are interviewed to understand their experiences and reactions to community changes. The residents' voices and opinions are coded according to the predominant themes emerging in the interviews. The interview data is augmented with information from articles on residents' responses to the community changes published in newspapers such as *the New Zealand Herald* and *the East and Bays Courier*. A systematic review of the media articles complements the limited number of interviews carried out by the researchers in order to better understand the residents' perspectives.

1.5 The Choice of Study Area

A conceptual exploration of spatial justice is carried out in relation to empirical research in Auckland, New Zealand, the fifth-largest city in Australasia. Spatial justice has mostly been used to understand cities in North America and Europe; it has been much less applied to cities in Australasia. However, many cities in Australasia have greatly diverse socio-cultural environments, which combined with their evolutionary processes provide ample opportunities to explore spatial justice. Analysis of these cities will highlight both the emergence of common trends internationally and regional variation in urban development. This book will both extend existing work internationally, as well as adding a much stronger New Zealand dimension to studies recently undertaken in Europe, North America, and Asia.

New Zealand, covering a total area of 268,021 km^2, is an island country in the southwestern Pacific Ocean. Polynesians began to settle in these islands perhaps as early as 1250 and subsequently developed a distinctive Māori culture. By the sixteenth century, the two main islands had largely been explored (Eldred-Grigg 2011, pp. 7, 12). Te Waipounamu (Jade River), the Māori name given to the South Island, shows the importance of jade, a hard green stone used for tools, weapons, and jewellery. Aotearoa (Long White Cloud) and Te Ika-a-Maui (Maui's fish) were among the Māori names given to the North Island. Of the 120,000 people thought to have lived in the country by the end of the eighteenth century, the great majority lived in the northern half of Aotearoa, with only a few thousand living in Te Waipounamu (Eldred-Grigg 2011, p. 15).

The discovery of New Zealand by Europeans has generally been attributed to Dutch navigator Abel Tasman, as early as 1642 (Yate 1970). In 1840, representatives of the UK and Māori chiefs signed the Treaty of Waitangi, which declared British sovereignty over New Zealand. Census figures from 2018 report that the majority (70.5%) of New Zealand's population of about 5 million is of European descent. Indigenous Māori account for 16.5% of the population and are the largest minority, followed by Asians (15.1%) and Pacific Islanders (8.1%) (Statistics New Zealand 2022).

For more than a century, the state has provided rental homes for tens of thousands of New Zealanders unable to afford a home of their own. Social houses are spread throughout the country. However, New Zealand's engagement with neoliberalism since the mid-1980s has profoundly changed the politics and praxis of national and local government, institutions, and organisations. Similar to the UK, the USA, Australia, and many other countries, redeveloping and replacing post-war social housing areas to achieve higher density and mixed-income neighbourhoods have become a major urban development focus (Arthurson 2001). Although, compared to many other countries, the pressing need for urban regeneration has emerged relatively recently in New Zealand, applying the spatial justice lens will enable a precise reconstruction and spatial understanding of social housing development projects, and therefore more informed discussion about justice theory and practice.

Auckland is New Zealand's most populous city, with approximately 1.72 million residents recorded in 2021. Located in the upper North Island, greater Auckland extends northward through coastal suburbs, westward to the bush-covered Waitakere ranges and sprawls over rolling hills to the south and east (Fig. 1.1). The administrative area of Auckland mainly occupies an isthmus between the Manukau and Waitemata harbours. Most of the isthmus had been surveyed by the 1860s and was being utilised to some degree by various forms of economic activity at that time (Bloomfield 1967, p. 11). By the 1960s, it was largely built up (Bloomfield 1967, p. 12).

As home to nearly a third of New Zealand's population, Auckland's demography is larger, denser, faster growing, and more ethnically diverse than the rest of the country. As one of the fastest-growing cities in Australasia, Auckland has experienced rapid population growth in recent years (John and Wynd 2008). This diversity and rapid growth have created urban planning challenges concerning social housing provision and redevelopment (The New Zealand Productivity Commission 2017). In response to the housing crisis, the New Zealand government has taken measures such as involving community housing providers and the wider housing sector in the provision of social housing and transforming social housing zones to mixed-tenure areas. The increasing pressure on land has seen many communities caught up in a process of urban renewal and regeneration in the form of more intensive and compact residential projects in the past two to three decades. Among these urban renewal projects, the Tāmaki regeneration programme is one of the most complex and controversial.

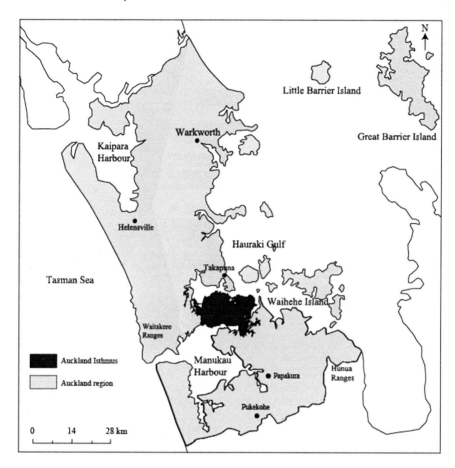

Fig. 1.1 Auckland and its isthmus (*Source* Based on Auckland Council 2022)

The Tāmaki area is located at the eastern end of the Auckland Isthmus by the banks of the estuarial Tāmaki River, which is an arm of the Hauraki Gulf (Fig. 1.1). Part of the Maungakiekie-Tāmaki local board area, it lies 11 kms southeast of Auckland's CBD (Fig. 1.2). It connects with the CBD and other suburbs via the Eastern Railway Line, primary arterial roads—Apirana Avenue, Pilkington Road, and Lagoon Drive, and collector roads or secondary arterial roads—West Tamaki Road, Taniwha Street, Point England Road, Tripoli Road, and Dunkirk Road. Comprising the suburbs Glen Innes, Point England, Panmure, and their town centre, the Tāmaki area covers approximately 6.58 square kilometres (Figs. 1.3, 1.4, and 1.5).

The New Zealand Wars took place from 1845 to 1872 between the New Zealand colonial government and allied Māori on the one side and Māori and Māori-allied settlers on the other. They were also referred to as the Land Wars or the Māori Wars (Belich 1986). To defend the infant city of Auckland from attacks by Māori in the 1840s, military settlements were established across the isthmus as a first line of

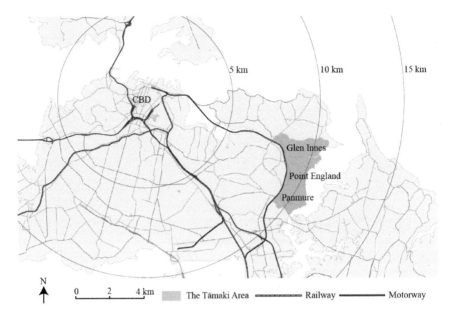

Fig. 1.2 Tāmaki area on the Auckland Isthmus (*Source* Based on Auckland Council 2022)

defence. The early development in Tāmaki was largely due to the creation and growth of the colonial 'fencible' settlement of Panmure. Its kernel already existed in mid-1848 (Baker 1987, p. 21). Tāmaki became a major state-housing area from the 1930s when the First Labour Government implemented policies intended to provide homes and stability for people in need (Housing New Zealand 2017). Designed by Reginald Hammond in the 1940s, the Point England development reflected his interest in garden city principles and formal and symmetrical planning. The modernist design of Ernst Plischke is evident in the north of Point England, with many loop roads, crescents, cul-de-sacs, and irregular shapes (Arps 2012) (Fig. 1.2). After World War II, a large number of immigrants from the Pacific Islands were introduced to New Zealand to supply cheap labour to the booming manufacturing sector (Scott et al. 2010). Many moved into state housing in the inner city and suburbs, including the Tāmaki area (Friesen 2015). Following the implementation of a major urban renewal programme in Freemans Bay in the 1950s, some of the residents displaced as a result moved into the Tāmaki area. State housing in Tāmaki increased by 479% between 1951 and 1956 (Jackson 1965).

The Tāmaki area is characterised by its cultural diversity—45% Pacific, 22% Māori, and 12% Asian. About 56% of houses are state-owned. Young people aged under 15 years make up nearly 30% of the local population. Over 60% of residents live in public housing (The Treasury 2018). According to Environmental Health Intelligence New Zealand, the deprivation index score for Glen Innes, Point England, and Panmure in 2013 was 9–10, the highest level of deprivation and much higher than in surrounding suburban areas such as Glendowie and St. Johns (Fig. 1.6).

Fig. 1.3 Ground plan of Tāmaki (*Source* Auckland Council 2022)

The area faces significant challenges as a result of the high level of deprivation, high unemployment rate, and low levels of educational achievement (The Treasury 2013).

The Tāmaki area has been targeted by multiple local and central government planning interventions (Scott 2013), including the systematic community renewal plans developed and implemented from 2000. Thus, over the past two decades, the area has been significantly influenced by the processes of community renewal and urban intensification. Housing prices have increased quickly, encouraging private landlords to capitalise by increasing ground rents, and also attracting investors seeking to create more houses for the commercial housing market (Schrader 2005). Because many large areas of land and concentrations of sections of various sizes are state-owned, large-scale planning interventions and urban design strategies have been realised.

The social housing redevelopment projects have led to extensive demolition of existing residential buildings, displacement of their residents, and the introduction of new residents and commercial activities (Gordon et al. 2017). It is not surprising that the process of change has encountered community resistance. The Tāmaki Housing

Fig. 1.4 An aerial view of the central part of Tāmaki. Maybury Reserve is in the foreground; Tāmaki River is in the background to the left (*Source* Authors' photograph, February 2022)

Fig. 1.5 Glen Innes town centre. Te Oro Youth Music and the Arts Centre is in the foreground in the middle, shops are in the mid-ground (*Source* Authors' photograph, February 2022)

Fig. 1.6 Deprivation index scores in the Auckland Isthmus and the Tāmaki area in 2018 (*Source* The Environmental Health Intelligence New Zealand 2022. Reproduced with permission)

Group organised many protests against the process of privatisation (Fig. 1.7). For example, on 28 April 2012, more than 4000 anti-asset sale protesters marched down Queen Street in Auckland to draw attention to the privatisation of state assets. In October 2015, the Tāmaki Housing Group marched through Panmure to protest against the transfer of ownership from the state to the Tāmaki Regeneration Company.

Alongside the delivery of medium-density and mixed-tenure housing, the Tāmaki area has endured changing configurations in built forms as well as residents' life experiences. Similar to elsewhere, a large portion of the existing research on social housing regeneration in the Tāmaki area has focused on changing housing policies and the impact of community transformation on social life. However, the interplay between policy interventions, place reconfiguration, and people's lived experience, which is crucial to understanding and reflecting on current planning practice, remains relatively neglected. The Tāmaki area is in a state of flux and presents major challenges to planning. This complex interplay between the community, policies, and the spatialisation of planning provides an environment conducive to exploring spatial justice as a conceptual and practical frame of reference for planning.

1.6 Book Structure

The introductory chapter introduces the rationale for this research. It presents and explains the research aims, objectives, research questions, and research process. Chapter 2 explores the development of research on justice, and the significance

Fig. 1.7 Protests against privatisation (*Source* Tokalau-Chandra and Maude 2017. Reproduced with permission)

of spatial justice for planning. While research in spatial justice has expanded and diversified, more clarity is required in terms of its intellectual content, methods, and application in practice. Chapter 3 establishes a theoretical framework and lays out a road map for the research project. It also describes the collection and analysis of data through morphological fieldwork and mapping, policy and plan analysis, and a social survey. Chapter 4 explores issues and challenges facing urban regeneration and social housing redevelopment in Aotearoa New Zealand. Based on historical and geographical information about the Tāmaki area, it further describes and justifies the choice of the study area. Based on an examination of morphological formation and change in social housing areas, Chapter 5 presents a historico-geographical interpretation of these spatial morphological processes. Chapter 6 seeks to uncover the underlying political and economic structures behind the Tāmaki redevelopment programmes by exploring representations of ideology, strategy, language, and practice in planning processes. Then, based on a social survey, Chapter 7 analyses individuals' responses and practices towards community change in the study area. Chapter 8 recaps the study and clarifies its research findings. Drawing on the information presented in the conceptual and empirical chapters, this final chapter develops a critical discussion about the issues and challenges facing planning for spatial justice. It also provides recommendations concerning urban justice research and practice in outlining an agenda for future research.

References

Arps J (2012) Rise, ruin and regeneration: an examination of the regeneration of post-war suburban state housing in New Zealand. Dissertation, Victoria University of Wellington

Arthurson K (2001) Achieving social justice in estate regeneration: the impact of physical image construction. Hous Stud 16(6):807–826

Auckland Council (2022) GeoMaps mapping service. https://www.aucklandcouncil.govt.nz/geospatial/geomaps/Pages/default.aspx. Accessed 25 Oct 2022

Baker RA (1987) From bush to borough: an illustrated history of the Mount Wellington area. Tāmaki City Council, Auckland, New Zealand

Belich J (1986) The New Zealand wars. Penguin, Auckland, New Zealand

Bloom ND, Umbach F, Vale LJ (2015) Public housing myths: perception, reality, and social policy. Cornell University Press, Ithaca, United States

Bloomfield GT (1967) The growth of Auckland 1840–1966. In: Whitelaw JS (ed) Auckland in ferment, a special publication of New Zealand Geographical Society, Miscellaneous Series No. 6. New Zealand Geographical Society, Auckland, pp 1–21

Bonner-Thompson C, Hopkins P (2017) Geographies of the body. In: Warf B. Oxford bibliographies of geography. https://www.oxfordbibliographies.com/view/document/obo-9780199874002/obo-9780199874002-0157.xml. Accessed 10 May 2019

Bratt RG, Stone ME, Hartman C (2013) Why a right to housing is needed and makes sense: editors' introduction. In: Tighe JR, Mueller EJ (eds) The affordable housing reader. Routledge, London, England, pp 53–71

Campbell H, Marshall R (2006) Towards justice in planning: a reappraisal. Eur Plan Stud 14(2):239–252

Campbell S (1996) Green cities, growing cities, just cities?: urban planning and the contradictions of sustainable development. J Am Plann Assoc 62(3):296–312

Cardoso R, Breda-Vázquez I (2007) Social justice as a guide to planning theory and practice: analysing the Portuguese planning system. Int J Urban Reg Res 31(2):384–400

Conzen MRG (1960) Alnwick, Northumberland: a study in town-plan analysis. Institute of British Geographers, London, England

Conzen MRG (1988) Morphogenesis, morphological regions and secular human agency in the historic townscape, as exemplified by Ludlow. In: Denecke D, Shaw G (eds) Urban historical geography: recent progress in Britain and Germany, vol 10. Cambridge University Press, Cambridge, England, pp 253–272

Davidoff P (1965) Advocacy and pluralism in planning. J Am Inst Plann 31(4):331–338

Dikeç M (2001) Justice and the spatial imagination. Environ Plann A: Econ Space 33(10):1785–1805

Doyal L, Gough I (1991) A theory of human need. Macmillan, London, England

Eldred- S (2011) People, people, people: a brief history of New Zealand. David Bateman Ltd., Auckland, New Zealand

Fainstein S (2000) New directions in planning theory. Urban Aff Rev 35(4):451–478

Fainstein S (2010) The just city. Cornell University Press, Ithaca, United States

Fairclough N, Muldenrring J, Wodak R (1997) Critical discourse analysis. In: van Dijk T (ed) Discourse studies: a multidisciplinary introduction. Sage, Los Angeles, pp 357–378

Fenster T (2013) Bodies and places in Jerusalem: gendered feelings and urban policies. Hagar 11:63–81

Ferrari E (2012) Competing ideas of social justice and space: locating critiques of housing renewal in theory and in practice. Int J Hous Policy 12(3):263–280

Forester J, Krumholz N (1990) Making equity planning work: leadership in the public sector. Temple University Press, Philadelphia

Foucault M (1975) Surveiller et punir. Gallimard, Paris. English edition: Foucault M (1977) Discipline and punish: the birth of the prison (trans: Sheridan A). Pantheon, New York

Friesen W (2015) Asian Auckland: the multiple meanings of diversity. Asia New Zealand Foundation, Wellington, New Zealand

Goetz EG (2013) The audacity of HOPE VI: discourse and the dismantling of public housing. Cities 35:342–348

Gooding T (2016) Low-income housing provision in Mauritius: improving social justice and place quality. Habitat Int 53:502–516

Gordon R, Collins FL, Kearns R (2017) 'It is the people that have made Glen Innes': state-led gentrification and the reconfiguration of urban life in Auckland. Int J Urban Reg Res 41(5):767–785

Gurstein P, Young M (2013) Housing justice: a human rights approach. In: Proceedings of World Academy of Science, Engineering and Technology (No. 76). World Academy of Science, Engineering and Technology, p 271

Hafeznia MR, Hajat MG (2016) Conceptualization of spatial justice in political geography. Geopolitics Quarterly 11(4):32–60

Harvey D (1973) Social justice and the city. Arnold, London, England

Harvey D (1998) The body as an accumulation strategy. Environ Plann D: Soc Space 16:401–421

Healey P (1997) Collaborative planning: shaping places in fragmented societies. UBC Press, Vancouver, Canada

Hastings A (2000) Discourse analysis: what does it offer housing studies? Hous Theory Soc 17(3):131–139

Housing New Zealand (2017) History of state housing. Retrieved from http://www.hnzc.co.nz

Howe E (1994) Acting on ethics in city planning. Centre for Urban Policy Research, New Brunswick, Canada

Israel E, Frenkel A (2017) Social justice and spatial inequality: toward a conceptual framework. Prog Hum Geogr 42(5):647–665

Jackson R (1965) State housing in Auckland. Dissertation, University of Auckland

Jacobs K (2006) Discourse analysis and its utility for urban policy research. Urban Policy and Research 24(1):39–52

John SS, Wynd D (2008) Left behind: how social and income inequalities damage New Zealand children. https://www.cpag.org.nz/assets/Publications/LB.pdf. Accessed 15 Oct 2022

Jonkman A (2019) Distributive justice of housing in Amsterdam. https://pure.uva.nl/ws/files/40291766/Backmatter.pdf. Accessed 15 Oct 2022

Kenn D (1995) Paradise unfound: the American dream of housing justice for all. Boston University Public Interest Law Journal 5(1):69–98

Lake RW (2016) Justice as subject and object of planning. Int J Urban Reg Res 40(6):1205–1220

Leckie S (1989) Housing as a human right. Environ Urban 1(2):90–108

Lees L (2004) Urban geography: discourse analysis and urban research. Prog Hum Geogr 28(1):101–107

Lefebvre H (1974) La production de l'espace, Paris: Anthropos. English edition: Lefebvre H (1991) The production of space (trans: Nicholson-Smith D). Blackwell, Oxford, England

Marcuse P (1976) Professional ethics and beyond: values in planning. J Am Inst Plann 42(3):264–274

Marcuse P (2009) Spatial justice: derivative but causal of social injustice. Spatial Justice 1:1–6

Nast H, Pile S (1998) Making places bodies. In: Nast H, Pile S (eds) Places through the body. Routledge, London, England

Rawls J (1971) A theory of justice. Harvard University Press, Cambridge, United States

Reeves P (2006) Introduction to social housing. Routledge, London, England

Sandercock L (2004) Towards a planning imagination for the 21st century. J Am Plann Assoc 70(2):133–141

Schrader B (2005) We call it home: a history of state housing in New Zealand. Reed, Auckland, New Zealand

Scott K (2013) The politics of influence: an anthropological analysis of collective political action in contemporary democracy. Dissertation, University of Auckland, Auckland

Scott K, Shaw A, Bava C (2010) Social equity and social housing densification in Glen Innes, New Zealand: a political ecology approach. In: Dürr E, Jaffe R (eds), Urban pollution: cultural meanings, social practices. Berghahn, Oxford, England, pp 178–197

Sen AK (2009) The idea of justice. Harvard University Press, Cambridge, Massachusetts

Shen G, Zheng W, Wang H, Lombardi P (2015) Critical issues in spatial distribution of public housing estates and their implications on urban renewal in Hong Kong. Smart and Sustainable Built Environment 4(2):172–187

Soja EW (1996) Thirdspace: journeys to Los Angeles and other real-and-imagined places. Blackwell, Madden, Leake

Soja EW (2000) Postmetropolis: critical studies of cities and regions. Blackwell, Oxford, England

Soja EW (2009) The city and spatial justice. Paper prepared at the Conference Spatial Justice, Paris. https://relocal.eu/wp-content/uploads/sites/8/2016/10/JSSJ1-1en4.pdf. Accessed 15 Oct 2022

Soja EW (2010a) Seeking spatial justice. University of Minnesota Press, Minneapolis

Soja EW (2010b) Spatializing the urban, Part I. City 14:629–635

Stanley A (2009) Just space or spatial justice? Difference, discourse, and environmental justice. Local Environ 14(10):999–1014

Statistics New Zealand (2022) 2018 census ethnic group summaries. https://www.stats.govt.nz/tools/2018-census-ethnic-group-summaries/. Accessed 25 Oct 2022

Talen E (2002) The social goals of new urbanism. Hous Policy Debate 13(1):165–188

Tett A, Wolfe JM (1991) Discourse analysis and city plans. J Plan Educ Res 10(3):195–200

The Environmental Health Intelligence New Zealand (2022) https://www.ehinz.ac.nz/indicators/population-vulnerability/ethnic-profile/. Accessed 15 Oct 2022

The New Zealand Productivity Commission (2017) Better urban planning. https://www.productivity.govt.nz/sites/default/files/Urban%20planning%20final%20web%20pdf_0.pdf. Accessed 15 Oct 2022

The Treasury (2013) Briefing to the incoming Minister of Housing: monitoring housing New Zealand Corporation and Tāmaki Redevelopment Company. http://purl.oclc.org/nzt/big-1530. Accessed 15 Oct 2022

The Treasury (2018) Treasury Report T2018/669: Tāmaki Redevelopment Company—budget bid options—16 March 2018—budget 2018 information release. https://treasury.govt.nz/sites/default/files/2018-08/b18-3931049.pdf. Accessed 15 Oct 2022

Thurber A, Fraser J (2016) Disrupting the order of things: public housing tenant organizing for material, political and epistemological justice. Cities 57:55–61

Tokalau-Chandra T, Maude S (2017) Glen Innes woman refuses to leave her home of over 30 years. https://www.stuff.co.nz/auckland/88498924/glen-innes-women-refuses-to-leave-her-home-of-37-years. Accessed 13 July 2023

Vale LJ (2013) Public housing in the United States: neighbourhood renewal and the poor. In: Carmon N, Fainstein SS (eds) Policy, planning, and people: promoting justice in urban development. University of Pennsylvania Press, Philadelphia, United States, pp 285–306

Vaughan L, Clark DLC, Sahbaz O, Haklay M (2005) Space and exclusion: does urban morphology play a part in social deprivation? Area 37:402–412

Wachs M (1985) Planning, organizations and decision-making: a research agenda. Transp Res Part A: Gen 19:521–531

Waldron J (1991) Homelessness and the issue of freedom. UCLA Law Rev 39:295–324

Yate W (1970) An account of New Zealand and of the church missionary society's mission in the North Island. A.H. and A.W. Reed, New Zealand

Young IM (1990) Justice and the politics of difference. Princeton University Press, Oxford, England

Chapter 2
An Enquiry into Planning for Justice

Abstract This chapter explores the development of research on justice and the significance of spatial justice for planning. The traditional (re)distributive, political-economic, and postmodern perspectives of justice have enriched studies of justice and invoked diverse research themes in planning. Supported by critical spatial consciousness, Soja's idea of spatial justice seeks to build a new understanding of justice that has the potential to connect aspirations and outcomes in the theory and practice of planning. While research in spatial justice has expanded and diversified, more clarity is required regarding its intellectual content, methods, and application in practice, in particular in what way and to what extent this conception can be applied in empirical studies, and how it can be integrated into the established planning system. In seeking answers to the questions, a new conceptual framework for spatial justice is needed to strengthen its intellectual basis and its use in urban planning.

Keywords Justice · Social justice · Space · Spatial justice · Planning

2.1 Social Justice, Space, and Planning

Much has been written about the concept of justice in the social sciences and humanities (Table 2.1). Although Soja was first to place greater emphasis on the ontological, epistemological, and practical significance of spatial justice, this does not mean space was not already important in theories of social justice. Space or place as a locale or backdrop to social, economic, and political processes has a long history in discussions on social justice. Different perspectives on social justice, including (re)distributive (Rawls 1971), political-economic (Harvey 1973), and postmodernist (Young 1990), present different understandings of the relationship between space and justice. This chapter traces the evolution of the notion of justice and space in relation to social justice to form the basis for a critical spatial perspective, following which spatial justice and its application in urban planning are explored.

Table 2.1 Development of notions of justice

Main author and thought	Theoretical source	Principle
Lefebvre (1968) *The Right to the City*		Demand…[for] a transformed and renewed access to urban life
Bleddyn Davies (1968) Territorial justice		The distribution of local services with respect to the needs of designated service areas
John Rawls (1971) *A Theory of Justice*		Justice has two principles: the liberty principle and the equality principle. The equality principle is further subdivided into the fair equality of opportunity and difference principles. The liberty has priority over the equality principle
David Harvey (1973) *Social Justice and the City*	John Rawls (1971) *A Theory of Justice*	Territorial social justice: a just distribution justly arrived at
Iris Marion Young (1990) *Justice and the Politics of Difference*		Justice is not only distributive, but also encompasses the institutional conditions that promote the self-development and self-determination of a society's members
David Harvey (1996) *Justice, Nature and the Geography of Difference*	John Rawls (1971) *A Theory of Justice* and Iris Marion Young (1990) *Justice and the Politics of Difference*	The just production of just geographical difference; space, time, place and difference
Leonie Sandercock (1998) *Towards Cosmopolis: Planning for Multicultural Cities*	Iris Marion Young (1990) *Justice and the Politics of Difference*	Fosters and celebrates diversity and difference
David Harvey (2008) The right to the city	Lefebvre (1968) *The Right to the City*	The freedom to make and remake our cities and ourselves; a common rather than an individual right since this transformation inevitably depends upon the exercise of a collective power to reshape the processes of urbanisation
Susan Fainstein (2010) *The Just City*	Harmonise the contractarian 'theory of justice' (Rawls 1971) with its post-liberal criticisms, particularly those of Young	Equity, democracy, and diversity
Edward Soja (2010) *Seeking Spatial Justice*	Lefebvre (1968) *The Right to the City* David Harvey (1973, 2008); John Rawls (1971); Iris Marion Young (1990)	The fair and equitable distribution in space of socially valued resources and the opportunities to use them

2.1.1 (Re)distributive Justice

According to contemporary philosopher Frankena (1962), at the centre of justice, whether social or otherwise, lies the notion of allotment—be that duties, goods, offices, opportunities, penalties, punishments, privileges, roles, and status. Moreover, at least in the case of distributive justice, the notion of comparative allotment is based on the principle that things are allotted to persons according to certain standards (Cohen 1987). In his 1968 book *Social Needs and Resources in Local Services*, Bleddyn Davies proposes the notion of 'territorial justice' in relation to the 'distribution of local services with respect to the needs of designated service areas' (as cited in Dikeç 2001, p. 1786). This is perhaps the first attempt to discuss justice in geography. While Davies combines distributive thought in relation to geographical regions, he is later criticised for ignoring social problems (Smith 1994).

John Rawls (1971) provides the theoretical foundation for distributive justice, the most influential of all twentieth-century theories of justice (Cohen 1987; Okin 1989). Using the notion of the social contract, Rawls (1971) derives two principles of justice, the liberty principle and the equality principle; the second is subdivided into the fair equality of opportunity and difference principles. These two principles are arranged in order of priority, with the first given priority over the second. This prioritising of basic liberties seeks to generate 'greater equality of opportunity or a higher level of material goods and services', even for the least advantaged (Lamont and Favor 2013). The justice paradigm has become the predominant perspective in justice studies in many disciplines, including philosophy, economics, sociology, psychology, anthropology, political science, education, and geography (Cochran-Smith 2010; Druckman and Albin 2011; Follesdal 2011; Harvey 1973; Sampson 1986). However, Rawls' theory clearly lacks social-spatial thought, which may explain why his 'paradigm tends to conceive of individuals as social atoms, logically prior to social relations and institutions' (Young 1990, p. 27).

Rawls (1971) and Nozick (1974) both emphasise the importance of libertarianism and self-ownership to achieving social justice. Based on these two concepts, Nozick (1974) developed the three principles of just distribution to form the framework of his 'entitlement theory of justice' (p. 150). The three principles are just acquisition, just transfer, and just rectification, with just rectification used to rectify violations of the first two principles. As a libertarian, Nozick insisted it is not possible to tell whether the distribution of goods is just simply by looking at its pattern. Just outcomes are achieved by the particular just actions of individuals rather than patterns of distribution (Lamont and Favor 2013). Amartya Sen's capacity approach further extends the distributive theory of social justice (Nussbaum 2003; Robeyns 2003). Sen argues that the design of social policies and institutions, and the evaluation of well-being, inequality, poverty, and justice, should focus primarily on people's capability to function. Although these theorists make different claims, they all accept the central tenets of distributive justice.

2.1.2   The Political-Economic Perspective to Social Justice

The formation of the political-economic perspective of social justice was influenced by Marxism. Henri Lefebvre (1974), David Harvey (1973) and Edward Soja (2009) have contributed to the development of this perspective in urban studies by redefining the role of space and by introducing production and economic relations into the traditional notion of social justice.

Lefebvre's concept of the production of space emphasises space as not just a container of social processes but a social process itself, providing the basis of the idea of spatial justice (Lefebvre 1974). Space is not a passive locus of social relations. On the contrary, it has been used to oppress, exploit, and dominate and to create forms of social control and discipline with the support of knowledge and technical expertise. Corresponding to the three interrelated levels of capitalist relations—biological reproduction, the reproduction of labour power, and the reproduction of the social relations of production—Lefebvre's spatial theory involves three propositions linking the physical, mental, and social aspects of space. The first is defined as *spatial practice*. It involves 'production and reproduction, and the particular locations and spatial sets characteristic of each social formation' (Lefebvre 1974, p. 33). This concept of space captures the continuity and cohesion in the relationship between social information and space in a given society. The second proposition is *representations of space*, which are linked to the relations of production and the order imposed by the knowledge of planners, urbanists, technocrats, social engineers, and other experts. The third and last is *representational space*, which relates to the symbolic representation of a particular lived space through complex symbolism, code, and art (Lefebvre 1974).

Through his absolute, relative, and relational notions of space, Harvey (1973) also presents a tripartite conceptualisation of space. If we regard space as absolute, it becomes a 'thing in itself' with an existence independent of matter. It then possesses a structure we can use to pigeonhole or individuate phenomena. His relative view of space proposes that space can be understood as a relationship between objects that exists only because objects exist and relate to each other. There is another sense in which space can be viewed as relative, and Harvey chooses to call this relational space. In the manner of Leibniz, here space is regarded as being contained in objects in the sense that an object can be said to exist only insofar as it contains and represents within itself relationships to other objects (Harvey 1973). In this view, 'space is neither absolute, [nor] relative [n]or relational in itself, but it can become one or all simultaneously depending on the circumstances' (Harvey 1973, p. 13). Regarding the relationship between space and social process, Harvey proposes that 'spatial forms are seen not as inanimate objects within which the social process unfolds, but as things which 'contain' social process in the same manner that social processes are spatial' (p. 10). These new interpretations of space have inspired scholars to reflect on the ways in which space is produced and the problems embedded in the process of producing space.

Spatial thinking has been deployed to understand the city and contribute to the development of theory on the right to the city, as proposed by Lefebvre (1996) and Harvey (2008). Their definition of the right to the city is not limited to basic human rights and access to urban resources and should not be understood as a visiting and return right. Rather, it is 'a transformed and renewed access to urban life' (Lefebvre 1996, p. 158). Harvey (2008) further develops this interpretation, arguing, 'the right to the city is far more than the individual liberty to access urban resources: it is a right to change ourselves by changing the city ... the freedom to make and remake our cities' (p. 1).

Harvey (1973) is particularly critical of neoliberal urban management that treats cities as a commodity to be consumed and for consumption. In this view, the city is the product of the perpetual need of capitalists to find profit while the freedom of citizens to make and remake their cities is ignored. This new understanding of the right to the city laid the foundation for subsequent justice studies in human geography and has also become an influential approach in urban planning (Cardoso and Breda-Vázquez 2007).

2.1.3 The Postmodernist Perspective

From the 1990s, the distributive paradigm began to face many challenges and criticisms from feminists, postmodernists, and other theorists. Among them, Nancy Fraser (1998) argues that distributive justice does not take the cultural dimensions of injustice into account. She also criticises theories of recognition for overlooking economic inequalities and claims for redistribution. Fraser (1998) claims that 'justice today requires both redistribution and recognition, as neither alone is sufficient'.

Focusing on difference and cultural issues in the city and emphasising the process and relationships that produce and reproduce distributive patterns, Iris Marion Young (1990) formulates a postmodern theory of justice. Here, justice is not only distributive, but also encompasses the institutional conditions that promote the self-development and self-determination of a society's members (Young 1990). This redefinition of social justice moves away from distribution and redistribution under capitalism; it is concerned with the social structure and social institutions that influence the process of achieving social justice. Young insists that the concept of distribution should be explicitly limited to material goods, like natural resources and money.

In Young's view, other important aspects of social justice such as decision-making power, division of labour, and culture can be addressed through the concept of institutional injustice. Institutional (in)justice takes two forms—institutionalised domination and oppression—which manifest in different social conditions and processes. Domination exists in the systematic institutional conditions that inhibit or prevent people from participating in determining their actions, or the conditions of their actions. Oppression results from systematic institutional processes that prevent some people from developing and exercising their capacities and expressing their experience. Domination and oppression are not exclusive but overlapped, and oppression usually includes or entails domination (Young 1990).

The rationales of universalism, impartial moral reasoning, normalising reasoning, and social atomism that are implicit in the distributive paradigm have brought problems and challenges to distributive justice. One significant problem is the distributive paradigm's emphasis on the morally proper distribution of material goods and allocation of social position, especially job opportunities among society's members. This emphasis on distribution obscures the social structures and institutional context often hidden in distributive patterns (Faust et al. 1992). As a result, issues of power, division of labour, and culture are poorly addressed, despite some distributive theories of justice explicitly extending the distributive paradigm to cover such goods as self-respect, opportunity, power, and honour. The 'scope of justice is wider than distributive issues' and should cover political issues and other social issues (Young 1990, p. 33).

Promoting the politics of difference is therefore proposed as the best way to eliminate injustice. Forester (1999) strongly advocates for an understanding of difference as fundamental, essential, unbridgeable, and contributing to long-standing conflict and mutual suspicion within social groups. According to Young (1990), rather than an essentialist attribute, group difference should be regarded as an outcome of social processes that are fluid and relational. Young's understanding of difference as not a fixed attribute of different social groups seeks to move beyond notions of otherness, exclusion, and oppression. While the existence of different skin colour, gender, abilities, and their related identities cannot be ignored or denied, different groups also share some common attributes, experiences, and goals. In a similar vein, in her work on the relationship between social justice and gender, Christine Littleton (1989) suggests that difference is generated by the interaction between persons and persons, or between persons and institutions, rather than existing in each individual person.

In urban planning, this approach has contributed to the recognition of marginalised social groups through communicative planning and public participation (Lane 2005; Porter and Barry 2015; Yiftachel and Huxley 2000). Inspired by Young (1990), David Harvey's rethinking of social justice proposes that uneven geographical development is an intrinsic feature of the capitalist mode of production (Dikeç 2001; Harvey 2005). One of the main differences between the political-economic approach and postmodernist and communicative approaches is that the former is outcome-oriented, while the latter pay more attention to process-oriented planning (Cardoso and Breda-Vázquez 2007).

This shift in theoretical perspectives on social justice, especially the works of Harvey (1973) and Iris Marion Young (1990), has significantly influenced the study of social justice in urban planning. Urban planning researchers have engaged with the discussion on social justice through theorising what the composition of a just city should be (Amin 2006). This discussion can be viewed as a debate between outcome- and process-related justice, with the potential to profoundly inform understandings of difference and diversity in cities (Fincher and Iveson 2012).

Susan Fainstein (2010) applies theoretical concepts of justice developed by contemporary philosophers to the concrete problems faced by urban planners and policymakers, arguing that despite structural obstacles, meaningful reform can be achieved at the local level. In her book *The Just City*, Fainstein (2010) draws on the work of John Rawls, Martha Nussbaum, Iris Marion Young, Nancy Fraser, and others to develop an approach to justice for twenty-first-century cities that incorporates three central concepts: diversity, democracy, and equity. Fainstein's concept of the just city encourages planners and policymakers to embrace a different approach to urban development. Her objective is to combine a progressive focus by city planners on equity and material well-being with considerations of diversity and participation towards fostering a better quality of urban life within the context of a global capitalist political economy. This work supports existing and potential programmes and institutions, such as urban renewal programmes and other urban development initiatives, by encouraging urban researchers to challenge injustice in urban policy and planning. Fainstein (2010) further argues that the planner's primary function is to listen to people's stories and assist in forging a consensus among differing viewpoints. To this end, many researchers have advocated process-related justice as a way of involving urban voice in the process of decision-making where marginalised social groups 'struggle for recognition' (Morrison 2003).

Extending the propositions of Fainstein and other communicative planners, Sandercock (1998) proposes a utopian cosmopolis that fosters and celebrates diversity and difference. Sandercock envisages a 'society in which difference can flourish—difference in all its multiplicity—as we continue to struggle for economic and environmental justice, for human community, and for the survival of the spirit in the face of the onslaught of a global consumer culture' (1998, p. 218). To achieve this society, planners need to apply the skills of knowing through dialogue, knowing through experience, and learning by doing (Sandercock 1998). In summary, academic work on (re)distributive justice from a postmodernist perspective pays more attention to the outcome of resource distribution and the process of decision-making within urban areas. Space is mostly regarded as a resource or the container for achieving social justice.

2.2 Spatial Justice and Thirdspace Theory

Soja's ideas about justice reflect significant influence from the work of Michel Foucault (1975), Henri Lefebvre (1974, 1991), David Harvey (1996, 1998), and Iris Marion Young (1990). As an active urban theorist, Soja (2010) does not simply combine these previous ideas in social justice; he picks up and develops their thoughts by giving space an equal role with society and time (Soja 2010).

Several terms were developed in the second half of the twentieth century by theorists seeking to add the spatial dimension to justice. Following Bleddyn Davies' (1968) discussion about 'territorial justice', Harvey (1973) uses the term in his book *Social Justice and the City*, defining it as 'a just distribution justly arrived at'.

However, this concept has not been further developed and is rarely used by other researchers (Soja et al. 2011).

One of the earliest attempts at theorising spatial justice was made by a political geographer John O'Laughlin in 1973, when he was the first to coin the term in his dissertation, *Spatial Justice and the Black American Voter: The Territorial Dimension of Urban Politics*. Subsequently, a book entitled *Société, Espace et Justice: Inégalites Régionales et Justice Socio-spatiale* by the French geographer Alain Reynaud was published in 1981. A paper by GH Pirie called simply 'On spatial justice' then appeared in 1983. While a significant attempt to conceptualise the notion of spatial justice, Pirie's understanding of space was limited to its traditional meaning as a physical container and entity consisting of individual locations and their distance relations; spatial justice was thus reduced to shorthand for 'social justice in space' (Pirie 1983, p. 471). Pirie acknowledged this limitation, suggesting that 'it would be worthwhile investigating the possibility of matching justice to notions of socially constructed space' (Pirie 1983, p. 472).

Unfortunately, the notion of spatial justice was then ignored by geographers and planners until the turn of the twenty-first century (Dikeç 2001; Soja 2009). However, as the spatial turn expanded and with the development of critical spatial consciousness, the spatialising of justice, democracy, community struggles, and civil society has since attracted increasing academic attention, and terms such as 'spatial justice' and 'right to the city' began to be used widely after 2000 (Soja et al. 2011).

Soja's publications, including *Postmetropolis: Critical Studies of Cities and Regions* (2000) and *Seeking for Spatial Justice* (2010), echo and enrich the concept of spatial justice by clarifying the meaning of space and foregrounding a spatial perspective (Soja 2010). Two sets of trialectics make up the critical spatial perspective and have further contributed to the development of the notion of spatial justice. The first trialectics, termed ontological trialectics, holds that human existence encompasses three ontological qualities: sociality (social/societal), historicity (temporal/historical), and spatiality (spatial/geographical), thus challenging the traditional coupling of historico-sociality. This new mode of spatial thinking is supported by a growing community of researchers who believe these three moments are inseparable and interdependent, working together as applied to epistemology, theory building, empirical analysis, and social practice (Soja 1996). In Soja's (2010) view, however, spatiality has remained relatively neglected.

By emphasising the spatiality of human life and the formation of spatially conscious politics, Soja explores 'how spatiality and spatial processes shape social relations of all kinds, from the immediacy of interpersonal interaction to relations of class and social stratification to long-term patterns of societal development' (Soja 2010, p. 18). Space is not a substitute for class, social relations, ideology, and political analysis; instead, 'the spatial shapes the social as much as social shapes the spatial' (Soja 1980, p. 207; 2009, p. 2).

Extending Lefebvre's triad of spatial practice (perceived space), representations of space (conceived space), and spaces of representation (lived space), Soja's *trialectics of spatiality* consists of three notions, namely 'Firstspace', 'Secondspace', and 'Thirdspace'. The Firstspace is physical, material, and empirical space in the real world, such as the office, the home, and other buildings. Firstspace, described as perceived space, is directly sensible and open to accurate measurement and description. In the Firstspace, space is understood as the result of history and sociality (Soja 1996). The process of producing the material form of a society is interpreted as the spatial practices that embrace 'production and reproduction, and the particular locations and spatial sets characteristic of each social formation. Spatial practice ensures continuity and some degree of cohesion' (Lefebvre 1974, p. 14). It is both the 'medium and outcome of human activates, behaviour, and experience' (Soja 1996, p. 66).

Secondspace is defined as mental/conceived space. It is the space of utopian thought and vision of the semiotician and decoder. Thus, it is conceptualised space, the space of scientists, planners, urbanists, technocratic subdividers, and social engineers, as of a certain type of artist with a scientific bent—all of whom identify what is lived and what is perceived with what is conceived (Lefebvre 1974). This space is the outcome of the relationships of production, that is, a representation of the power and ideology that create space via 'control over knowledge, signs, and codes: over the means of deciphering spatial practice and hence over the production of spatial knowledge' (Soja 1996, p. 67).

Thirdspace is lived space, a space of inhabitants and users. Both Soja and Lefebvre believe Thirdspace, or the space of representation, encompasses all three moments of spatiality—perceived, conceived, and lived, representing the interaction between different spatialities. Thirdspace comes into being through the productive tension between 'real' and 'imagined' space. Lived space does not exist without these other two moments of spatiality. Its existence is dominated by conceived space and also relies on the existing perceived space. This space is 'filled with politics and ideology, with the real and the imagined intertwined, and with capitalism, racism, patriarchy, and other material spatial practices that concretize the social relations of production, reproduction, exploitation, domination, and subjection' (Soja 1996, p. 68). It is also a space that embodies inhabitants and users' behaviour and experience, and their social struggle against the power underlying the impositions and operation of perceived and conceived space.

Soja creatively incorporates these moments of spatiality within an epistemological typology. Firstspace epistemology is the most dominant form of spatial analysis and spatial knowledge. Focusing on the analytical deciphering of spatial practice, it privileges objectivity, the materiality of human occupancy of the surface of the earth, and the distribution patterns of the built environment. Studies carried out under the Firstspace epistemology can be divided into two categories: The focus of the first category is the accurate description of physical appearances; studies in the second category explore spatial explanations of social, psychological, and biophysical processes (Soja 1996).

Secondspace epistemology searches for explanations of conceived space and the ways in which 'spatial knowledge is primarily produced through discursively devised representations of space, through the spatial working of the mind' (Soja 1996, p. 79). The minds of architects, urban utopianists, spatial poets, idealist philosophers, and other roles produce subjective imaginaries and ideational constructions about what a space should be. For example, the utopian urbanist seeks to achieve social and spatial justice by applying better ideas, good intentions, and improved social learning (Soja 1996). Compared to the Firstspace epistemology, Secondspace epistemology extends arguments from subjectivity to objectivity, idealism to materialism, agency to structure, and abstract space to concrete space (Allen 1997).

Thirdspace epistemology involves the 'sympathetic deconstruction and heuristic reconstitution of the Firstspace-Secondspace duality' (Soja 1996, p. 81). Concerned with the interplay between Firstspace, Secondspace, and Thirdspace, it concentrates on exploring new intersectionalities between spatiality, historicity, and sociality alongside the ontological assertion of space. This new spatial thinking has enriched research and practice in space-focused disciplines such as geography, architecture, urban planning as well as others that have tended to concentrate on the traditional dialectics of sociality–historicity.

There are obvious and intertwined connections between Firstspace, Secondspace, and Thirdspace. None of the three can exist alone, and space cannot be sliced up like a pie. The Firstspace (perceived) we see every day is a result of the historical advent of Secondspace (conceived). The physical forms and their accompanying characteristics are historically and socially produced. They impact everyday activities within the wider socioeconomic context and specialised practice helps to ensure continuity and a certain degree of cohesion towards a 'guaranteed level of competence and a specific level of performance' in terms of every member of society's social relationship in space (Lefebvre 1974). The Thirdspace is a hybrid of perceived, conceived, and lived moments. It contains users' embodied experiences and social encounters during the everyday activities of life. Their struggles and negotiation with the dominating power coming from the Secondspace and built physical environment (Firstspace) shape space as an organic and evolutionary process, rather than a fixed and pure outcome.

Theoretically, these three moments simultaneously and equally constitute spatiality, with none privileged over the others. However, in reality, the power of each of the moments, especially the power of Secondspace and Thirdspace, is distinct with regard to the means by which it is operated, and its influence. As Soja argues, 'the speculative primacy of the conceived [space] over the lived [space] causes [spatial] practice to disappear along with life, and so does little justice to the 'unconscious' level of lived experience per se' (Lefebvre 1974). This spatial order is embodied by policies and plans (conceived spaces), with the result that it serves simply as 'a tool of thought and of action', 'a means of production', and 'a means of control, of domination, of power' (Lefebvre 1974).

Combining the concept of justice with the epistemology of spatial triads, Soja argues that spatial justice is not a substitute for social, economic, or other forms of justice. Instead, it is a new and crucial way to rethink justice from a critical spatial perspective. Emphasising the spatial or geographical aspects of justice and injustice, spatial justice 'involves the fair and equitable distribution in space of socially valued resources and the opportunities to use them' (Soja 2009, p. 10).

It echoes other forms of justice, such as social, economic, and environmental justice, framing these forms of justice in particular spatial contexts, where historical and present policy and planning decisions are produced and implemented (Prange 2009). However, Marcuse (2009a, b) warns against a strong spatial focus, believing that while most problems have a spatial aspect, it is just a side effect in relation to problems in the economic, social, and political arenas. For Marcuse, spatial justice is derivative not causal (Marcuse 2009a). However, for Soja, spatial causes play an equivalent role to other causes, making spatial justice equal to social justice.

Soja's critical spatial perspective and spatial justice have laid the foundation for subsequent discussion of justice and space. Dikeç's dialectical formulation—the spatiality of injustice and the injustice of spatiality—is inspired by the critical spatial perspective. The spatiality of injustice considers physical or locational dimensions as a way of exploring the more abstract aspects of the social and economic relationships expressed by physical space that sustains the production of injustice. This view of the injustice of spatiality focuses on existing structures in their capacities to produce and reproduce injustice through space. Similarly, the theory of spatial justice does not merely aim to achieve the descriptive exploration of geographical dimensions of social justice; it is a comprehensive attempt to spatialise the concept of justice from ontology, epistemology, theory building, empirical study, and community actions. It involves interpretive, generative, and explanatory thinking to define and investigate the spatiality of justice in theory and practice by deploying the inherent power of critical spatial consciousness and spatialisation of justice and participatory democracy.

2.3 Spatial Justice and Planning

Strengthening spatial justice in planning has become an active field of enquiry. Concerning spatial outcomes, Prange (2009) applied the concept of spatial justice to investigate the city of Somerville, Massachusetts, which was seeking to become a spatially just city. The study evaluated the potential utility of spatial justice for a city on its way to becoming just. Towards understanding spatial justice in planning actions, Bailey et al. (2012) lay out a framework of spatial injustice with three categories: spatial claim (ability to live, work, or experience space); spatial power (opportunities to succeed in and contribute to space); and spatial link (access and connect to and with other spaces). They then use this framework to reveal the production of spatial injustice in urban renewal programmes in Georgia and California.

In other research using data collected through a survey of residents and observations of visible social cohesion and accessibility, Bassett (2013) examines the role of spatial justice in urban regeneration processes. The study reveals that achieving spatial quality, which includes usage value—organisation and efficiency; experience value—value attachment and identity; and future value—functionality and adaptability, is essential to achieving spatial justice. In this case, local spatial planning policies failed to reduce spatial injustice in Groningen, the subject of the study. Steven Flusty (1994) argues for 'an equitable distribution of spatial resources for all' (p. 51) as space is a limited resource and a foundation of other rights. However, Flusty focuses only on the built form, ignoring the structural dynamics of spatialisation (Dikeç 2001).

Urban spatial causality and the generative force of cities are two main themes in urban studies influenced by critical spatial consciousness, which emphasises the spatialisation of process, contradiction, and internal relationships in urban generation and regeneration. Uneven geographical development, spatial segregation, and social movements with spatial strategies have become key topics and approaches to rethinking generative effects in cities.

In relation to planning policy, the notion of spatial justice has been applied to interrogate and criticise the spatial distribution qualities of European polycentric development policy and examine to what extent elements of (in)justice are inherent in this policy (Connelly and Bradley 2004). In another example, Ferrari (2012) sketches a conceptual framework of social-spatial justice with four structuring principles: territory, place, scale, and network, to rethink the critiques and justifications of the English government's policy of housing market renewal. Further, Bouzarovski and Simcock (2017) introduce the concept of spatial justice and inequality to reveal and evaluate energy justice according to three aspects: landscapes of material deprivation; ways in which spatially uneven exposure to energy poverty is driven by deeper socio-material inequalities; and spaces of misrecognition.

Inspired by the critical spatial perspective, these studies highlight the relationship between justice and space. In particular, the spatiality of injustice starts with physical or locational aspects to then explore the more abstract spaces of the social and economic relationships that are expressed in physical space and sustain the production of injustice. The injustice of spatiality focuses on 'existing structures in their capacities to produce and reproduce injustice through space' (Dikeç 2001, pp. 1792–1793).

By analysing policy and plans, these previous studies have undoubtedly contributed to the empirical substantiation of spatial justice for planning and the understanding of how and why a particular place is (un)justly produced and changed (Dabinett 2010). Although translating geographical thinking into spatial principles of justice is challenging, previous studies have sought answers to some key research questions about spatial scale and the nature of justice as follows: From the perspective of spatial scale, should a theory of justice in space encompass the city, the metropolis, or the region? Moreover, how can we measure justice? Focusing on the theme of justice, is it distributive in nature, or is it specific, emphasising matters of discrimination, oppression, and political access? Finding answers to these questions requires more research work (Israel and Frenkel 2017).

The use of the term spatial justice has been and still is somewhat vague and ambiguous. Most studies are concerned with metrics for assessing development outcomes. The research methods used are not consistent and studies in this area are poorly connected, and lack a concerted effort to link analytical interests in outcome and process. More specifically, the integration of geographical urban morphology, policy analysis, and embodied research is virtually absent in the extant literature on spatial justice and planning.

Nevertheless, spatial justice is an emerging field of enquiry in urban planning and the extant literature has foregrounded its relevance to urban regeneration programmes in particular. To promote spatial justice, matrix indexes of accessibility and mobility have been built and applied to either the implementation or evaluation of programmes. Concerning urban regeneration, it is evident that in large part, the research focus remains on spatial outcomes such as location and distribution of resources, which are the main themes under Firstspace and Secondspace epistemology. Much less attention has been paid to the nature of spatial justice, which is based on critical spatial consciousness. This has led to the inter-relationships between the three moments of spatiality being neglected in most studies, as well as the process and outcome of this interplay.

2.4 Summary

Discussions about justice have long been a feature of the urban planning literature (Campbell 2006). Prompted by Susan Fainstein's (2010) book *The Just City* and other publications (Campbell 2006; Fincher and Iveson 2012), the idea of the just city has emerged as a planning rationale alongside (or counter to) competing rationales such as the sustainable city, the smart city, the creative city, the entrepreneurial city, and other logics connecting goals to outcomes and means to ends in the theory and practice of planning (Lake 2016). Some have argued that justice is becoming central to planning theory and practice rather than a side consideration (Campbell 2006; Campbell and Marshall 2006).

The notion of justice is now recognised as more imperative to planning than ever before, with the main approaches including (re)distributive justice, political-economic justice, and postmodernist justice. The evolution of these approaches has enriched studies of justice from different perspectives and invoked diverse research themes in planning. Emphasising the city as a particular space, Lefebvre's right to the city and Fainstein's just city are now among the most influential approaches in urban planning. These two concepts are regarded as more practical and concrete than spatial justice. While the spatial thinking underlying the right to the city has been recognised in many academic accounts, the term spatial justice is not explicitly used.

Soja argues that the ontological role of the spatial for understanding human existence and justice has been relatively neglected. Elaborating on the difference between his view of spatial justice and the just city, he explains: 'Being assertively spatial, seeing justice as essentially spatial in all its aspects, is what distinguishes what I have written from the closely related writings on the just city, for example. I'm exploring very specifically how a spatial perspective can add new insights at a political-theoretical level to understand and to struggle against the social injustice of every kind. But even more concretely, I look at how a critical spatial consciousness can stimulate new strategies for political organizations and activists to work towards greater social justice, greater equality, and to fight against the most oppressive forces that are operating in the world today' (Soja 2009, p. 3).

Soja's notion of spatial justice, supported by critical spatial consciousness, seeks to build a new understanding of justice at the ontological and epistemological levels. At the ontological level, spatial justice is equal, rather than subordinate to social justice. As with other urban issues, justice should also be interpreted in its social, spatial, and temporal dimensions. At the epistemological level, (in)justice is embedded in the interplay between Firstspace, Secondspace, and Thirdspace. To develop a deeper understanding of the (in)justice in social housing redevelopment, it is therefore necessary to understand the production and reproduction of these three spaces, and their interaction within the process of redevelopment.

An overview of recent studies concerning spatial justice reveals a twofold distinction: first are those studies aimed at providing explanations or developing explanatory frameworks, or both; second are those investigations aimed at determining the modalities according to which the city should be planned or built in the future. This duality creates new questions about how spatial justice knowledge can be operationalised in applied circumstances and, conversely, how planning issues can be problematised for research. There is a need to propose new conceptual formulations to build bridges between the two heuristic poles.

References

Allen R (1997) What space makes of us: thirdspace, identity politics, and multiculturalism. Paper presented at the American Educational Research Association Conference, Chicago, IL, March 24–28

Amin A (2006) The good city. Urban Stud 43(5/6):1009–1023

Bailey K, Lobenstine L, Nagel K (2012) Spatial justice: a frame for reclaiming our rights to be, thrive, express and connect. http://www.ds4si.org/blog/2012/1/23/spatial-justice-a-frame-for-reclaiming-our-rights-to-be-thri.html. Accessed 25 Oct 2022

Bassett SM (2013) The role of spatial justice in the regeneration of urban spaces: Groningen. MUP Capstone, Groningen, Netherlands

Bouzarovski S, Simcock N (2017) Spatializing energy justice. Energy Policy 107:640–648

Campbell H (2006) Just planning: the art of situated ethical judgment. J Plan Educ Res 26(1):92–106

Campbell H, Marshall R (2006) Towards justice in planning: a reappraisal. Eur Plan Stud 14(2):239–252

Cardoso R, Breda-Vázquez I (2007) Social justice as a guide to planning theory and practice: analysing the Portuguese planning system. Int J Urban Reg Res 31(2):384–400

Cochran-Smith M (2010) Toward a theory of teacher education for social justice. In: Hargreaves A, Lieberman A, Fullan M, Hopkins D (eds), Second international handbook of educational change, vol 23. Springer Science and Business Media, pp 445–467

Cohen RL (1987) Distributive justice: theory and research. Social Justice Res 1:19–40

Connelly S, Bradley K (2004) Spatial justice, European spatial policy and the case of polycentric development. Paper presented for the ECPR Workshop on European Spatial Politics or Spatial Policy for Europe, Uppsala, Sweden. https://ecpr.eu/Filestore/PaperProposal/acf96714-7941-4f8c-a6a4-4680370473d3.pdf

Dabinett G (2010) Spatial justice and the translation of European strategic planning ideas in the urban sub-region of South Yorkshire. Urban Stud 47(11):2389–2408

Davies B (1968) Social needs and resources in local services: a study of variations in standards of provision of personal social services between local authority areas. Michael Joseph, London, England

Dikeç M (2001) Justice and the spatial imagination. Environ Plann A: Econ Space 33(10):1785–1805

Druckman D, Albin C (2011) Distributive justice and the durability of peace agreements. Rev Int Stud 37(3):1137–1168

Fainstein SS (2010) The just city. Cornell University Press, Ithaca, United States

Faust D et al (1992) Collective response: social justice, difference, and the city. Environ Plann D: Soc Space 10(5):589–595

Ferrari E (2012) Competing ideas of social justice and space: locating critiques of housing renewal in theory and in practice. Int J Hous Policy 12(3):263–280

Fincher R, Iveson K (2012) Justice and injustice in the city. Geogr Res 50(3):231–241

Flusty S (1994) Building paranoia: the proliferation of interdictory space and the erosion of spatial justice. LA Forum for Architecture and Urban Design, West Hollywood, CA

Follesdal A (2011) The distributive justice of a global basic structure: a category mistake? Polit Philos Econ 10(1):46–65

Forester J (1999) The deliberative practitioner: encouraging participatory planning processes. MIT Press, Cambridge

Foucault M (1975) Surveiller et punir. Gallimard, Paris. English edition: Foucault M (1977) Discipline and punish: the birth of the prison (trans: Sheridan A). Pantheon, New York

Frankena WK (1962) The concept of social justice. In: Brandt RB (ed) Social justice. Prentice-Hall, Englewood Cliffs, pp 1–29

Fraser N (1998) Social justice in the age of identity politics: redistribution, recognition, participation. https://www.ssoar.info/ssoar/bitstream/handle/document/12624/ssoar-1998-fraser-social_justice_in_the_age.pdf?sequence=1. Accessed 25 Oct 2022

Harvey D (1973) Social justice and the city. Arnold, London, England

Harvey D (1996) Justice, nature and the geography of difference. Blackwell, Oxford, England

Harvey D (1998) The body as an accumulation strategy. Environ Plann D: Soc Space 16(4):401–421

Harvey D (2005) Spaces of neoliberalization: towards a theory of uneven geographical development. Verso, New York, United States

Harvey D (2008) The right to the city. New Left Rev 53:23–40

Israel E, Frenkel A (2017) Social justice and spatial inequality: toward a conceptual framework. Prog Hum Geogr 42(5):647–665

Lake RW (2016) Justice as subject and object of planning. Int J Urban Reg Res 40(6):1205–1220

Lamont J, Favor C (2013) Distributive justice. In: Zalta EN (ed), Stanford encyclopaedia of philosophy. https://plato.stanford.edu/entries/justice-distributive/. Accessed 25 Oct 2022

Lane MB (2005) Public participation in planning: an intellectual history. Aust Geogr 36(3):283–299

Lefebvre H (1968) Le Droit à la ville. Anthropos, Paris

Lefebvre H (1974) La production de l'espace. Anthropos, Paris

Lefebvre H (1991) The production of space (trans: Nicholson-Smith D), original work published 1974. Blackwell, Oxford, England

Lefebvre H (1996) Writings on cities (trans: Kofman E, Lebas E). Blackwell, Cambridge, MA

Littleton CA (1989) Book review: feminist jurisprudence: the difference method makes. Stanford Law Rev 41(3):751–784

Marcuse P (2009a) Spatial justice: derivative but causal of social injustice. Spatial Justice 1(4):1–6

Marcuse P (2009b) From critical urban theory to the right to the city. City 13:185–197

Morrison Z (2003) Recognising 'recognition': social justice and the place of the cultural in social exclusion policy and practice. Environ Plann A: Econ Space 35(9):1629–1649

Nozick R (1974) Anarchy, state, and utopia. Basic Books, New York, Unite State

Nussbaum M (2003) Capabilities as fundamental entitlements: Sen and social justice. Fem Econ 9(2/3):33–59

Okin SM (1989) Justice, gender, and the family. Basic Books, New York

Pirie GH (1983) On spatial justice. Environ Plann A: Econ Space 15(4):465–473

Porter L, Barry J (2015) Bounded recognition: urban planning and the textual mediation of Indigenous rights in Canada and Australia. Crit Policy Stud 9(1):22–40

Prange J (2009) Spatial justice: a new frontier in planning for just, sustainable communities Dissertation, Tufts University

Rawls J (1971) A theory of justice. Harvard University Press, Cambridge, United States

Reynaud A (1981) Société, espace et justice: inégalités régionales et justice socio-spatiale (vol 6). Presses Universitaires de France, Paris, France

Robeyns I (2003) Is Nancy Fraser's critique of theories of distributive justice justified? Constellations 10(4):538–554

Sampson EE (1986) Justice ideology and social legitimation: a revised agenda for psychological inquiry. In: Bierhoff HW, Cohen RL, Greenberg J (eds) Justice in social relations. Plenum Press, New York, United States, pp 87–102

Sandercock L (1998) Towards cosmopolis: planning for multicultural cities. Wiley, London

Smith DM (1994) Geography and social justice. Blackwell, Oxford

Soja EW (1980) The socio-spatial dialectic. Ann Assoc Am Geogr 70(2):207–225

Soja EW (1996) Thirdspace: journeys to Los Angeles and other real-and-imagined places. Blackwell Publishing, Madden, Leake

Soja EW (2000) Postmetropolis: critical studies of cities and regions. Blackwell, Oxford, England

Soja EW (2009) The city and spatial justice. Paper prepared at the Conference Spatial Justice, Paris. https://relocal.eu/wp-content/uploads/sites/8/2016/10/JSSJ1-1en4.pdf. Accessed 25 Oct 2022

Soja EW (2010) Seeking spatial justice. University of Minnesota Press, Minneapolis, United States

Soja E, Dufaux F, Gervais-Lambony P et al (2011) Spatial justice and the right to the city: an interview with Edward Soja. Justice Spatiale/spatial Justice 3:1–8

Yiftachel O, Huxley M (2000) Debating dominance and relevance: notes on the 'communicative turn' in planning theory. Int J Urban Reg Res 24(4):907–913

Young IM (1990) Justice and the politics of difference. Princeton University Press, Oxford, England

Chapter 3
From Aspirational to Operational: Towards an Integrated Approach to Spatial Justice

Abstract Spatial (in)justice is concerned with both outcome and process in planning. It has the potential to promote justice as both an end to be achieved and a means for achieving desired ends. However, it faces criticism as a concept for being too abstract and not suitable for application in research and practice. The operational aspects of the triad and its epistemological orientations need clarification. Social housing redevelopment entails the changing configuration of built forms and community life. Drawing on geographical urban morphology, policy analysis, and embodiment research, a new conceptual framework for spatial justice is established to investigate the spatiality of (in)justice and the (in)justice of spatiality in the context of community renewal.

Keyword Spatial justice · Geographical urban morphology · Policy analysis · Embodiment research

The interplay and negotiation between Firstspace, Secondspace, and Thirdspace make up the spatiality of justice. The three spatial dimensions are not exclusive, but rather three different perspectives informing the understanding of a particular place. Firstly, following Soja's emphasis on physical space, geographical morphological analysis is used to articulate the spatial characteristics of the city. More specifically, evolutionary and configurational investigations of the spatial composition of urban structures reveal the relationship between spatial forms and urban processes in the production of (in)justice. Secondly, with a focus on the ideologies and values at play in Secondspace (conceived space), public housing policy and plans are analysed from a political-economic perspective. Secondspace is dominating space representing power and ideology that exercise social control over knowledge. Influenced by this tradition, the political-economic analysis concentrates on the ways in which policies and plans define an area and what the underlying ideologies and values are. Thirdly, following Soja's emphasis on socialised lived space in spatial justice, Thirdspace is explored from the perspective of embodiment research. Drawing on postmodernist thinking, embodiment studies focus on the experience and resistance embodied by individuals and their influences on urban spatial change. In summary, an integrated analytical framework comprising a geographical morphological study, housing policy analysis, and embodiment research is established to investigate the spatiality of (in)justice and the (in)justice of spatiality in relation to community regeneration in Auckland.

3.1 Geographical and Morphological Evolution of Firstspace (Perceived Space)

As Soja indicates, physical space, which can be understood in terms of human spatiality, embodies the social relations that play an essential role in spatial trialectics. Spatial forms, structure, and design are outcomes of social relations and in turn impact the reproduction of social relations, subjective imaginaries and representations, and everyday life experience. From the standpoint of physical space analysis, an examination of the evolution of built form offers a starting point from which to develop a holistic picture of the interwoven relationships between the three moments of spatiality.

3.1.1 Morphological Periods and Plan Units

Geographical urban morphology explores the spatial and physical characteristics of urban areas through their history and the agents and ideas involved in their creation and transformation. In his seminal work 'The morphology of landscape', Sauer (1925) points out that the term 'morphology' has its origins in eighteenth-century biological science, although the concept of morphology appears in classical Western thought (Bowen 1981). Its etymology can be traced back to Greek, in which the root word 'morph' means 'shape' or 'form', and thus, morphology refers to the study of forms.

The morphological method was introduced to geography by Ritter (1779–1859) in relation to the study of the forms and structure of the landscape (Sauer 1925). Subsequently, Von Richthofen (1883) undertook pioneering work on the morphology of the natural landscape. In parallel, Schlüter was drawing attention to the morphology of the cultural landscape at the end of the nineteenth century (Whitehand 1981). He called for a detailed description of visible and tangible man-made forms on the ground, and a genetic and functional explanation of the aims and actions of human beings over the course of history and in the context of nature. Not content with mere descriptive morphology, Schlüter envisaged an explanatory morphology, fully aware of the interdependence between the three aspects of form, function, and development in geography through time (Whitehand 1981). Urban morphology, as it took shape at the end of the nineteenth century and in the early twentieth century, was essentially about the study of the urban landscape as a subdivision of the cultural landscape (Whitehand 1981).

The historico-geographical approach to urban morphology, in particular as it relates to town-plan analysis, was developed by MRG Conzen (1960) in his book *Alnwick, Northumberland: A Study in Town-Plan Analysis* in the mid-twentieth century. Further refined in the course of well over a century (Conzen 1960; Whitehand 2001), urban morphology provides a systematic framework for distinguishing and characterising the spatial structure of urban landscapes according to their processes of development (Whitehand 2009).

Morphological analysis has a number of tenets. Firstly, the urban landscape comprises three interrelated urban form complexes or elements—the ground plan (including plots, streets, and blocks), building fabric (the 3-dimensional form), and land and building utilisation (Conzen 1960). The ground plan, which is the most resistant to change, provides the framework for the building forms and patterns of land utilisation. The plot, as the fundamental unit in the ground plan, is identified as 'a parcel of land representing land-use unit defined by boundaries on the ground' (Conzen 1960). Additionally, Conzen also refers to the plot as a unit of property holding. A plot is not only an area of land, but also a unit combining an area of land and the building on the land to show the attribute of land use and property (Kropf 2018). Secondly, the morphological structures of the urban landscape are the products and expressions of particular social, political-economic, and techno-logical processes. Thirdly, urban developments can be conceptualised as a series of morphological periods that leave distinct residues in the urban landscape (Conzen 1960). Finally, recognition of the residues of past periods, varying from one part of an urban area to another, gives rise to spatial groupings of form ensembles (Whitehand 2009).

Geographical urban morphology provides a dynamic approach to the spatial struc-ture of the urban landscape. Over 100 specific concepts have been developed in morphological analysis to expose and explain the integrated complexity of the urban landscape—largely in Britain and central Europe. Among the most frequently cited conceptual constructs are plan units, morphological periods, morphological regions, morphological frames, plot redevelopment cycles, and fringe belts. The notions morphological periods and plan units are directly relevant to the practice of spatial justice and are therefore applied in this research to investigate the process of urban development and the urban landscape as a mosaic of interrelated forms, as well as how they fit together. Morphological periods and plan units are interrelated: Plan units are a direct outcome of processes and, in a real sense, the embodiment of the attitudes prevailing at the time and in the place of their creation (Conzen 1966).

It has long been recognised in Western countries that change takes place within a series of morphological periods. Architectural historians speak of 'architectural periods' and Italian architects, notably of the Caniggian School, recognise 'phases' (Caniggia and Maffei 2001). Each morphological period is characterised by the widespread introduction of new forms, for example, new types of street layout, building types, and architectural styles. These new forms are then reproduced over varying amounts of time before being succeeded by different predominant forms in the next morphological period (Conzen 1960). Morphological periods leave their distinctive residues, both created and adapted, in the urban landscape (Conzen 1969);

these form the basis of plan units—the spatial groupings of form ensembles. A plan unit is an area with unity in respect of its combination of streets, plots, and buildings, which distinguish it from surrounding areas.

In his study of Alnwick, MRG Conzen (1969) clearly states that 'it is important to realize that town plans originate, develop and function within a physical and human context without which they remain incomprehensible' (p. 5). This focus on the continuity of the evolutionary process of the urban landscape, as well as its social-cultural development, is central to urban morphology. It provides a powerful tool for understanding how current landscape forms have come into being and how they fit together. It also forms a basis for spatial characterisation and assessment.

Geographical urban morphology has mostly been used to understand urban land-scape transformation in cities with a long history. It has, hitherto, seldom been applied to cities in Australasia. Indeed, the stratification of urban form within cities is an observable record of changes in society over time. In morphological research on cities with a short history, the application of morphological techniques generally allows more precise reconstructions of the historical development of the urban land-scape. In recent morphological research in New Zealand in particular, the wider practical implications of morphological analysis are becoming increasingly evident. What started essentially as academic research is now also being recognised for its implications for urban landscape management (Gu 2010; Wang and Gu 2020), urban coding and planning (Gu 2014), urban design (Gu 2018), and tourism planning (Xie and Gu 2015). Spatial justice, however, has hitherto not been studied in association with urban morphology.

3.1.2 Urban Morphology and Critical Spatial Thinking

Researchers in urban morphology are seeking to extend morphological analysis from purely physical and absolute space to the political, economic, and cultural layers of a society, as evidenced in the earlier discussion of the philosophical foundations of urban morphology. This debate presents possibilities for this study in relation to integrating geographical morphological analysis into an exploration of critical spatial thinking and spatial justice.

As early as 1998, MRG Conzen (1998) initiated a discussion concerning the need for a philosophical base for urban morphology in the journal *Urban Morphology*, arguing that urban morphology should be linked with Ernst Cassirer's philosophy of human culture. In Conzen's view, the evolution of urban forms involves a dynamic complex of physical, biotic, and social causality, thus requiring Cassirer's cognition theory. Conzen's appeal for a philosophical base gained support from international morphologists in subsequent issues of the journal (Kropf 1999; Gerosa 1999; Varela et al. 2017; Mugavin 1999).

Mugavin (1999) offers two paths to a philosophical base—with origins in different periods. In the modern era when Cassirer's Kantian 'knowledge of culture' prevailed, space was seen as an object that emerges from location, and a part or aspect of place. Influenced by Heidegger, modernists paid considerable attention to place, region, and location. The social aspects of space were also noted by researchers and epistemologists in this period and conceptualised as 'social space'. However, as described by Mugavin (1999), the influence of postmodernism led to a divergence from Cassirer's path, with philosophical thought moving in a different direction. Researchers in the postmodern era have enriched the meaning of place according to their respective fields. Instead of looking at place as a fixed entity, it is seen as a continuing dynamic made up of many components, including history, nature, power relations, gender, poetics, geographic reality, urban sociology, nomadism, and architecture, among others.

These new threads and arguments, particularly the theories of Michel Foucault and Henri Lefebvre, are relevant to the study of urban morphology. Foucault (1975) provides historical and political perspectives on the built environment, emphasising the institutions of a site and how space is occupied by buildings. Two main ideas underpin Foucault's theory. Firstly, he proposes the notions 'space of domination' and 'knowledge as power', as exemplified by modern institutional buildings, the prison, the school, and the factory, where urban form reflects institutional regimes in the built environment. Secondly, Foucault suggests that 'place itself has a history', as also believed by urban morphologists. Both these propositions are explicitly or implicitly included in the work of morphologists. A Foucauldian morphologist will tend to systematically analyse the relationship between social and spatial aspects of space/place and explore the ways in which these relationships, and broader societal patterns, permeate individual sites (Mugavin 1999). Analysing the influence of social, cultural, and institutional changes on historical and physical circumstances is another topic implied in urban morphology studies. Morphologists pay attention to the isomorphic patterns between urban form, institutional regimes, owners, and residents. Lefebvre's *The Production of Space* also provides a potential path for urban morphology by integrating space with people, the constructed environment, and other social aspects of urban change.

These theoretical discussions initiated by Conzen in 1998 extended urban morphology and inspired empirical studies connecting urban form and social, cultural, and political aspects of human existence. Although suggestions varied concerning the philosophical foundation most relevant to urban morphology, they share one main similarity: They not only considered purely physical form, but physical form in combination with cultural, social, and political aspects of a society. Introducing Lefebvre's work led to the re-recognition by researchers of the role of space in urban form. However, few morphological studies have been conducted under this new understanding of space and form.

Soja (1996) notes that 'all social relations become real and concrete, a part of our lived existence, only when they are spatially "inscribed" that is concretely represented in the social production of space. Social reality is not just coincidentally spatial, existing "in" space. It is presuppositionally and ontologically spatial. There is no unspatialised social reality. There are no aspatial social processes. Even in the realm of pure abstraction … there is a pervasive and pertinent, if often hidden, spatial dimension' (p. 46).

Concerning Firstspace and spatial justice, morphological analysis provides a powerful tool to understand spatial characteristics of the city and the characteristics of the city in space. In particular, the idea of plan units effectively bridges analyses of spatial outcomes and processes. The key point is the way in which these units embody local historical development to 'objectivate the spirit of a society' (Conzen 1988). Plan units can be used as a basis for prescriptions in which future changes are justly incorporated into the existing landscape.

Morphological analysis has the potential to contribute to planning for spatial justice that seeks more contextualised decision-making and ensures new changes are incorporated justly and harmoniously into existing urban areas. In turn, this study will contribute to the development of plan analysis by exploring the relationship between changing built forms and embodiment research, and the changing morphology of social housing units.

3.1.3 Morphological Data Collection and Analysis

Archival searches, a property information database, and fieldwork were deployed to obtain primary and secondary research data for morphological analysis. The morphological fieldwork was carried out in the study areas. This involved noting initial impressions and then taking sequential photographs along the fieldwork route to record land utilisation, building types, construction status, and landscape characteristics.

Secondary data collection was undertaken by searching online archival resources provided by the General Library at the University of Auckland, Auckland Libraries, and the National Library of New Zealand, and gathering historical plans and design frameworks provided by Auckland Council, Housing New Zealand, and the Tāmaki Regeneration Company. Current and historical maps, aerial photographs, existing plans, and design evidence were collected and documented in this process. In particular, a database of property information—Property Guru (CoreLogic 2020)—provided an important resource for this research. Property Guru provides a compilation of Auckland property information. Data include the land area, floor area, property type, land and building value, the names of occupants and owners, and the uses and sales histories of properties. The building ages of most of the properties are also available in this database. A plot-by-plot survey of the study area in conjunction with the historical maps and plans and Property Guru data provided the basis for the morphological analysis. Both the primary and secondary data were recorded and organised using ArcGIS, a tool for geo-spatial analysis. Property information obtained from Property Guru was analysed and presented in ArcGIS.

Studies of morphological periods are based on various official records containing information about the urban landscape at different times. Sources of information that allow comparisons to be made over time include maps and plans, photographs, and verbal descriptions. In recent times, more continuous records of change have become available, notably governmental and other administrative records, such as building and planning applications. Explanations for changes can sometimes be revealed by making comparisons with data for other sorts of change over time, such as indicators of economic and social change. In a study of the expansion of Auckland's isthmus, Gu (2010) recognises four morphological periods: pioneer development (1840s–1880s), late Victorian and Edwardian (1890s–1910s), inter-war (1920s–1930s), and early post-war (1950s–1960s). Each period is characterised by distinctive planning and building ideologies and techniques that have left observable material residues in the urban landscape.

The urban landscape comprises three morphological elements: the ground plan, the building fabric, and land and building utilisation. In the process of identifying plan units, it is possible to divide an urban area, based on the ground plan and building fabric, into landscape divisions that each has a unity distinguishing them from adjoining areas. The physical geographical and natural landscape elements (e.g., topographical features and vegetation) and building materials can also be taken into consideration (Gu 2010). Geographical plan units are then used to map the physical manifestations of these morphological periods (Conzen 1958).

According to the arguments presented for spatial justice, the distribution and pattern of the social housing units in the Tāmaki area will reflect the spatial structure of the social landscape. This research therefore sought to reconstruct the changing processes of the plan and social housing units with the expectation of not only revealing the effects of planning decisions on the community's character, but also to help to understand residents' experiences of community changes.

3.2 Ideologies and the Understanding of Secondspace (Conceived Space)

Social housing redevelopment as a type of urban regeneration involves a range of urban policies, in particular housing policies and plans enacted by the state. Following Lefebvre and Soja's spatial thinking, it can be argued that the policies and plans that explicitly conceived new images of the Tāmaki area reflect objectives and goals influenced by the political and economic ideology of the time. As Gunder (2010) claims, 'planning is inherently ideological, because ideology constitutes our chosen and dominant belief, or value, systems. These in turn, shape what we want, what is important, and hence our planning objectives and goals' (p. 299).

Planning as a profession specifically attempts to achieve 'a 'successful' ordering of the built environment' (Harvey 1985, p. 165). This focus on spatial ordering is about the proper location and appropriate mix of the spatial elements constituting the built environment, such as houses, offices, hospitals, schools, and other facilities. As a form of urban policy formulation and implementation, this spatial ordering serves the processes of social production and reproduction and reflects social relations (Harvey 1985). Planning ideas and practices related to spatial ordering cannot be excluded from the social and property relations of capitalist society. It is thus impossible for planning to be an unbiased or innocent value-free profession. As a 'site' or 'position', it is dominated by the beliefs and values of a certain social group (Scott and Roweis 1977).

National housing policy is profoundly driven by ideologies that are 'socially and historically constructed bundles of contested and contingent ideas, values and beliefs with recurring, yet fluid and dynamic, patterns' (Davoudi et al. 2020, p. 32). Housing policies themselves and the role of planning in housing provision, especially under the influence of the 'housing crisis' narrative and demand for affordable housing, have changed over time with evolving shifts in political ideology (Navarro-Rivera 2015). As an important part of the state welfare system, state-housing provision and management is significantly impacted by these ideological changes.

New Zealand has experienced three ideological shifts, from liberalism (1891–1934) to Keynesianism (1935–1984) and then to neoliberalism (post-1984), which have significantly impacted state-housing provision and planning policy and practice in different periods (Coleman 1958; Larner 2000; Jock 2014; Roper 2006). These shifts are evidenced in three major political and economic reforms, namely the Liberal Government reforms starting with their election to power in 1891, the Labour Government programme implemented between 1935 and 1949, and neoliberalist reform from 1984 (Table 3.1).

Table 3.1 A list of key state-housing policies and planning documents

	Social housing policy	Planning regulatory act
Liberalism between 1891 and 1934 (Liberal government reform from 1891)	Workers' Dwelling Act 1905	Town Planning Act 1926
	Housing Act 1919	
Keynesianism between 1935 and 1984 (Labour Government programme 1935–1949)	Housing Act 1936	
	Housing Act 1955	Town and Country Planning Act 1953
	Health Act 1956	Town and Country Planning Act 1977
Neoliberal turn after 1984 (Neoliberalist reform from 1984)	Residential Tenancies Act 1986	
	Housing Restructuring Act 1992	Resource Management Act 1991
	Accommodation Supplement 1993	
	Housing Corporation Amendment Act 2001	
	Building Act 2004	
	Housing Accords and Special Housing Area Act 2013	

3.2.1 Planning and Development in the Liberal and Keynesian Periods

The Liberals came to power and proposed reforms based on liberalism in the year 1891. Their mission was to build a new world that reproduced all that was good from the old world while avoiding its social ills, such as land monopoly, poverty, slums, unemployment, and other problems produced by the agricultural and industrial revolutions. The government was committed to implementing experimental legislation to achieve an equitable distribution of national income and true democracy, thus setting an example for the rest of the world (Coleman 1958). They targeted class politics and associated social inequality. Their main aim was to abolish class and class politics altogether, thus putting labour and capital on an equal footing and promoting the interests of all people (Hamer 1988).

The reforms initiated by the Liberal Government addressed different aspects of society. One of the most important measures was land reform aimed at breaking down the land monopoly and encouraging settlement by enacting land laws for purchasing Māori land and then selling it to smallholder farmers. Other reforms such as establishing a new basis for industrial relations, extending voting rights to women, developing the system of old-age pensions, and providing state housing to workers were also initiated during this period. In combination, these reforms established the model for subsequent New Zealand administrations and modern New Zealand politics, including party government and the welfare state. The resulting image of New Zealand as a 'social-democratic laboratory' attracted the interest of international progressives. Visitors from overseas spread the image of an egalitarian paradise, among them Americans who pushed for similar changes in their country (Coleman 1958; Marcetic 2017; Phillips 2012).

From the early 1900s, successive New Zealand governments have actively intervened in the state rental housing market. As early as 1905, the Liberal Government passed the Workers' Dwellings Act, subsequently building the first state houses for inner-city workers to rent (Kāinga Ora—Homes and Communities 2020). However, this Act was subsequently viewed as a failure because only 646 houses were constructed, falling far short of the initial target of 5,000 and failing to solve the housing crisis. Further, criticisms were also raised in relation to the excessive rent and poor location of the houses that were built. After World War I, the housing crisis in New Zealand deepened, catalysing the launch of the Housing Act in 1919. This new Act supported deeper engagement by the government in housing construction, and low-interest loans for both residents and local government. Both strategies typified government housing initiatives through the 1910s and 1920s (Hargreaves et al. 1985; Martin 1996).

In the field of urban planning, the idea of garden cities was introduced into New Zealand during the period 1900–1926. It contributed to public and official awareness of the need for planning. Town planning bills were proposed in 1911 and again in 1917. Although these two bills were not put into practice, they were the earliest attempts to enact legislation for urban planning, marking town planning's arrival on the political and legislative agenda. In 1919, the government sponsored the Town Planning Conference and Exhibition, which brought together town planning enthusiasts, experts, and officials from the central and local level for the first time. Meanwhile, an increasing number of clubs and societies were becoming involved with planning and planting projects. Politically, the early years of this period were strongly influenced by the Liberals, who claimed that collective action was necessary for the market to function adequately (Miller 2000). These activities and initiatives culminated in the enactment of the first comprehensive town planning legislation in 1926. The Town Planning Act was intended to regulate and limit land-use activities. The main features of the Act were centralised control over planning and zoning and planning schemes. Although achieving only limited uptake in planning schemes, the passing of the 1926 Act moved planning from a concept into practice.

The legacy of liberal reform was substantial. For a long period after 1912, the core aspects of liberal policy were extended or modified, but no radical revisions were made (Hamer 1988). New Zealand's progressive reputation as a 'social-democratic laboratory' continued through the twentieth century until the mid-1980s. Taking power in 1935 at the end of the great depression, the First Labour Government initiated a programme of restoring living salaries and wages, providing full employment for everyone, and improving working conditions. It also promised to strengthen the system of compulsory arbitration, extend the scope of pensions, and expand welfare services into a broad system of social security. This whole programme emphasised ethical rather than scientific concerns with words such as adequate, just, fair, and reasonable (Hillman 1960).

By 1938, the First Labour Government had established a welfare state (Briggs 2006) including a housing agenda, signing off on building high-quality 'state housing' in 1935. About 5,000 state houses were built in 1939. Since then, state houses have played a major role in providing secure accommodation for people in need (Olssen et al. 2010). The number of state houses boomed after World War II, with the government building around 10,000 state houses each year. At the same time, through a combination of tax policies, specific housing initiatives, and a programme of funding, the government was also assisting first homebuyers to purchase newly built houses as a way of encouraging people to move into newly developed suburbs.

Up until the 1970s, the state was the largest source of mortgage funds in New Zealand (Murphy 2004). The Housing Corporation was formed in 1974 to develop and allocate houses in inner-city areas. By the mid-1980s, the state was providing 5% of the housing market and accounted for 25% of the total rental market. Meanwhile, supported by the government, homeownership reached 74%. During this period, state houses were allocated based on residents' needs. Under the income-related rent subsidy, tenants were charged a maximum of 25% of their income for rent. The government increased state intervention through the large-scale provision of housing according to a zoning-based land-use planning system (Austin et al. 2014). As Murphy (2004) describes, 'early state houses have assumed something of an iconic status within the New Zealand imagination, being a material manifestation of the country's early and innovative welfare state' (p. 119).

After World War II, New Zealand experienced rapid urban expansion, which was accompanied by a revival of interest in urban planning. Urban expansion outside administrative boundaries resulted in the phenomenon of suburban sprawl, while the deterioration of old residential areas raised concerns about the development of slums (Gatley and Walker 2014; Perkins et al. 1993). Meanwhile, environmentalists were claiming that town planning could improve the quality of city life. All these factors combined to highlight the importance of town planning and promote its acceptance. The state housing built in the post-war period put these environmental ideals into practice. State-housing suburbs were constructed according to the principles of garden cities, with curved streets, reserves, community centres, and single dwelling houses on quarter-acre plots.

Rapid urban expansion and advocacy by environmentalists led to the Town and Country Planning Act 1953. Under this Act, powers concerning the preparation and approval of planning schemes were transferred from the Town Planning Board to local authorities. The Board was abolished. Each local authority was required to provide a district-planning scheme and submit it to the Minister of Works for approval. The Act instituted regional planning focusing on development and the co-ordination of public improvements, services, and amenities belonging to different municipal areas (Perkins et al. 1993).

The Town and Country Planning Act 1953 was subsequently reviewed in 1970. The review committee identified the following important changes: The Act needed to be simplified and arranged in a more logical form; the Act should be extended to enable third-party rights to participate; environmental considerations should be considered in the planning process; and links between planning at the national, regional, and local level should be more clearly established. The outcome of the review was the Town and Country Planning Act 1977. The Act incorporated both centralised control and empowerment of local authorities. The Ministry had responsibility for approving regional schemes and the provision of public works; however, there was flexibility in land-use zoning as planning tribunals reviewed local decisions. Another feature was increased community participation. The Act introduced community councils and extended objection rights to any person or body affected by proposed plans. Any person representing relevant aspects of the public interest could thus object to a scheme or planning application. The Act also acknowledged Māori and their culture and traditions concerning ancestral land (The New Zealand Productivity Commission 2015). These initiatives made planning more politically oriented with protest and conflict around land and development becoming a feature of local government politics (Perkins et al. 1993).

Similar to many other new-world countries, public housing in New Zealand cities since the 1980s has been influenced by neoliberal policies centred on processes of privatisation, marketisation, commodification, financialisation, and individualisation (Clapham 2019; Aalbers et al. 2017). The resulting economic and political reforms have had far-reaching effects on the welfare system. Welfare spending was curbed due to a popular view that high levels and the duration of benefit support were supporting unemployment. Treasury argued that welfare should be spent more effectively and only provided for people truly in need (Massey 1995). Other effects involved changes to the delivery of education, health, housing, science, transport, justice, as well as provisions around land use. The most common strategy was separating policy and operations. Separating funding, purchasing, and the provision of services increased competition between service providers. Responsibilities were reallocated between government departments, and there was wholesale transfer of responsibilities from the government to private or non-government organisations. As a result, new systems of service delivery were established. Social housing provision, as a part of the welfare system, was significantly impacted by the movement towards privatisation (Flynn 1988; Murphy and Kearns 1994).

3.2.2 Critical Discourse Analysis: A Political-Economic Perspective

The political-economic approach to critical discourse analysis developed by Norman Fairclough (1992) was applied to understand Secondspace or perceived space in the development and regeneration in Tāmaki. For the purposes of this research, critical discourse analysis has advantages compared to other approaches to discourse because it has been further developed in urban geography, urban planning, and urban studies. In particular, it has been used in these fields to interpret the implementation process for urban policies and plans, and understand how key political actors, both individual and collective, get involved in policy, and how they exercise their power. Consistent with critical spatial thinking and spatial justice as deployed in this research, the political-economic approach helped to understand and reveal how the policies and plans behind the Tāmaki Regeneration Programmes have defined the community and informed how it should be redeveloped.

As a social practice, discourse first provides a model of action and representation that reflects people's actions upon the world and each other. Secondly, there is a dialectical relationship between discourse and social structure. Discourse is shaped by social structure. The structural factors determining a particular discursive event vary according to the kind of social domain or institutional framework in which discursive events are generated. As Fairclough (1992) points out: '...discourse is shaped and constrained by the social structure in the widest sense and at all levels: by class and other social relations at a societal level by the relations specific to particular institutions such as law or education, by systems of classification, by various norms and conventions of both a discursive and a non-discursive nature, and so forth' (p. 64).

The Marxist tradition of political, economic, and ideological critique created a foundation for the political-economic approach to critical discourse analysis (Lees 2004). This approach emphasises the dialectical interconnectivity of language and other elements of society. From this perspective, the production of social life 'is based within the articulation together of diverse elements and aspects of sociality into relatively stable configurations which always essentially and inherently include language (or more generally, discourse)' (Fairclough and Graham 2002, p. 303). This changed the view of language underpinning some earlier approaches to critical discourse analysis, where language and society were seen as separately constituted realities and language was considered an 'ideal' and non-material entity, thus ignoring the relationship 'between' language and sociality. Accepting the dialectical interconnectivity of language and other elements of society provides a way to understand the relationship between policies and the wider political, economic, and social context at the epistemological level.

At a practical level, this approach uses discourse analysis as a tool to uncover 'certain hegemonic ways of thinking and talking about how things should be done that serve certain vested interests' (Lees 2004, p. 102). Researchers adopting this approach are aware of the constraints imposed by linguistic structures, as well as the potential for using those structures purposively in a dialectic manner reminiscent of structuration theory. In urban studies, it is well acknowledged that the normative discourse of urban policy and planning documents reflects power relations (Campbell 2006; Gunder 2010). Rather than reflecting a rational scientific or deliberative process, such documents are an object constructed by these power relations, which can be found on different scales from the body to the global. As Scott and Roweis (1977) point out, 'planning does not, and cannot, transcend the social and property relations of capitalist society, but is contained within and is a reflection of those same relations' (p. 1118). The ideologies inherent in capitalist social orders permeate planning (Harvey 1978). Just as the language or rhetoric used in policy reflects the political ideologies and interests of the actors, it also influences how the policies are implemented (Lees 2004). As Rydin (1998) explains, 'as a result, language can influence the policy process in a variety of ways: it can alter perceptions of interests and issues; it can define the object of policy attention; it can promote particular policy agendas; it can shape the nature of communication between actors; …it can cement coalitions or differences between actors; and it can be diversionary, resulting in a form of symbolic politics' (p. 178).

Two ideas are highlighted by researchers when undertaking discourse analysis in urban studies: (1) the interpretative context, which can be understood as the social setting in which the discourse is located; and (2) the rhetorical organisation of the discourse, which functions as the argumentative schema by which to approach a text and establish its authority (Tonkiss 1998, as cited in Lees 2004). With regard to the specific research method, Fairclough (1989) builds an analytical model tied to three interrelated dimensions of discourse: the object of analysis (including verbal, visual or verbal and visual texts); the means by which the object is produced and received (writing/speaking/designing and reading/listening/viewing) by human subjects; and the socio-historical conditions that govern these processes (Janks 1997). Correspondingly, the model used in this research comprises text analysis (description), processing analysis (interpretation), and social analysis (explanation).

The plans, strategies, policy statements, vision documents, and design frameworks analysed in relation to development and regeneration in Tāmaki mainly cover the period spanning the 1950s to 2020. This research is also informed by a review of previous research outcomes for social housing policies and urban generation, which provide a frame of reference for assessing the Tāmaki experience.

3.3   Embodiment Research and Thirdspace (Lived Space)

Lived space is not owned by its habitants, or policymakers and planners. It encompasses the experience of people living in the Firstspace as mediated through the ideologies of the Secondspace. It is also where power relations and social encounters take place within the daily routines of life. Both Young (1990) and Harvey (1998) recognise the role of the body in the development of injustice. Young (1990) argues that oppression is the result of creating despised groups through constructions of ugly bodies that inspire unconscious fear of these groups. Situating the concept of the body in the background of Marx's representations, Harvey (1998) explores how bodies are treated as a circulation and accumulation of variable capital. Based on Harvey's analysis of the politics of bodily practices in relation to Marx's representations, the study of the body has provided a significant approach to understanding the real spatiotemporal relations between practices occurring in physical space and representations, imaginaries, institutions, social relations, and the prevailing structures of political-economic power. As 'a site of contestation for the very forces that create it', the body can be viewed as the 'measure of all things' (Harvey 1998, p. 421).

Thinking about lived space from the perceptive of the body helps to understand both these dimensions. Drawing largely on Foucault's (1975) argument that social structure and modern power inscribe and imprint upon the body, and Merleau-Ponty's (1945) research on how the body acts and reacts with the environment, studies on the geographies of embodiment have been providing rich conceptualisations of bodies since the early 1990s. In particular, they offer a unique spatial perspective, arguing that bodies are places where discourse and power relations are simultaneously mapped, embodied, and resisted, and where identities are performed and constructed (Bonner-Thompson and Hopkins 2017; Harvey 1998). The corporeal nature of the body makes it both a dimension and object of space, power, and social relations. At the same time, the body has the intentionality and capacity to act as a subject, but largely expresses itself preconsciously and involuntarily in a way that is normally hidden in the time–space routine and repeated conscious or unconscious movements (Johnston 2009; Seamon 2013).

A small but compelling collection of literature has developed conceptual models of the body in contemporary planning. Fenster (2013) uses the body as an approach to understanding women's discomfort, dis-belonging, and detachment in the Jewish ultraorthodox Mea Shearim neighbourhood of East Jerusalem. Urban policy is seen as reinforcing their emotional status by enforcing patriarchal norms that restrict women's use of urban space. Fenster (2013) concludes that as a form of embodied subjective knowledge, these personal everyday feelings are local knowledge and should be considered in urban planning. Buser (2014) argues that non-representational theory and the 'affective turn', both based in embodiment research, provide useful concepts and theories for planning. Providing further insights from the body as a geographical space, Sweet and Ortiz (2015) explore explicitly embodied experiences, in this case women's fear of violence, thus compensating for the shortcomings of planning by collecting information in the private realm.

While this existing literature emphasises that emotions, feelings, and the physical senses contribute to enriching local knowledge for planning, most studies have examined marginalised social groups. There are thus few examples illustrating a clearly formulated methodology for embodiment analysis that is both *exogenous* and *endogenous* to a particular social group.

The body is both a spatial and social subject involved in generating, producing, and creating difference (Lefebvre 1974). These attributions mean the body can complement democratic proceduralism in the pursuit of a just planning process. Three reasons necessitate involving bodily practices and experiences in the planning process. Firstly, the logic of democratic proceduralism leaves the production of the city in the hands of the capitalist class. This devalues the value of the city for users. Secondly, both democratic proceduralism and political liberalism exclude the 'person' from 'political' action. However, the city is also produced by the everyday activities of its citizens and inhabitants, rather than being solely the result of the political actions of local government. Thirdly, for Lefebvre, the city dweller can only enjoy their right to the city and fair access to the city's space if their role in the daily production of the city is recognised and valued (Bell and Davoudi 2016). Concerning planning for spatial justice, three interrelated aspects of the body—the body of power, the experiencing body, and the embodied encounter—are recognised as the basis of embodied knowledge.

First, 'the body is placed geopolitically' (Nast and Pile 1998, p. 2) in power relations created by social norms and structures. The skin, feelings, emotions, habits, and physical capacities of embodied subjects are inscribed and imprinted by these power relationships (Foucault 1975), and it is through subjugating and disciplining bodies that dominant cultures designate and control certain groups (Johnston 2009). Subordinate groups with different bodily attributes to the mainstream culture are dismissed and degraded as ugly and impure, providing the basis for privileged groups to justify their control over such groups. The body is therefore recognised as a site of struggle and contestation.

Rooted in Foucault's genealogy of power, knowledge, and body (Foucault 1975), bio-power in the form of 'numerous and diverse techniques for achieving the subjugation of bodies and the control of populations' plays an indispensable role in the processes of the modern nation state for regulating humans in large groups (Foucault 1975, p. 140). One form of oppression is defining some social groups as 'the other', according to their bodily characteristics, which may be constructed as ugly, dirty, defiled, impure, or sick. Such constructions result in unconscious fear of and aversion to the despised group. The dominant culture thus devalues and excludes some groups in a process of oppression (Young 1990).

Secondly, the experiencing body provides an approach to understanding individuals' perspectives and reactions to changing space, the body of others, and power relations. The role of sensual experience in planning has been highlighted in previous studies (Bild et al. 2016; Pugh 2013; Sweet and Ortiz 2015). Human beings above all are seen as corporeal. This corporeality makes the body both a dimension and object of spatial, power, and social relations.

The built environment produced by planning directly impacts bodily experience of certain places, encounters with others, and the reactions of residents. Therefore, the affect, feelings, emotions, conscious or unconscious behaviours, place attachment, and identity of individuals are closely tied to planning practice and form important components of the production of local knowledge.

This research strand has its origins in phenomenology, which treats the body as the starting point for experiencing and perceiving the world. The phenomenological tradition is characterised by its rejection of the idea of the body as just a physical object. For phenomenologists, the body and consciousness are not separate, but integrated; the body is always an embodiment of consciousness (Turner 2008). Maurice Merleau-Ponty (1945) introduced the concept of the lived body, describing a mind–body–world system and asserting that the three aspects are integrated. As the lived body contains material and self-conscious aspects and stays connected to the outside world in a constant flow, human beings and life are essentially corporeal. This corporeality means the body is a dimension and object of spatial relations, as without the body there would be no space. In Merleau-Ponty's phenomenology, the body is given intentionality and the capacity to act as a subject, which can express itself preconsciously and involuntarily (Johnston 2009). The intentionality and capacity are usually hidden in the time–space routines and repeated movements enacted by the body without conscious thought.

These unconscious time–space routines and repeated bodily movements are seen as choreographed by environmental and people–place relations. Building on the ideas of Maurice Merleau-Ponty (1945), David Seamon's (2013) concepts of body-ballet, time–space routine, and place-ballet expand the connection between body studies and studies of natural and built environments, thus opening up a new approach for urban studies. His work explores how people act and react to the environment.

Drawing on the concept of the lived body, Young (1980, 1990) is primarily concerned with women's bodily existence. In her essay 'Throwing like a girl' (1980), she discusses the outcomes for women of gender socialisation processes constructed by patriarchal social structures. Applying a phenomenological, embodied, and 'fleshy' perspective, Hockey and Collinson (2009) argue that bodily senses play an important role in the process of workers becoming skilled. As shown in these works, the phenomenology of the body is very relevant to theorising the way in which people come to understand and react to the world around them.

Spatial justice seeks to promote more progressive and participatory forms of democratic politics and social activism, and to provide new ideas about how to mobilise and maintain cohesive collations and regional confederations of grassroots social activists (Soja 2010, p. 10). For planners, skills including storytelling, listening, and interpreting visual clues and body language are necessary to communicate and negotiate with groups from diverse backgrounds (Sandercock 2004). Meanwhile, highlighting the importance of human capabilities, the agency embodied by individuals calls for a re-examination of planning outcomes through investigating how embodied practices reconstruct the built environment, redefine its use, and transform 'space' into 'place'. This process reflects the 'resistance-acceptance spectrum' in relation to individuals and planning practices (Beall and Kanji 1999).

Thirdly, the body in social relations examines how embodied practices and social relations impact each other. It incorporates two main topics. One is the way in which the body acts upon social relations as participants maintain their connection through embodied practices; the other is how social relations act upon body image, appearance, and practices. This interaction is re-defined by Merleau-Ponty and Erving Goffman from the perspective of body movement, subject perception, and orientation. They believe that interaction is simultaneously about consciousness and embodiment. It is not only based on physical body action, but a fluid process that involves the interaction of mind, emotions, and understanding. This means that actors' minds, emotions, and intentions are accessible through examining embodied actions (Crossley 1996).

Since the late nineteenth century, multiple ways of knowing in planning have been emphasised by the notions recognition of difference, democratic deliberation, and participation (Feinstain 2010). Correspondingly, paradigms of participatory and communicative planning have been incorporated into and developed in planning theory and practice (Forester 1999; Healey 1999). Both paradigms purport to make the voices of poorly represented groups heard by professionals. In particular, the idea of 'recognition of difference' underlines the role played by the lived body in the production of personal identity and subjectivity.

Although these three dimensions of the body have been used separately for different purposes, in this study they are integrated into a conceptual framework that links planning policies, places, and individuals, and the other actors surrounding them. The urban environment produced by planning directly impacts body experience, encounters with others, and the reactions of residents. Individuals' emotions, conscious or unconscious behaviours, place attachment, and identity are therefore closely linked with planning practices.

3.3.1 Interpreting Lived Experience

Described as 'a conversation with a purpose', interviews are sensitive and people-oriented, supporting deep understandings and explanations of certain phenomena through gathering detailed descriptions of interviewees' lives and experiences (Burgess 1988, p. 102). An in-depth interview provides a way for the researcher and interviewee to understand each other more deeply and broadly than other research methods. Unlike questionnaires and other quantitative methods, interviews do not attempt to propose universal and representative descriptions and explanations, but rather to 'understand how individual people experience and make sense of their own lives' (Valentine 2005, p. 111).

In-depth semi-structured interviews were used to obtain a richer understanding of the perceptions, motivations and experiences of people living in Glen Innes. Unlike structured interviews and unstructured interviews, a semi-structured interview follows a guide, but also provides opportunities for the interviewer to spontaneously explore topics that arise with particular participants. A semi-structured interview differs from a non-structured interview because it consists of a certain number of pre-determined questions. Moreover, unlike a structured interview, it does not ask the same questions in the same order. Between 24 September and 19 December 2019, a total of 17 interviews were conducted with both long-time residents and new residents, referred to by some researchers as gentrifying residents. All the participants were recruited through advertisements posted on Facebook or in public areas such as the Glen Innes Library and two local supermarkets, Pak'nSave and Countdown.

General ethical considerations include ensuring participants' privacy, anonymising interviews and redacting commercially sensitive information. Given the implications of the research for Māori and Pasifika, the survey process followed *Te Ara Tika: Guidelines for Māori Research Ethics. Te Ara Tika* principles are drawn from tikanga Māori and its philosophical base of mātauranga Māori. In addition, a Māori planning expert was consulted to ensure the investigation was consistent with Māori protocols and practices and Te Tiriti o Waitangi.

Residents were categorised according to how long they had lived in Glen Innes, and whether they were property owners. Participants were identified as long-time tenants if they were living in social housing in Glen Innes before regeneration, long-time private owners if they owned private property in Glen Innes before regeneration, and newcomers if they had recently moved into a property purchased in a redeveloped area such as Northern Glen Innes, Fenchurch, and Wai O Taki Bay. Interviews ranged in length from 40 to 90 min.

The interview protocol for the semi-structured interviews comprised three sets of approximately 15 questions, which had been developed before the interviews. After first collecting basic information about the participants, the main question themes were: (1) the connections between the participant and their neighbourhood, the ways in which they interacted with fellow residents, and their activities; (2) the characteristics of the Glen Innes area, including social and physical changes; and (3) the impact of regeneration programmes on their lives and their feedback about these programmes.

The order of questions and the time and attention given to questions on particular topics varied depending on the participants' life stories. Extra questions were asked to deepen understanding of participants' experiences and opinions. Interviews were audiotaped and then transcribed into text by the researcher prior to analysis in NVivo 12 to identify themes and produce categories by which the responses could be organised (Braun and Clarke 2013). Responses were coded by predominant interview themes in relation to residents' experiences. Vague responses were sorted according to the most relevant category, which ensured that each response was allocated to only one theme.

To better understand residents' experiences of change, this project also used published news reports as supplementary material. Eighty-two news reports pertinent to residents' responses to the community changes were collected by searching *The New Zealand Herald* and the *East and Bays Courier* for articles published in the period 2000 to 2018. All supplementary information is cited and acknowledged. The resident voices and opinions revealed in these sources were coded according to the themes revealed by the analysis of the interviews. This systematic review of news articles substantially complemented the limited number of interviews carried out.

Incorporating geographical morphological analysis, housing policy analysis, and the perspective of the body, Fig. 3.1 presents an integrated conceptual framework for characterising the processes and outcomes of social housing redevelopment, in particular the delivery of medium-density housing and its results. More broadly, the aim of this study is to understand the issues and challenges of planning for quality community life for everyone in New Zealand. Through the creation of the new conceptual framework, this project contributes to the development of spatial justice through articulating how such a conception can be applied to the analysis of enactments of (in)justice in planning practice. It is also expected to advance geographical morphological analysis and embodiment research by extending their use in planning for social housing redevelopment.

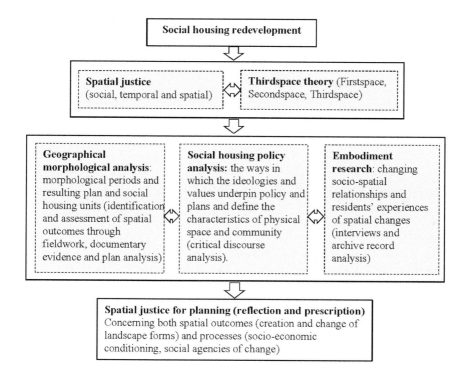

Fig. 3.1 Conceptual framework for research

3.4   Summary

This chapter has developed an analytical framework for the examination of social housing redevelopment in New Zealand. Geographical urban morphology provides an evolutionary approach to spatial landscape forms. Housing policy analysis articulates the ways in which the ideologies and values underlying policy and plans define the characteristics of physical space and community. Influenced by Lefebvre and Soja, discussing the body within space offers possibilities for rethinking just planning by exploring residents' reactions to community changes. Used in combination, urban morphology, policy analysis, and embodiment research provide field-based and original evidence for critical spatial analysis.

This study used analytical generalisation (Gobo 2013; Polit and Beck 2010) to extend the findings and results to support a discussion of theory. The mix of techniques used to collect and analyse data follows the logic described for extending a case study. Morphological analysis was used to distinguish, characterise, and explain the spatial structure of the urban landscape of Tāmaki. The urban morphology fieldwork not only pays attention to changes in the spatial pattern on the ground and in maps, but also collects historical and new plans and documentary and archival records to systematically explain the form complexes and sequences of urban fabric types in Tāmaki. Critical discourse analysis was used to understand how planning and policies have defined Tāmaki social housing redevelopment. Interviews explored how residents have reacted, coped, and adapted to physical and social changes in this area. These three data sets and methods complement each other and, in combination, target outcomes and process in the evolution and interplay of Firstspace, Secondspace, and Thirdspace in Tāmaki. The resulting research findings from a case study of Tāmaki regeneration are expected to contribute to planning that promotes social equity and spatial cohesion.

References

Aalbers MB, Loon JV, Fernandez R (2017) The financialization of a social housing provider. Int J Urban Reg Res 41(4):572–587

Austin PM, Gurran N, Whitehead CME (2014) Planning and affordable housing in Australia, New Zealand and England: common culture; different mechanisms. J Housing Built Environ 29(3):455–472

Beall J, Kanji N (1999) Households, livelihoods and urban poverty (working paper). International Development Department, University of Birmingham. https://citeseerx.ist.psu.edu/viewdoc/download?doi=10.1.1.201.7888&rep=rep1&type=pdf. Accessed 26 Oct 2022

Bell D, Davoudi S (2016) Understanding justice and fairness in and of the city. In: Davoudi S, Bell D (eds) Justice and fairness in the city: a multi-disciplinary approach to 'ordinary' cities. Policy Press Bristol, pp 1–20

Bild E, Coler M, Pfeffer K, Bertolini L (2016) Considering sound in planning and designing public spaces: a review of theory and applications and a proposed framework for integrating research and practice. J Plan Lit 31(4):419–434

Bonner-Thompson C, Hopkins P (2017) Geographies of the body. In: Warf B (ed) Oxford bibliographies of geography. Oxford University Press, Oxford

Bowen ID (1981) Techniques for demonstrating cell death. In: Trump BF, Berezesky IK, Osornio-Vargas AR (eds) Cell death in biology and pathology. Springer, Dordrecht, pp 379–444

Braun V, Clarke V (2013) Successful qualitative research: a practical guide for beginners. Sage, Los Angeles

Briggs SV (2006) Integrating policy and science in natural resources: why so difficult? Ecol Manag Restor 7(1):37–39

Burgess R (1988) Conversations with a purpose: the ethnographic interview in educational research. In: Burgess R (ed) Studies in qualitative methodology, vol 1. JAI Press, London, pp 137–155

Buser M (2014) Thinking through non-representational and affective atmospheres in planning theory and practice. Plan Theory 13(3):227–243

Campbell H (2006) Just planning: the art of situated ethical judgment. J Plan Educ Res 26(1):92–106

Caniggia G, Maffei GL (2001) Interpreting basic building: architectural composition and building typology. Alinea, Florence, Italy

Clapham D (2019) Remaking housing policy: an international study. Routledge, Abingdon, Oxon, New York

Coleman PJ (1958) The spirit of New Zealand liberalism in the nineteenth century. J Mod Hist 30(3):227–235

Conzen MRG (1958) The growth and character of Whitby. In: Daysh GHJ (ed) A survey of Whitby and the surrounding area. Shakespeare Head, Stratford-up-Avon

Conzen MRG (1960) Alnwick, Northumberland: a study in town-plan analysis. Institute of British Geographers, London, England

Conzen MRG (1966) Historical townscapes in Britain: a problem in applied geography. In: House JW (ed) Northern geographical essays in honour of G.H.J. Daysh. University of Newcastle upon Tyne Newcastle upon Tyne, England, pp 56–78

Conzen MRG (1969) Alnwick, Northumberland: a study in town-plan analysis, 2nd edn. Institute of British Geographers Special Publication 27, Institute of British Geographers, London

Conzen MRG (1988) Morphogenesis, morphological regions and secular human agency in the historic townscape, as exemplified by Ludlow. In: Denecke D, Shaw G (eds) Urban historical geography: recent progress in Britain and Germany, vol 10. Cambridge University Press. Cambridge, England, pp 253–272

Conzen MRG (1998) Apropos a sounder philosophical basis for urban morphology. Urban Morphol 2(2):113–114

CoreLogic (2020) CoreLogic New Zealand. https://www.corelogic.co.nz/. Accessed 26 October 2022

Crossley N (1996) Body-subject/body-power: agency, inscription and control in Foucault and Merleau-Ponty. Body Soc 2(2):99–116

Davoudi S, Galland D, Stead D (2020) Reinventing planning and planners: ideological decontestations and rhetorical appeals. Plan Theory 19(1):17–37

Fairclough N (1989) Language and power. Longman, London, England

Fairclough N (1992) Discourse and social change, vol 10. Polity Press, Cambridge, England

Fairclough N, Graham PW (2002) Marx as critical discourse analyst: the genesis of a critical method and its relevance to the critique of global capital. Estudios de Sociolinguistica 3(1):185–229

Feinstain S (2010) The Just City. Cornell University Press, Ithaca

Fenster T (2013) Bodies and places in Jerusalem: gendered feelings and urban policies. Hagar-Studies in Culture, Politics and Identities 11(1):63–81

Flynn R (1988) Political acquiescence, privatisation and residualisation in British housing policy. J Soc Policy 17(3):289–312

Forester J (1999) The deliberative practitioner: encouraging participatory planning processes. MIT Press, Cambridge, England

Foucault M (1975) Surveiller et punir. Gallimard, Paris. English edition: Foucault M (1977) Discipline and punish: the birth of the prison (trans: Sheridan A). Pantheon, New York

Gatley J, Walker P (2014) Vertical living: the architectural centre and the remaking of Wellington. Auckland University Press, Auckland, New Zealand

Gerosa PG (1999) The philosophical foundations of urban morphology. Urban Morphol 3(1):44–44

Gobo G (2013) Sampling, representativeness and generalizability. In: Seale C, Gobo G, Gubrium JF, Silverman D (eds) Qualitative research practice. Sage, London, England, pp 405–427

Gu K (2010) Urban morphological regions and urban landscape management: the case of central Auckland, New Zealand. Urban Design Int 15(3):148–164

Gu K (2014) From urban landscape units to morphological coding: exploring an alternative approach to zoning in Auckland, New Zealand. Urban Design Int 19(2):159–174

Gu K (2018) The teaching of urban design: a morphological approach. J Plan Educ Res 40(4):472–481

Gunder M (2010) Planning as the ideology of (neoliberal) space. Plan Theory 9(4):298–314

Hamer DA (1988) The New Zealand liberals: the years of power, 1891–1912. Auckland University Press, Auckland, New Zealand

Hargreaves RP, Hearn TJ, Little S (1985) The state and housing in New Zealand to 1919. NZ Geogr 41(2):46–55

Harvey D (1978) The urban process under capitalism: a framework for analysis. Int J Urban Reg Res 2(1–3):101–131

Harvey D (1985) The geopolitics of capitalism. In: Gregory D, Urry J (eds) Social relations and spatial structures. Palgrave, London, England, pp 128–163

Harvey D (1998) The body as an accumulation strategy. Environ Plan d: Soc Space 16(4):401–421

Healey P (1999) Institutionalist analysis, communicative planning, and shaping places. J Plan Educ Res 19(2):111–121

Hillman J (1960) The welfare state in New Zealand. Am J Agr Econ 42(3):718–720

Hockey J, Allen-Collinson J (2009) The sensorium at work: the sensory phenomenology of the working body. Sociol Rev 57(2):217–239

Janks H (1997) Critical discourse analysis as a research tool. Discourse Stud Cult Politics Educ 18(3):329–342

Jock P (2014) Ideas in New Zealand—the new right. Te Ara—the Encyclopedia of New Zealand. http://www.TeAra.govt.nz/en/ideas-in-new-zealand/page-7. Accessed 26 Oct 2022

Johnston L (2009) Body. In: Kitchin R, Thrift N (eds) International encyclopaedia of human geography. Elsevier, Amsterdam, Netherlands, pp 326–331

Kāinga Ora—Homes and Communities (2020) https://kaingaora.govt.nz/. Accessed 26 Oct 2022

Kropf K (1999) Wandering around the foundations: on Cassirer, signs, Peirce and Chance. Urban Morphol 3(1):45–46

Kropf K (2018) Plots, property and behaviour. Urban Morphol 22(1):5–14

Larner W (2000) Neo-liberalism policy, ideology, governmentality. Stud Polit Econ 63:5–25

Lees L (2004) Urban geography: Discourse analysis and urban research. Prog Hum Geogr 28:101–107

Lefebvre H (1974) La production de l'espace. Anthropos, Paris. English edition: Lefebvre H (1991) The production of space (trans: Nicholson-Smith D). Blackwell, Oxford, England

Marcetic B (2017) New Zealand's neoliberal drift. Jacobin. https://www.jacobinmag.com/. Accessed 25 Oct 2022

Martin JE (1996) Holding the balance: a history of New Zealand's Department of Labour, 1891–1995. Canterbury University Press, Christchurch, New Zealand

Massey P (1995) New Zealand: market liberalisation in a developed economy. Macmillan, London, England

Merleau-Ponty M (1945) Phénoménologie de la perception. Gallimard, Paris. English edition: Merleau-Ponty M (1962) Phenomenology of perception (tans: Smith C). Routledge and Kegan Paul, London, England

Miller CL (2000) Town planning in New Zealand, 1900–1933: the emergent years: concepts, the role of the state, and the emergence of a profession. Dissertation, Massey University

Mugavin D (1999) A philosophical base for urban morphology. Urban Morphol 3(1):95–99

Murphy L (2004) To the market and back: housing policy and state housing in New Zealand. GeoJournal 59(2):119–126

Murphy L, Kearns RA (1994) Housing New Zealand Ltd: privatisation by stealth. Environ Plan A: Econ Space 26(4):623–637

Nast H, Pile S (1998) Makingplacesbodies. In: Nast H, Pile S (eds) Places through the body. Routledge, London, England

Navarro-Rivera J (2015) The diversity of Latino ideology. Dissertation, University of Connecticut

Olssen A, McDonald H, Grimes A, Stillman S (2010) A state housing database: 1993–2009. Motu Economic and Public Policy Research. New Zealand. http://motu-www.motu.org.nz/wpapers/10_13.pdf. Accessed 25 Oct 2022

Perkins HC, Memon PA, Swaffield SR, Gelfand L (1993) The urban environment. In: Memon PA, Perkins HC (eds) Environmental planning in New Zealand. Dunmore Press, Palmerston North, New Zealand

Phillips J (2012) Visitors' opinions about New Zealand. Te Ara—the Encyclopedia of New Zealand. http://www.TeAra.govt.nz/en/visitors-opinions-about-new-zealand. Accessed 25 Oct 2022

Polit DF, Beck CT (2010) Generalization in quantitative and qualitative research: myths and strategies. Int J Nurs Stud 47(1):1451–1458

Pugh J (2013) Speaking without voice: Participatory planning, acknowledgment, and latent subjectivity in Barbados. Ann Assoc Am Geogr 103(5):1266–1281

Roper B (2006) Business political activity in New Zealand from 1990 to 2005. Kōtuitui: New Zealand J Soc Sci 1(2):161–183

Rydin Y (1998) The enabling local state and urban development: resources, rhetoric and planning in East London. Urban Stud 35(2):175–191

Sandercock L (2004) Towards a planning imagination for the 21st century. J Am Plann Assoc 70(2):133–141

Sauer CO (1925) The morphology of landscape. Univ Calif Publ Geogr 22:19–53

Scott AJ, Roweis ST (1977) Urban planning in theory and practice: a reappraisal. Environ Plan a: Econ Space 9(10):1097–1119

Seamon D (2013) Lived bodies, place, and phenomenology: implications for human rights and environmental justice. J Hum Rights Environ 4(2):143–166

Soja EW (1996) Thirdspace: journeys to Los Angeles and other real-and-imagined places. Blackwell Publishing, Madden, Leake

Soja EW (2010) Seeking spatial justice. University of Minnesota Press, Minneapolis, Unite State

Sweet EL, Ortiz ES (2015) Bringing bodies into planning: visceral methods, fear and gender violence. Urban Studies 52(10):1826–1845

The New Zealand Productivity Commission (2015) Using land for housing. https://www.productivity.govt.nz/sites/default/files/using-land-for-housing-final-report-full%2C%20PDF%2C%204511Kb.pdf. Accessed 20 Oct 2022

Turner BS (2008) The body and society: explorations in social theory. Sage, Los Angeles, Unite State

Valentine G (2005) Tell me about…: using interviews as a research methodology. In: Flowerdew R, Martin D (eds) Methods in human geography: a guide for students doing a research project. Longman, Essex, England, pp 110–126

Varela FJ, Thompson E, Rosch E (2017) The embodied mind: cognitive science and human experience. MIT Press, MA, United States

Von Richthofen F (1883) Aufgaben und Methoden der heutigen Geographie. Veit

Wang S, Gu K (2020) Pingyao: the historic urban landscape and planning for heritage-led urban changes. Cities 97, 102489. https://doi.org/10.1016/j.cities.2019.102489

Whitehand JWR (1981) Background to the urban morphogenetic tradition. In: Whitehand JWR (ed) The urban landscape: historical development and management: papers by M.R.G. Conzen. Institute of British Geographers Special Publication, No 13. Academic Press, London, England, pp 1–24

Whitehand JWR (2001) British urban morphology: the Conzenian tradition. Urban Morphol 5(2):103–109

Whitehand JWR (2009) The structure of urban landscapes: strengthening research and practice. Urban Morphol 13(1):5–27

Xie PF, Gu K (2015) The changing urban morphology: waterfront redevelopment and event tourism in New Zealand. Tourism Manage Perspect 15:105–114

Young IM (1980) Throwing like a girl: a phenomenology of feminine body comportment motility and spatiality. Hum Stud 3(1):137–156

Young IM (1990) Justice and the politics of difference. Princeton University Press, Oxford, England

Chapter 4
Urban Regeneration and Social Housing Redevelopment in Aotearoa New Zealand: Issues and Challenges

Abstract Urban regeneration is the act of improving a place or system, especially by making it more lively and successful, and has long been an active field of research in urban studies. Much has been written about urban regeneration, including the associated gentrification, displacement and resistance, and social-spatial justice. Moreover, different theories have been developed to reveal the underlying logic of these processes. This chapter clarifies the characteristics of housing-led urban regeneration in the New Zealand context. A review of previous research on social housing redevelopment in Tāmaki, Auckland, suggests the potential of spatial justice as an integrative/unifying theory for connecting place, policies, and people. Spatial justice offers a timely contribution to tackling planning problems in social housing provision in New Zealand and also adds a new dimension to international efforts to promote social inclusion.

Keywords Urban regeneration · Neoliberalist planning · Social housing redevelopment · Tāmaki · Glen Innes

4.1 Urban Regeneration

The notion of regeneration is nearly always applied to the process of bringing vitality and energy back to urban settings in decline, for example, residential neighbourhoods, manufacturing sites, and commercial precincts. The terms urban renewal, renovation, redevelopment, and revitalisation carry similar meanings (Rossi and Vanolo 2013). Urban regeneration has been a major target of urban policies since the 1950s when it emerged as a solution to the many problems facing urban neighbourhoods in towns and cities.

Researchers have debated the origins of urban regeneration and related topics such as partnership, social exclusion, and sustainability (Atkinson 1999; Hemphill et al. 2004; Hibbitt et al. 2001). Urban regeneration is defined differently across urban studies. According to Dalia Lichfield Associates (1992), it is 'comprehensive and integrated vision and action which seeks to resolve urban problems and bring about a lasting improvement in the economic, physical, social and environmental condition of

© The Author(s), under exclusive license to Springer Nature Switzerland AG 2023
S. Wang and K. Gu, *Spatial Justice and Planning*, The Urban Book Series,
https://doi.org/10.1007/978-3-031-38070-9_4

an area that has been subject to change or offers opportunities for improvement' (cited in Korkmaz and Balaban 2020, p. 2). This definition has been adopted and extended by other scholars to consider the processes of decline and how they can be addressed (Roberts and Sykes 2000). Evans and Shaw (2004) define urban regeneration as 'the transformation of a place (residential, commercial or open space) that has displayed the symptoms of environmental (physical), social and/or economic decline […] to breathe new life and vitality into an ailing community, industry and area (bringing) sustainable, long-term improvements to local quality of life, including economic, social and environmental needs' (p. 4).

Urban regeneration is by its nature an intervention in the existing urban system (Roberts and Sykes 2000). It is a complicated process involving decision-making, implementation of urban policies, and evaluation of outcomes. The main topics of interest arising in the process of urban regeneration concern strategy and partnership, the physical aspects, environmental and sustainability aspects, and social and community issues. The most common models of urban regeneration are housing-led, event-led, infrastructure-led, and culture-led regeneration. Housing-led regeneration is targeted at neighbourhoods with a high concentration of sub-standard houses and justified by its stated intention of addressing issues of potential crime, poor health conditions, and other social problems (Bailey 2005; Woo 2014; Evans and Shaw 2004).

Government strategies and partnerships between government, the private sector, and local residents have been explored in geography and urban planning. Increasingly, researchers and decision-makers believe that an effective and successful urban regeneration programme requires a framework that is strategically designed, locally-based, and involves multi-agency partnerships. Influenced by neoliberalism, urban regeneration normally involves collaboration between government and the market. In order to attract investment from the private sector in the process of urban regeneration or increase the vitality of commercial activities in regenerated areas, regeneration strategies need to take into account land and building supply and demand characteristics, including the quality of the existing housing stock, sources of future demand in the industrial sector, and property trends in terms of location and type of premises. Displacement of people as residents lose their homes in regeneration areas is another problem that needs to be addressed in the process of urban regeneration. Various actors such as policymakers, planners, designers, developers, and residents should thus all be involved in the process of defining delivery mechanisms and institutional arrangements (Carter and Roberts 2000).

Some main factors concern the physical built environment. Firstly, the components of the built environment—buildings, land and sites, utilities and services, and transport infrastructure—constitute the existing physical stock. Secondly, socioeconomic changes and the corresponding new requirements of the built environment are also significant issues. The rate of socioeconomic change is more rapid than physical change. In the early stages of urban regeneration, it is necessary to develop a well-founded understanding and close integration of what realistic and sustainable social and economic conditions will look like. Thirdly, physical reconfiguration can contribute to removing constraints, leading changes, building on opportunities, increasing supply side investments, and integrating socioeconomic and physical renewal (Roberts and Sykes 2000).

The environment and sustainable development are also crucial issues in urban regeneration. Global environmental concerns have promoted studies of sustainability and regeneration. Urban form plays an important role in sustainable development. For example, notions of the compact city and new urbanism have become popular among policymakers, planners, designers, and architects (Roberts and Sykes 2000).

Concerning the social and community aspects of urban regeneration, themes and topics generally relate to the needs of local people in communities and provision for meeting those needs (Fernback 2005), the needs of particular community groups (Speak 2000), social inclusion and exclusion in regenerated areas (Sharp et al. 2005), community empowerment, effective community participation and involvement (Atkinson 2003), and capacity-building employment, education, and training programmes (Krüger 1993). Critical urbanists have raised the issue of gentrification and displacement-related urban regeneration (Smith 2006). By their very nature, these topics emphasise the importance of the voice, experience, and power of local residents and call for the prioritisation of social cohesion and justice in the process of urban regeneration.

4.2 Social Housing Redevelopment: An International Perspective

Social housing redevelopment is one of the urban regeneration activities that has targeted public/social housing neighbourhoods that were mostly built in the early post-war period when the Keynesian ideology had dominated the social, economic, and political systems. Different from North European cities where social housing comprised a larger proportion of the housing stock and housed a far larger number of households who belong to diverse social and income groups, social housing provision has been regarded as a residual model or experienced a long period of revisualisation in the USA, Canada, Australia, and New Zealand (Harloe 2008; Watt and Smets 2017). Revisualisation has been defined as 'the process whereby public housing (and other social housing) moves towards a position in which it provides only a 'safety net' for those who for reasons of poverty, age or infirmity cannot obtain suitable accommodation in the private sector' (Malpass and Murie 1982, p. 174). Under this residual model, social housing provision serves the poorest and most vulnerable residents in a society and social housing tenants have the chance to exit their tenure in social housing when they can afford the housing price in the private market. In this case, social housing neighbourhoods have gradually been associated with poverty, welfare dependency, high unemployment rates, crime, drugs, disorder, and other social problems.

Some key social housing redevelopment programmes, including Hope VI in the USA (Vale 2018; Hanlon 2010), Five Estates of Peckham regeneration in the UK (Jackson and Butler 2015; Glucksberg 2017), Regent Park revitalisation in Canada (Rowe and Dunn 2015; August 2014a, b), and Bonnyrigg Living Communities project in Australia (Rogers 2012, 2013) have aimed to physically replace previous run-down social houses with modernist houses and endeavoured to shift the image and status of state housing away from its association with concentrated poverty and other social problems. Towards achieving this aim, these programmes share some commonalities in their objectives, rationales, approaches, and outcomes (Table 4.1).

The Regent Park revitalisation programme is representative of issues and challenges facing most recent public housing redevelopment programmes. The Regent Park site is located on the eastern edge of Toronto's downtown covering a land area of about 69 hectares. Before revitalisation, 2,083 rent-geared-to-income social housing units housed about 7,500 residents. Regent Park was regarded as a low-income neighbourhood with poor housing conditions. In addition to the problems of criminal activities and public safety, issues and challenges facing the physical environment included the poor relationship between buildings and the surrounding open spaces and poorly designed public spaces. Regent Park has gradually become an area with many urban problems in the public's perception and thus isolated from the surrounding areas and the rest of the city (James 2010; Greaves 2011). In 2002, the Toronto Community Housing Corporation (TCHC) launched a multi-phase transformation plan to replace old residential buildings with high-quality new housing units. Regent Park's cultural diversity and the strong sense of community among its residents provided both opportunities and challenges to the process of urban regeneration.

The Regent Park revitalisation programme began in 2002 and headed to phases four and five in 2020. It has been the largest neighbourhood regeneration project in Canada. The initial plan in 2005 planned to construct approximately 5,400 social and market housing units and projected to house about 12,500 residents at the completion of all phases (Fig. 4.1). In 2014, the approved rezoning plan allowed the land to increase the total number of new units up to 7,500. The number of residents would be more than 17,000 once phase five is completed. By the fall of 2021, this programme had built 1,350 social housing units, 364 new affordable rental housing units, and 989 rent-geared-to-income replacement units (Brail et al. 2021).

Since the beginning of this programme, there have been discussions and debates about how this programme justified the urban revitalisation's objectives (August 2014a, b; Jahiu and Cinnamon 2022), what are the ideological drivers of the urban revitalisation (Hackworth 2002), whether residents of Regent Park have been involved in the decision-making process (De Schutter and Riemer 2009), and how residents respond to territorial stigmatisation and resist the revitalisation (Purdy 2003). The Regent Park revitalisation programme has significantly reflected the neoliberalism premise which downsizes the responsibility of the government's role in welfare provision by obtaining profits from gentrification and real estate speculation

Table 4.1   Examples of social housing redevelopment programmes

	Hope VI of Orchard Park	Five Estates of North Peckham regeneration	Regent Park Revitalisation	Bonnyrigg Living Communities project
Location	Boston, USA	London, UK	Toronto, Canada	Sydney, Australia
Building time	1942	1966	1948	Late 1970s
Building typology before redevelopment	A superblock consisted of 28 garden-style apartment buildings	65 five-storey blocks in all on a 40-acre site, comprising 1444 homes	69-acre housing complex with high- rise and walk-up apartment buildings	81-hectare front-to-back houses; Radburn urban design principles applied
Redevelopment dates	1993–1998	1994–2008	2002–undergoing	2004
Redevelopment objectives	Reduce the concentrated poverty; improve public safety; attract more moderate- and middle-income groups;	Improve the urban environment; increase the area's tenure mix; foster social interaction	Alleviate the socioeconomic gap; revitalised mixed-income, mixed-use, and residential neighbourhood	
Redevelopment rationale	New Urbanism; social mix	Social mixing	Social mixing; right of return applied before 2006	Public–private partnership Social mix policies
Redevelopment outcomes	Garden-style apartments and row houses; mixed-income community; reducing the total number of dwelling units from 711 to 446; mixed-tenure housing stock (85% is public housing and 15% market-rate apartments)	Reducing density; tenure diversification	Build a total of 7,500 new units; increase density; mixed tenure	Increased housing density; mixed tenure (30% public and 70% private); mixed home typological types

(Hackworth and Moriah 2006). Deconcentrating poverty and social mix were used as a solution to the social problems and justification for the need for redevelopment and revitalisation (August 2014b). However, this programme failed to achieve its promise to resolve social problems and promote social inclusion. Residents have experienced the hardship associated with relocation, gentrification, and displacement. Local residents have been organised to resist the urban revitalisation programme (Sahak 2008). There is limited interaction between pre-redevelopment public housing tenants and

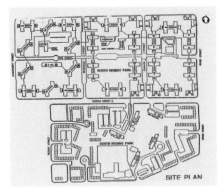

Fig. 4.1 Plans of Regent Park before and after redevelopment (*Source* Based on Toronto City Council 2007)

post-redeveloped new residents. Even though public consultation was undertaken in the process, the residents were not fully involved in the decision-making process and they are not true partners in the process of urban redevelopment (De Schutter and Riemer 2009).

4.3   Urban Regeneration in New Zealand

In contrast to the UK, other European countries, and the USA, the pressing need for urban regeneration in New Zealand has emerged relatively recently and there is limited significant and comprehensive New Zealand urban regeneration research (Jones 2009; Perkins et al. 2019). Among large urban redevelopment projects, the urban renewal programme initiated in Freemans Bay in the 1950s, the redevelopment of the Viaduct Harbour on Auckland's commercial waterfront in the late 1990s, and community renewal in Talbot Park, Tāmaki, in the early 2000s are noteworthy. In particular, 'if importance can be measured in column inches, Freemans Bay is the undisputed sovereign of New Zealand suburbs' (Dodd 1972a, p. 13). The issues and problems in the implementation of the urban renewal programme initiated in Freemans Bay have influenced many other community redevelopment projects in New Zealand in the years since.

Freemans Bay is one of the oldest suburbs in Auckland. It sits just to the west of Auckland's CBD, cradled below the Ponsonby and Karangahape Road ridgelines (Fig. 4.2). Land purchased for subdivision from the chiefs of Ngāti Whātua in 1842 was first developed along the shoreline (Terrini 1972). Freemans Bay evolved over the following few decades into a seaside village with a range of small marine industries and a growing number of workers' cottages along Sale Street, Ireland Street, and

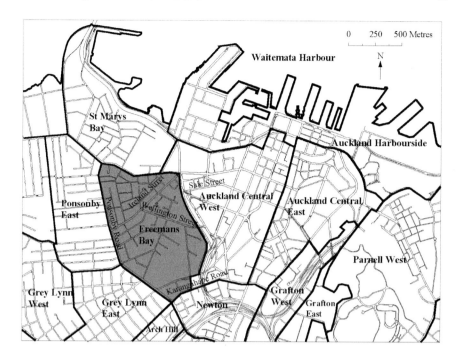

Fig. 4.2 Freemans Bay and Auckland's CBD (*Sources* Auckland Council 2022)

Wellington Street (Auckland City Council 1976; Terrini 1972). Renall Street still possesses many well-preserved old houses (Fig. 4.3).

At the turn of the twentieth century, the bay was reclaimed and converted into what is now Victoria Park. As commercial and industrial activity in the inner city expanded, Freemans Bay was chosen as the site for a number of industrial buildings and municipal services. The effect of these changes was to sever Freemans Bay residents from their local places of work and encroach on their environment with mostly unpleasant developments such as the gas works and night soil dump (Dodd 1972a, b; Nairn 2013). Subdivision had occurred to such an extent that section sizes in Freemans Bay were among the smallest in Auckland (Terrini 1972). Materials used in construction were often of poor quality and dwellings were erected at speed to make development as quick and profitable as possible (Bland 1942). Houses in the lower bay were closer to the industrial and commercial centre of the city, which was constantly expanding and encroaching on the eastern boundary of the suburb (Auckland City Council 1976).

By the 1920s, Freemans Bay had reached its peak in terms of building density with a population of 10,500 (Terrini 1972). In 1935, the slum issue in Auckland had become so acute it warranted an investigation by Auckland City Council into almost 11,000 dwellings across the inner-city suburbs of Grey Lynn, Ponsonby, Arch Hill, Newton, Eden Terrace, Grafton, Parnell, and Freemans Bay, carried out under the Housing Survey Act 1935 (Forrest 1967; Bland 1942). An official report was

Fig. 4.3 Renall Street in Freemans Bay (*Source* Authors' photograph 2017)

released in 1937 revealing that 35% of the 10,698 'buildings' surveyed did not meet the government's prescribed baseline for structural fitness, and overcrowding was linked to poorer socioeconomic groups (Bland 1942; Nairn 2013). The government programme of urban renewal in Freemans Bay responded to the issue of slumification as a holistic condition. Up until the time the programme was implemented in 1950, previous interventions had attempted to revive Freemans Bay by attacking isolated symptoms of the poor housing conditions site by site (Nairn 2013).

Freemans Bay became the first New Zealand suburb to be officially declared a 'reclamation area' under the provisions of the Housing Improvement Act 1945 (Dodd 1972a, p. 13). This enabled the local authority to completely replan and rebuild an area based on wide powers for land acquisition, demolition, subdivision, reconstruction, and resale (Dodd 1972a, p. 16). In 1950, the Council presented its planned solution, a comprehensive scheme to rebuild the entire suburb. The original 1950 scheme involved completely demolishing and redeveloping 221 acres of Freemans Bay. An additional 102 acres were added to this area in 1951 (Auckland City Council 1971). In essence, the plan was for five 'superblocks', arranged according to theories of pedestrian-vehicular segregation and with reference to the existing street and topographic patterns. Each superblock was to be a large high-density housing estate comprised of terrace housing and multi-unit apartment blocks and containing a central 'green' where community facilities would be located (Terrini 1972).

The 1950 plans to renew the entire area of Freemans Bay were only made feasible by the prospect of significant financial contributions from central government (Cook 1966). The programme was planned in a series of stages, with the clearance and redevelopment of the most run-down areas first.

The Auckland District Scheme 1953 provides a number of illustrations setting out the original vision for Freemans Bay. Two main styles of multi-unit housing were planned: 'flats' towards the top of the ridgeline and 'row houses' scattered everywhere. The first stage of redevelopment was to be the 12.3 acres making up the Phillips Street and Whitson Terrace blocks, both cleared in 1950. Redevelopment began in the Whitson Terrace block in accordance with the Council's original vision. By the time the Auckland District Scheme was released in 1953, the 3.8 acres known as the Whitson Terrace block had already been completed: In terraced two-storey buildings on concrete foundations, there are now 54 flats. Where originally 134 people lived in slum conditions, 214 people now enjoy good living accommodation with ample light, air, and open space at a density of 71 persons per acre on a landscaped site with a building coverage of only 15.4% (Nairn 2013) (Fig. 4.4).

Star flats were among a range of designs created by Fred Newman, chief architect of the Ministry of Works (Schrader 2005) (Fig. 4.5). Although not the same as the apartments developed by Simpson (1938), the star blocks were derived from a similar vision centred on maximum efficiency of density while minimising building coverage and maximising exposure to open space and sunlight. Similar blocks were subsequently used for state housing in Talbot Park in Glen Innes, and so became a staple typology of publicly owned multi-unit housing (Schrader 2005).

By the end of the 1950s, only two of the original 'superblocks' had been completed, with the remainder of Freemans Bay experiencing virtually no spontaneous renewal or further government clearance after the Phillips Street block (Terrini 1972). The cost of acquiring properties for clearance was highly prohibitive, and the fragmentation of land titles meant that alternatives to the star block pattern of redevelopment would be needed that aligned more closely with the pre-existing allotment structure. Critics of the 1950s scheme for Freemans Bay redevelopment focused on its formal mannerisms, its magnitude, and its necessity (Dodd 1972a, p. 17).

Due to the high cost of land acquisition and the drawn-out nature of the process, a new, more moderate scheme was adopted in 1968, where only a fifth (22 acres) of the remaining land was designated for total clearance (Terrini 1972). This slowing trend was being felt in urban renewal projects internationally (Terrini 1972). The Council softened its approach to urban renewal by adopting a more graduated approach, which included removing a large portion of the inner-city side of Freemans Bay. Specific policies were applied to different parts of the renewal area, ranging from complete clearance to rehabilitation.

In the Council's Freemans Bay Operative Plan 1973, the emphasis had shifted to the provision of better neighbourhood facilities, new play spaces, shopping areas, improved roading, citizens advisory services, and improved educational opportunities. Auckland City Council's initial solution to the housing problem in Freemans Bay was 'an over-simplification of heroic proportions' (Terrini 1972, p. 18). There were conflicting expectations around urban renewal: to the layman, urban renewal probably meant slum clearance; to the social worker, improved social conditions; and to the developer, increased land values. The planner's expectation of increased density can be added to this list. Implicit to all the above expectations was the construction of new buildings, as if new buildings represent an inherent good. Urban renewal

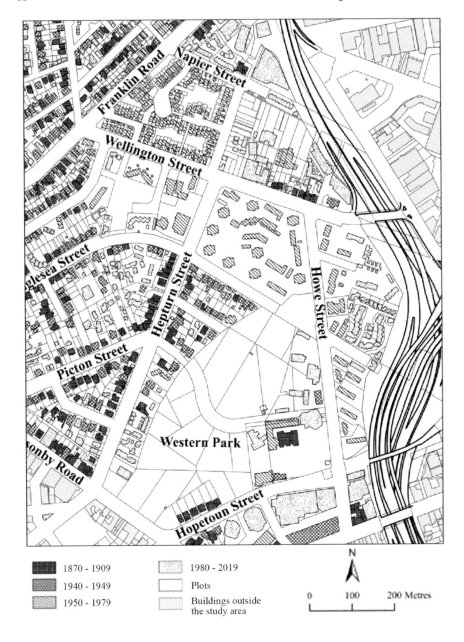

Fig. 4.4 Building forms and the ground plan of redeveloped areas in Freemans Bay 2022 (*Source* Based on An 2022)

Fig. 4.5 A star flat in Howe Street, Freemans Bay (*Source* Authors' photograph, February 2020)

is the restructuring of the urban environment to meet contemporary social needs. The urban renewal programme in Freemans Bay offered no guarantee that it would actually fulfil the social needs of the community. First and foremost was the need to be housed, irrespective of the size of their section.

By no means was this problem unique to Auckland. Plans for the comprehensive renewal of Freemans Bay were influenced by government action in Australian cities, where similar experiences with slum conditions had emerged only a few decades earlier (Flood 2003). In Australia, these slum conditions were beginning to be seen as an issue of national responsibility (Forrest 1967), while urban renewal on a large scale had been considered as an option by the central government in New Zealand since at least 1935 (NZ Committee on Housing 1935). At the time, the opposition Labour Party were actively promoting a comprehensive solution (Simpson 1938), a vision that never fully eventuated and would later be replaced by the 1950 programme.

Freemans Bay occupies an important place in New Zealand's planning history as the first substantial attempt at urban renewal, albeit one that never fully eventuated (Nairn 2013).

What was once seen as a comparatively simple project of clearance and redevelopment became a complex and convoluted renegotiation of expectations based on practicability (particularly regarding the acquisition of lots), and intense public opposition (Terrini 1972). The following reflections on planning have influenced community redevelopment in many ways in New Zealand, including recent plans for the Tāmaki area.

4.4   Social Housing Redevelopment in New Zealand

In New Zealand, social houses are spread throughout the country. As distinctive as villas and bungalows, this housing type is a legacy of the First Labour Government of 1935–1949, with over 30,000 built during this period, and even more built after that (McKay and Stevens 2014). The current concentration of low-income households in state housing in New Zealand cities is a direct result of government housing policies since 1991. Between the 1960s and the 1980s, a considerable number of state houses were deliberately developed in relatively wealthy suburbs—under a policy known as pepper-potting (Bikey 2010). However, the National governments of 1991–2000 and 2008–2017 implemented a policy of selling state housing in wealthier suburbs as well as reducing maintenance on dwellings in lower-income suburbs, requiring Housing New Zealand Corporation to return a substantial annual dividend to the Crown. As a result, the concentration of low-income households in deteriorating dwellings increased, and Housing New Zealand Corporation redevelopments involved the sale of some houses in order to meet annual dividend payments (Austin 2017, personal communication). As this brief history of social housing in New Zealand shows, changing government housing policies play a crucial role in planning and planning outcomes concerning social housing.

Six community renewal projects have been initiated and led by Housing New Zealand Corporation since 2001, in partnership with local communities, councils, and other government agencies (Macdonald and Peel 2005). These six projects involve former Housing New Zealand Corporation housing areas in Northcote (North Shore, Auckland), Tāmaki (Auckland), Clendon (Manukau), Fordlands (Rotorua), Eastern Porirua (Wellington), and Aranui (Christchurch). The projects vary in scale and scope. The redevelopment approach and initiatives mainly focus on revitalising neighbourhoods by using strength-based approaches, improvement to the physical environment and amenities, and helping residents build networks and establish a community spirit. Other initiatives include supporting employment and training opportunities, improving access to affordable community services, and supporting initiatives that increase neighbourhood safety and reduce crime (Bernacchi 2007).

Social needs are high in all project areas, which are characterised by low incomes, high unemployment, and above average crime statistics. Each of the projects has identified safety and crime as priorities to be addressed. While the community engagement and capacity-building interventions used in each of the projects vary, the philosophy behind the approach is to increase community participation in the project and develop community capacity. The community development approach is based on the belief that involving local people and resources in addressing local problems will effectively improve the well-being of individuals and increase the amount of social capital within a community. A strengths-based approach is used to identify and prioritise the strength and needs of each community (Bernacchi 2007).

Northcote, Eastern Porirua, Aranui, and Talbot Park (part of the Tāmaki project) all entail major physical redevelopment. These projects are larger in size than Fordlands and Clendon, and the sites mainly have older housing in poor condition built in the

1960s. Clendon was developed in the 1980s, and many of the issues there can be partly attributed to the construction type and design layout. For example, many properties have shared driveways, right of ways, and high fencing (Bernacchi 2007).

Talbot Park and Northcote have issues around the density and under-utilisation of land. Eastern Porirua and Aranui have ageing housing stock no longer suited to current demand. All the project sites have a large number of houses in multi-unit configurations. The units are mainly 3-bedroom, but demand has shifted to larger family homes of 4–6 bedrooms or smaller 1–2 bedroom units (Bernacchi 2007). Clendon and Fordlands are not intended for major housing redevelopment. The focus is on developing community capacity and initiating a range of minor capital improvements, for example, carports, fencing and security, landscaping, driveways, decks, and insulation and energy efficiency interventions (Bernacchi 2007).

The Housing Restructuring (Income Related Rents) Amendment Act 2000 restored the balance between social and commercial objectives in state housing. The Community Renewal Programme was one of several initiatives introduced by the then Labour Government to give greater emphasis to social outcomes. The programme goes beyond the boundaries of traditional housing redevelopment by adopting a community approach to area-based regeneration. Resident participation leads to better solutions for local circumstances. As part of the programme, the housing stock of Housing New Zealand may either be renovated, reconfigured to better meet the needs of tenants, or demolished and replaced with new dwellings (Bernacchi 2007).

4.5 The Historico-Geographical Development of the Tāmaki Area

The Tāmaki area in Auckland, which is one of the largest social housing areas in Aotearoa New Zealand, is undergoing rapid change. It stretches from the Tāmaki River in the east to St Johns and Mt Wellington in the west, and from the boundary with Glendowie in the north to Mt Wellington and the Panmure Basin (Baker 1987). It is about a 15–20 min drive from Auckland's CBD.

Te Wai o Taiki (Tāmaki River) on the eastern side of Tāmaki has sustained human life over history. Local iwi and hapu, Ngāti Pāoa, Ngāti Tai ki Tāmaki, and Ngāti Whātua Ōrākei, built thriving pa and tended kumara plantations there in pre-European times. It is estimated that at its peak, the Māori population in Tāmaki reached tens of thousands (Tāmaki Regeneration Company 2022).

The land between West Tamaki Road and Point England Road was mostly farmland until 1950 when the government began to gradually buy it (Fig. 4.6). By the late 1940s, attempts were being made to realise a vision for suburban growth in New Zealand. In 1954, the Ministry of Works published a manual for local authorities making recommendations for neighbourhood units and grouping of houses around common green space. The intention was to convince government authorities and subdividers of the need for more enlightened planning (Housing Corporation of New Zealand 1954, pp. 41–45). The original Point England, West Tamaki roads, and Taniwha Street were retained in the new plan. The area is approximately 2,000 acres and was designed for a population of over 30,000 people, with some 8,000 houses (Firth 1949, p. 79) (Fig. 4.7).

The development plan was prepared by Ernst Plischke during the period 1943–1947, when he worked for the Department of Town Planning at the Ministry of Housing. Ernst Plischke was born in 1903 in the town of Klosterneuburg near Vienna,

Fig. 4.6 Ground plan of Tāmaki in the 1930s (*Source* Based on Whitcombe and Tombs 1930s)

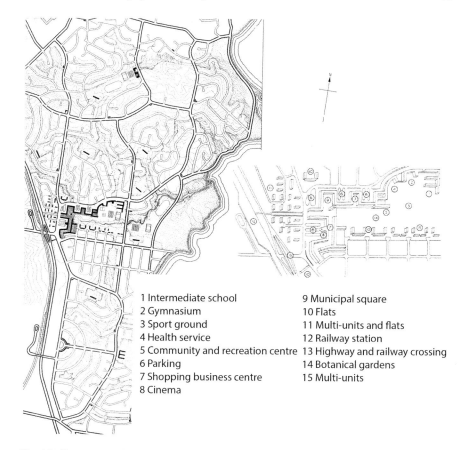

1 Intermediate school
2 Gymnasium
3 Sport ground
4 Health service
5 Community and recreation centre
6 Parking
7 Shopping business centre
8 Cinema

9 Municipal square
10 Flats
11 Multi-units and flats
12 Railway station
13 Highway and railway crossing
14 Botanical gardens
15 Multi-units

Fig. 4.7 Street system in the plan for Tāmaki and the proposed Tāmaki shopping and community centre (*Source* Based on Firth 1949, pp. 84–85)

Austria, and studied at Vienna's College of Arts and Crafts. By the time he moved to New Zealand in 1939 because of the German occupation, he was already recognised as a leader in modernist architectural design (Firth 1949). Loop roads, cul-de-sacs, and recessed courts were favoured by the planners of the time. They are particularly evident in the ground plan of the Tāmaki area. Modernist buildings and community facilities in the town centre were shown in Plischke's proposed plan. However, a large part of them were not realised.

According to Emami (2002), the plan for the Tāmaki area was influenced by the idea of neighbourhood units. While there is evidence that the concept of the neighbourhood unit emerged as early as 1923, at a joint meeting of the National Community Center Association and the American Sociological Society in Washington, DC, it was the publication of Clarence Perry's paper in the 1929 Regional Plan of New York and its Environs that led to its promotion as a planning tool (Perry 1929). Clarence Perry's monograph, entitled 'The neighborhood unit, a scheme for the arrangement for the family-life community', offered a diagrammatic model of the ideal layout for a neighbourhood of a specified population size. The model provided specific guidelines for the spatial distribution of residences, community services, streets, and businesses.

Perry's concept of the neighbourhood unit employs a variety of institutional, social, and physical design principles, influenced by popular notions from the 1920s such as separating vehicular and pedestrian traffic, and implementing arterial boundaries demarcating the inwardly focused neighbourhood cell from the greater urban lattice. The cellular nature of the neighbourhood unit allowed it to be utilised as a building block in the development of neighbourhood arrays, leading to its systematic modular usage during periods of rapid residential expansion in many countries.

The Tāmaki area was planned as a series of integrated neighbourhood units of different sizes (Emami 2002, p. 224), with single, double, and multi-family housing clustered around large areas of commonly held parkland. The dispersal of schools followed no particular pattern, with schools in the centre of the neighbourhood with access to pedestrian footpaths, and others located on the border to cover two neighbourhoods. A primary school in Tāmaki covers a neighbourhood block containing about 370 houses, which is less than the British and US examples (Emami 2002, p. 227). There are also small neighbourhoods that lack primary schools.

Green strips with a maximum width of 70 feet linked the reserves with children's playgrounds, houses, and the social and business centre of the development, providing convenient pedestrian access free from traffic hazards. It is noteworthy that in New Zealand where detached houses on big sections were favoured and so density was very much lower, these walkways or green strips did not work as they were originally designed. Generally, the distance between the houses and the shopping centre or schools was greater, and because the area was not self-contained or linked with the city by public transport, people preferred to use their own vehicles, as this provided freedom to choose schools, shopping centres, and work places further afield.

Each cul-de-sac was lined with 5–17 houses on sections averaging about a quarter acre (1000 m^2). This created a density of about 4–5 houses per acre, roughly 1/3 the density of a contemporary British new town (Emami 2002, p. 224). Like other state developments, suitable house types were selected from among the standard plans, with due consideration paid to topography, prevailing wind and view (Firth 1949, p. 66). Because houses were chosen from standard plans rather than planned according to neighbourhood principles, there was no tangible difference between Tāmaki and other developments in Auckland, or even wider New Zealand. Plischke's designs for the multi-units and flats around the town centre were not built (Fig. 4.6). Instead, detached houses with low density gave the area its special character.

Tāmaki was the first application of neighbourhood design principles in New Zealand (Emami 2002). The segregation of the town into neighbourhood units was embraced by New Zealand planners, although they made changes in the size and density of neighbourhood units. As a planned neighbourhood, the Tāmaki area is an outcome of national housing policies. The evolution of its physical characteristics reflects the prevailing New Zealand ideologies of the time as well as socioeconomic conditions. Over history, the Tāmaki area has experienced the transformation from

Māori land to rural settlement, to low density suburb, and then to medium-density suburb.

The Ministry of Works published a manual for local authorities in the 1950s recommending neighbourhood units and the grouping of houses around common green spaces (Housing Corporation of New Zealand 1954, pp. 41–45). However, the modernist development model and the associated creation of winding streets and cul-de-sacs have since come to symbolise the problems of suburbia.

4.6 Glen Innes and Its Relevant Research

Situated in the northern part of the Tāmaki area, Glen Innes is the largest neighbourhood in the area and currently experiencing intensive change, thus warranting a more detailed investigation (Figs. 4.8 and 4.9). Glen Innes was developed as a statehousing area in the 1950s and 1960s, and had the first comprehensively planned town centre in Auckland. The suburb has a significant Māori and Pacific population compared with other areas of Auckland. By 2013, Housing New Zealand was the major landowner, managing 57% of the houses in Glen Innes. In some streets, this figure is over 90%. The housing type is mainly single dwellings, and duplex and multi-unit blocks (Scott et al. 2006, 2010). Owing primarily to the unique combination of a highly connected and accessible location ripe for economic development in an area with a high proportion of state housing and high ethnic diversity (Tāmaki Regeneration Company 2017), major redevelopment projects have already taken place in Glen Innes, and more are proposed.

The redevelopment and regeneration activities in Glen Innes are project based (Fig. 4.10). Since 2000, four main programmes have been implemented: the Community Renewal Programme (2001), the Glen Innes Liveable Community Plan (2004), the Northern Glen Innes Redevelopment Project (2013), and the Tāmaki Transformation Programme (2016). These programmes vary in terms of their redevelopment scale, partnerships, decision-making processes, operations, and objectives and outcomes in relation to the physical and social environment. The evolution of these four programmes and their impacts on both the built environment and residents' experience are representative of many community renewal projects in New Zealand.

Land values and house prices in the Glen Innes area have increased quickly. The average price for a three-bedroom house was $400,000 in 2010 and $693,000 in 2014, and had risen to $1,008,590 in December 2019 (Gordon 2015; Barfoot and Thompson 2019). Three factors are contributing to this growth in land values and house prices. Firstly, Glen Innes is close to the Auckland Central area and coast, and is also well connected to the south and east Auckland. Secondly, the surrounding suburbs of St Heliers, St Johns, Glendowie, Meadowbank, Mission Bay, and Remuera are desirable places to live and home to largely well-off people. This proximity to wealthy neighbourhoods boosts Glen Innes's real estate prices. Thirdly, the ongoing regeneration is reshaping the image of Glen Innes to appeal to a demographic with

Fig. 4.8 An aerial view of Glen Innes in the northern part of the Tāmaki area, 2022. Rangitoto Island is in the background. Heatherbank Street can be seen bisecting the community in the foreground (*Source* Authors' photograph February 2022)

more disposable income than the majority of state-housing tenants. The suburb has become increasingly desirable to the middle-class market.

Figure 4.11 shows the European population has increased overall between 2006 and 2018, with some fluctuation. It increased from 34.4% in 2006 to 40.7% in 2013 and then dropped to 39.4% in 2018. Beginning in 2000, redevelopment activities implemented in northern Glen Innes and parts of Wai O Taiki Bay produced a new private housing market for buyers. Over the same period, the Māori population increased slightly, perhaps reflecting a higher birth rate and natural increase (births minus deaths). As reported by Statistics NZ, the total fertility rate for Māori women was 2.5 births per woman in the period 2012–2014, compared to the overall New Zealand rate of 2 births per woman (Statistics NZ 2016). The Pacific population in Glen Innes has declined by around 3.2% since 2006, while the area has witnessed growth in the Asian population. This can be explained by incremental gains from Asian immigration, in particular the influx of Burmese (Cooke 2010; Tan 2013).

Social housing-led urban regeneration is a dynamic process involving changes in place, policy, and social housing residents. The Tāmaki area has witnessed a long history of conflict and resistance with regard to who should govern the development and how. Cole (2015, 2017) analyses the ways in which capital displaces community, and how the local community has responded to this in Glen Innes. She argues that

Fig. 4.9 Street system in Glen Innes, 2021 (*Source* Auckland Council 2021)

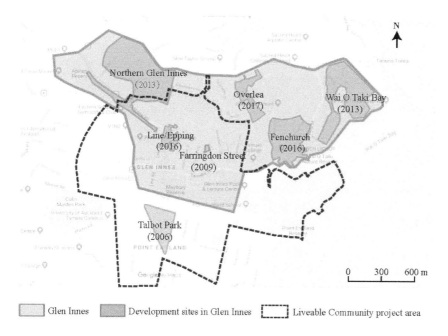

Fig. 4.10 Locations of social housing redevelopment sites in Glen Innes in 2020 (*Source* Based on Tāmaki Regeneration Company 2020a, b)

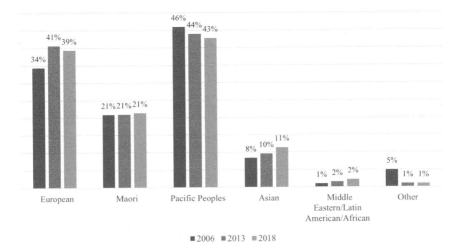

Fig. 4.11 Ethnic breakdown and change between 2006 and 2018 in Glen Innes (*Source* Statistics New Zealand 2018)

capital achieves its aim through evicting local residents from their community and land, using discursive devices to justify its actions. In response, the local community has formulated collective resistance to the process of capital accumulation. In another study based on local residents' narratives, Gordon (2015; Gordon et al. 2017) explores the implementation of two state-led gentrification programmes, Tāmaki Redevelopment and Creating Communities in Glen Innes, concluding that gentrification has resulted in a rapid rate of displacement and threatened residents' right to the city. With regard to the power of collective action, Scott (2013) explores how voluntary associations have successfully influenced the process of urban renewal in the Tāmaki area.

These critiques present a good understanding of community changes in Tāmaki based on an analysis of gentrification and displacement, and promote reflection on current regeneration programmes. However, the primary focuses are social and community issues and the research falls mainly within the fields of geography and sociology. As such, the physical changes and the interaction between physical changes, policy and planning, and local residents' experiences are not fully examined.

Research undertaken in the field of urban planning in response to the types of social conflict and issues discussed above is limited. The built environment in urban and rural areas changes over time. Urban planning is by its very nature an intervention in these changes. Providing linkages between knowledge and action, and policies and future outcomes, planning is an essential element of policy and administrative systems confronting challenges related to how to deal with the relationship between places and the people living in them (Pugh 1980). Its role is to effectively achieve the goals and objectives set out in policies through making various kinds of plans, such as regional plans, unitary plans, and community-based regeneration plans (Alterman and MacRae 1983; Friedmann and Hudson 1974; Solesbury 2013). Therefore, understanding the role of planning in the process of urban regeneration requires placing it in the broader context of urban policies made by local and/or central government.

To understand how the social conflict and problems described above are both produced by and responded to in the planning and policy fields, this study deploys the theory of justice and, more precisely, spatial justice to critically review and reflect on the process of social housing redevelopment in Glen Innes. Although many researchers argue that justice should help guide planning practice, the extent to which current planning policies themselves help to achieve justice requires further clarification.

4.7 Summary

Social housing-led regeneration policies and planning seek the redistribution of society's benefits and burdens through the reconstruction of the physical environment. The community renewal and regeneration projects in Tāmaki are part of the planning and housing policy targeted at former state-housing developments. The aim is to replace existing state housing with a medium-density mix of social housing, affordable housing, and higher-cost homes (Tāmaki Regeneration Company 2017).

Not surprisingly, there is a tension between people- and place-based policies in terms of distinguishing the aims and intended beneficiaries of state intervention in housing and regeneration programmes (Dabinett et al. 2001; Griggs et al. 2008). Researchers in favour of place-based policies argue that it is unjust for people to be 'worse-off simply because of where they live' (Turok 2004, p. 406), while those in favour of people-based policies insist that spatial concentrations need to be understood and tackled as the outcome of more fundamental problems (Ferrari 2012).

Critics also question the high social cost of privatisation by stealth, displacement of marginalised people, and for whom the 'healthier and safer community' is intended (Johnson 2014, p. 11). For example, in 2013, in the Northern Glen Innes redevelopment in Tāmaki, a net loss of at least 39 social housing units occurred in the process of replacing the existing 156 state houses with 260 new homes, which included 78 state houses and 39 other social housing properties. While Housing New Zealand (2017) believes that redevelopment is essential to improve our houses and to help build a healthier and safer community, the question remains—for whom?

Another criticism relates to the relocation of poor people from state-housing areas. Redeveloping state-housing areas is regarded as a way of reducing the concentration of disadvantaged and anti-social behaviours. However, this process raises the question: 'Where do you decant these poor people to if you are also concerned about concentrations of poor people in such places as South Auckland?' (Johnson 2014, p. 11).

The third criticism, stemming from the policymaking process for social housing redevelopment, questions the rushed nature of programmes. For example, Johnson (2014) points out that the original home and household report for the government was written in five weeks, arguing that such a short period is inadequate for the purpose of making recommendations.

Critiques of these measures and the driving force behind them—neoliberalism—have been advanced over the past two decades by sociologists, geographers, and political philosophers (Johnson 2014). It is evident that the mission to provide affordable housing and social housing for low-income families is more difficult in a neoliberalist context, which privileges profit based on real estate (Santoro 2015).

In Auckland, urban redevelopment and revitalisation have been implemented in the Tāmaki area with the aim of replacing existing state housing with a mix of social housing, affordable housing, and higher-cost homes (Tāmaki Regeneration Company 2017). In relation to a spatial examination of the processes of social and physical reconfiguration in the Tāmaki area, this book not only documents and explains New Zealand planning experiences and lessons in state-housing community renewal, but also advances spatial justice research and practice.

References

Alterman R, MacRae JD (1983) Planning and policy analysis converging or diverging trends? J Am Plann Assoc 49(2):200–215

Atkinson R (1999) Discourses of partnership and empowerment in contemporary British urban regeneration. Urban Stud 36(1):59–72

Atkinson R (2003) Addressing urban social exclusion through community involvement in urban regeneration. Urban Renaissance 1:101–119

Auckland City Council (1971) Freemans Bay planning review. Auckland City Council, Auckland

Auckland City Council (1976) Auckland's historical background, 3rd edn. Auckland City Council, Auckland

Auckland Council (2022) GeoMaps mapping service. https://www.aucklandcouncil.govt.nz/geospatial/geomaps/Pages/default.aspx. Accessed 25 Oct 2022

August M (2014a) Speculating social housing: mixed-income public housing redevelopment in Toronto's Regent Park and Don Mount Court. Dissertation, University of Toronto, Canada

August M (2014b) Challenging the rhetoric of stigmatization: the benefits of concentrated poverty in Toronto's Regent Park. Environ Plan a: Econ Space 46(6):1317–1333

Bailey N (2005) Housing-led regeneration: the Glasgow experience. In: Özdemir TÖ (ed) Istanbul 2004 International Regeneration Symposium: Workshop of Küçükçekmece District. Kucukcekmece Municipality Publication, Istanbul, Turkey, pp 207–213

Baker RA (1987) From bush to borough: an illustrated history of the Mount Wellington area. Tāmaki City Council, Auckland, New Zealand

Barfoot and Thompson (2019) Suburb report: rent, house prices and yield. https://www.barfoot.co.nz/market-reports/2019/december/suburb-report. Accessed 2 Oct 2019

Bernacchi A (2007) Housing New Zealand community renewal programme. International Cities, Town Centres and Communities Society Inc. 2007 Conference 'Cities on the Edge', North Shore City, Auckland, New Zealand, 26–29 June 2007

Bikey J (2010) Welfare state: the state of New Zealand social welfare housing. Dissertation, University of Auckland, Auckland, New Zealand

Bland WB (1942) Slums of Auckland. The Progressive Publishing Society, Wellington

Brail S, Lorinc J, Louis-Mcburnie K, Sanz L (2021) Regent Park: a progress report. https://metcal ffoundation.com/publication/regent-park-a-progress-report/. Accessed 18 Mar 2023

Carter A, Roberts P (2000) Strategy and partnership in urban regeneration. In: Roberts P, Sykes H (eds) Urban regeneration: a handbook. Sage, London, England

Cole V (2015) 'We shall not be moved': community displacement and dissensus in Glen Innes, Tamaki Makaurau. Dissertation, University of Auckland

Cole V (2017) Why landlords and investors love the Auckland unitary plan, and why you shouldn't. Economic and Social Research Aotearoa. https://www.google.com/search?client=safari&rls= en&q=Why+landlords+and+investors+love+the+auckland+unitary+plan,+and+why+you+sho uldn%27t&ie=UTF-8&oe=UTF-8. Accessed 20 Oct 2022

Cook N (1966) Freemans Bay maisonette flats. City Architect's Department, Auckland City Council, Auckland

Cooke D (2010) Corporate colonizing. In: Cooke D, Hill C, Baskett P, Irwin R (eds) Beyond the free market: rebuilding a just society in New Zealand. Dunmore, Auckland, New Zealand, pp 37–41

Dabinett G, Lawless P, Rhodes J, Tyler P (2001) A review of the evidence base for regeneration policy and practice. Office of the Deputy Prime Minister, London, England

Dalia Lichfield Associates (1992) Urban regeneration for the 1990s. Dalia Lichfield Associates, London, England

De Schutter J, Riemer M (2009) Participatory decision-making models in the context of environmental justice: are they working? In: Proceedings of the 2009 Amsterdam conference on the human dimensions of global environmental change. Amsterdam, Netherlands

Dodd R (1972a) Urban renewal: a case history of Freemans Bay, Auckland, Part 1. Town Plan Q 28(August):13–19

Dodd R (1972b) Urban renewal: a case history of Freemans Bay, Auckland, Part 2. Town Plan Q 29(September):7–16

Emami M (2002) Neighbourhood planning: from Radburn to Tamaki. In: Haarhoff E, Brand D, Aitken-Rose E (eds) Southern crossing: proceedings for the sixth Australasian urban history/ planning history conference. University of Auckland, Auckland, pp 217–229

Evans G, Shaw P (2004) The contribution of culture to regeneration in the UK: a review of evidence. DCMS, London, England

Fernback J (2005) Information technology, networks and community voices: social inclusion for urban regeneration. Information, Community and Society 8(4):482–502

Ferrari E (2012) Competing ideas of social justice and space: locating critiques of housing renewal in theory and in practice. Int J Hous Policy 12(3):263–280

Firth CH (1949) State housing in New Zealand. Ministry of Works, Wellington

Flood J (2003) The case of Sydney, Australia. In: Understanding slums: case studies for the global report on human settlements, United Nations Habitat, Nairobi, Kenya

Forrest J (1967) Residential renewal in Australia: comparisons with New Zealand. Proceedings from the Fifth New Zealand Geography Conference, Auckland

Friedmann J, Hudson B (1974) Knowledge and action: a guide to planning theory. J Am Inst Plann 40(1):2–16

Glucksberg L (2017) 'The blue bit, that was my bedroom': rubble, displacement and regeneration in inner-city London. In: Watt P, Smets P (eds) Social housing and urban renewal. Emerald Publishing Limited, Bingley, United Kingdom, pp 69–103

Gordon R (2015) State-led gentrification and impacts on residents and community in Glen Innes, Auckland. Dissertation, University of Auckland

Gordon R, Collins FL, Kearns R (2017) 'It is the people that have made Glen Innes': state-led gentrification and the reconfiguration of urban life in Auckland. Int J Urban Reg Res 41(5):767–785

Greaves A (2011) Urban regeneration in Toronto: rebuilding the social in Regent Park. Dissertation, Queen's University, Kingston, Canada

Griggs J, Whitworth A, Walker R et al (2008) Person-or place-based policies to tackle disadvantage? Not knowing what works. Joseph Rowntree Foundation, York, England

Hackworth J (2002) Postrecession gentrification in New York city. Urban Affairs Review 37(6):815–843

Hackworth J, Moriah A (2006) Neoliberalism, contingency and urban policy: the case of social housing in Ontario. Int J Urban Reg Res 30(3):510–527

Hanlon J (2010) Success by design: HOPE VI, new urbanism, and the neoliberal transformation of public housing in the United States. Environ Plan a: Econ Space 42(1):80–98

Harloe M (2008) The people's home?: social rented housing in Europe and America. Wiley, Hoboken, NJ

Hemphill L, Berry J, McGreal S (2004) An indicator-based approach to measuring sustainable urban regeneration performance: Part 1, conceptual foundations and methodological framework. Urban Stud 41(4):725–755

Hibbitt K, Jones P, Meegan R (2001) Tackling social exclusion: the role of social capital in urban regeneration on Merseyside—from mistrust to trust? Eur Plan Stud 9(2):141–161

Housing Corporation of New Zealand (1954) Housing the citizen: a manual for local authorities. Government Printer, Wellington, New Zealand

Housing New Zealand (2017) Annual report 2016/17. https://kaingaora.govt.nz/assets/Publications/Annual-report/HNZ16117-Annual-Report-2016-2017.pdf. Accessed 20 Oct 2022

Jahiu L, Cinnamon J (2022) Media coverage and territorial stigmatization: an analysis of crime news articles and crime statistics in Toronto. GeoJournal 87(6):4547–4564

Jackson E, Butler T (2015) Revisiting 'social tectonics': the middle classes and social mix in gentrifying neighbourhoods. Urban Studies 52(13):2349–2365

James RK (2010) From 'slum clearance' to 'revitalisation': planning, expertise and moral regulation in Toronto's Regent Park. Plan Perspect 25(1):69–86

Johnson A (2014) The new politics of social housing. http://www.salvationarmy.org.nz/sites/default/files/uploads/20140723SPPUAlanJohnsonspeechMar14.pdf. Accessed 20 Oct 2022

Jones D (2009) (Almost) Everything old is new again as New Zealand embraces urban regeneration. https://www.calibregroup.com/engage/article/2019/03/04/almost-everything-old-is-new-again-as-new-zealand-embraces-urban-regeneration. Accessed 20 Oct 2022

Korkmaz C, Balaban O (2020) Sustainability of urban regeneration in Turkey: assessing the performance of the North Ankara urban regeneration project. Habitat Int 95:1–4

Krüger A (1993) Local communities and urban regeneration: the contribution of community education. Commun Dev J 28(4):342–354

Macdonald J, Peel K (2005) New Zealand's community renewal programme in an international context: a literature review. http://www.hnzc.co.nz/. Accessed 20 October 2022

Malpass P, Murie A (1982) Housing policy and practice. Macmillan, London

McKay B, Stevens A (2014) Beyond the state: New Zealand state houses from modest to modern. Penguin, Auckland, New Zealand

Nairn R (2013) The ownership of multi-unit housing: unit title and how we got there. Dissertation, University of Auckland

Perkins HC, Mackay M, Levy D, Campbell M, Taylor N, Hills R, Johnston K (2019) Revealing regional regeneration projects in three small towns in Aotearoa-New Zealand. NZ Geogr 75(3):140–151

Perry CA (1929) The neighborhood unit, a scheme of arrangement for the family life community. Regional Survey of New York and its Environs. Monograph 1, vol 7. Russell Sage Foundation, New York

Pugh C (1980) Housing in capitalist societies. Gower, Farnborough, England

Purdy R S (2003) From place of hope to outcast space: territorial regulation and tenant resistance in Regent Park housing project, 1949–2001. Dissertation, Queen's University, Kingston, Canada

Roberts P, Sykes H (eds) (2000) Urban regeneration: a handbook. Sage, London, England

Rogers D (2012) The politics of time and space within market-centric urban policy: the case of the Bonnyrigg Living Communities project. Polymath: Interdisc Arts Sci J 2(3):16–34

Rogers D (2013) Urban and social planning through public–private partnership: the case of the Bonnyrigg Living Communities project, Sydney, Australia. Int Soc City Reg Planners Rev 9:142–155

Rossi U, Vanolo A (2013) The politics and geographies of actually existing regeneration. In: Leary ME, McCarthy J (eds) The Routledge companion to urban regeneration. Routledge, London, England, pp 159–167

Rowe DJ, Dunn JR (2015) Tenure-mix in Toronto: resident attitudes and experience in the Regent Park community. Hous Stud 30(8):1257–1280

Sahak J (2008) Race, space and place: exploring Toronto's Regent Park from a Marxist perspective. Dissertation, Ryerson University Toronto, Canada

Santoro PF (2015) Urban planning instruments for promoting social interest housing: from zoning to obligatory percentages in São Paulo, Brazil, in dialog with Bogotá, Colombia. Revista Brasileira de Estudos Urbanos e Regionais (RBEUR) 17(2):99–117

Schrader B (2005) We call it home: a history of state housing in New Zealand. Reed, Auckland, New Zealand

Scott K (2013) The politics of influence: an anthropological analysis of collective political action in contemporary democracy. Dissertation, University of Auckland

Scott K, Shaw A, Bava C (2006) Liveable communities, healthy environments or 'slumification' in Glen Innes, Auckland, New Zealand. http://citeseerx.ist.psu.edu/viewdoc/download?doi=10.1.1.527.2560&rep=rep1&type=pdf. Accessed 20 Oct 2022

Scott K, Shaw A, Bava C (2010) Social equity and social housing densification in Glen Innes, New Zealand: a political ecology approach. In: Dürr E, Jaffe R (eds) Urban pollution: cultural meanings, social practices. Berghahn, Oxford, England, pp 178–197

Sharp J, Pollock V, Paddison R (2005) Just art for a just city: public art and social inclusion in urban regeneration. Urban Studies 42(5–6):1001–1023

Simpson WR (1938) Workers' housing—a scheme for New Zealand. Auckland University Labour Club Bulletin, Unicorn Press, Auckland

Smith N (2006) Gentrification generalized: from local anomaly to urban 'regeneration' as global urban strategy. In: Fisher M, Downey G (eds) Frontiers of capital: ethnographic reflections on the new economy. Duke University Press, Durham, England, pp 191–208

Solesbury W (2013) Policy in urban planning: structure plans, programmes and local plans, vol 8. Elsevier, Oxford, England

Speak S (2000) Children in urban regeneration: foundations for sustainable participation. Commun Dev J 35(1):31–40

Statistics New Zealand (2016) http://archive.stats.govt.nz/browse_for_stats/population/estimates_and_projections/projections-overview/nat-maori-proj.aspx. Accessed 20 Oct 2022

Statistics New Zealand (2018) 2018 Census ethnic group summaries. Retrieved from https://www.stats.govt.nz/tools/2018-census-ethnic-group-summaries/. Accessed 20 Oct 2022

Tāmaki Regeneration Company (2017) Briefing to incoming ministers. https://www.tamakiregeneration.co.nz/sites/default/files/site-files/T%C4%81maki%20Redevelopment%20Company_Briefing%20to%20Incoming%20Ministers.pdf. Accessed 20 Oct 2022

Tāmaki Regeneration Company (2020a) Statement of performance expectations 2020–2021. https://www.tamakiregeneration.co.nz/sites/default/files/site-files/TRC%20SPE%2020a20-2021_FINAL.pdf. Accessed 20 Oct 2022

Tāmaki Regeneration Company (2020b) Tāmaki is where Auckland's story began. https://tamakiregeneration.co.nz/. Accessed 20 Oct 2022

Tāmaki Regeneration Company (2022) Tāmaki is where Auckland's story began. https://tamakiregeneration.co.nz/. Accessed 20 October 2022

Tan L (2013) Burmese largest group of refugees and least likely to leave. The New Zealand Herald, 3 April 2013. http://www.nzherald.co.nz/nz/news/article.cfm?c_id=1&objectid=10875026. Accessed 20 Oct 2022

Terrini V (1972) Freemans Bay—notes on urban renewal. Town Plan Q 44:17–19

Toronto City Council (2007) Regent Park secondary plan. Toronto City Council City Planning, Toronto

Turok I (2004) The rationale for area-based policies: lessons from international experience. In: Robinson P, McCarthy J, Foster C (eds) Urban reconstruction in the developing world. Heinemann, Sandown, Australia, pp 405–412

Vale LJ (2018) 'The fall of Orchard Park, the rise of Orchard Gardens', after the projects: public housing redevelopment and the governance of the poorest Americans. https://doi.org/10.1093/oso/9780190624330.003.0009. Accessed 10 Mar 2023

Watt P, Smets P (2017) Social housing and urban renewal: an introduction. In: Watt P, Smets P (eds) Social housing and urban renewal: a cross-national perspective. Emerald Publishing Limited, United Kingdom, pp 1–36

Woo Y (2014) Two tails of housing-led urban regeneration policy network: the UK and South Korea. Int Plan Stud 19(1):77–98

Chapter 5
Historico-Geographical Analysis of Spatial Differentiations

Abstract Historico-geographical mapping and geo-spatial techniques seek to reveal the spatial structure of both physical and social urban landscapes. Through examining the existing physical fabric of the city, maps, and ground plans, geographical morphological analysis helps to characterise urban manifestations and decipher the inherent information they contain about the social agents of change responsible for urban (re)development. Ground plan analysis, which is specifically used to distinguish and characterise the spatial differentiation of the urban landscape, leads to the identification of plan units. The analytical map of plan units then provides a template against which other layers of the community, including social, economic, environmental, and transport, can be mapped and analysed. For instance, the capital values of individual properties in Glen Innes were relatively homogenous before redevelopment. The community redevelopment has induced an uneven distribution of capital values, a pattern that coincides with the configuration of plan units. The map of plan units also provides an informed understanding of the structure of the urban landscape to support the formulation of process strategies for achieving both valued spatial–temporal and representational outcomes.

Keywords Urban morphology · Spatial differentiations · Social housing redevelopment · Tāmaki · Glen Innes

Soja (2000) notes that 'we look to the past, then, with decidedly contemporary eyes, and with the primary goal of enhancing our practical and theoretical understanding of the most recent episode in the social production of city space' (p. 4). The notion of space is more valued in the theory of spatial justice than in previous theories of justice. As a product, space bears the traces of the past, and is inscribed historically by what has happened in a particular spot or place. Present space is also immediately impacted by current actuality. Social housing redevelopment, as a form of urban development, generates a series of results. Spatial results enable us to recognise the intentions and outcomes of policies, market activities, and urban planning, and the impact on individuals and society. Therefore, understanding the generative process of space is a necessary dimension of exploring the production of justice and injustice. Geographical morphological analysis provides an opportunity to explore spatial practices by systematically examining the historical and geographical changes in space.

5.1 Geographical-Morphological Analysis of Perceived Space

In the early part of the nineteenth century, the political and economic system in New Zealand was shaped by British traditions and laissez-faire economic ideas prevailed. Commercial imperatives were manifested in all aspects of the political and economic system, including the process of urban development. Although some surveyors attempted to propose alternative layouts to embrace public space, these ideas were not taken up due to the dominant belief that public use land was a waste of a profit-making resource. The early colonial cities experienced square-grid town development that continued well into the twentieth century. However, this type of development quickly produced complex town planning problems in these cities (Barry-Martin 1956).

The resulting problems led to a growing realisation of the need for town planning and enactment of legislation regulating land use. Drawing on examples from England and Australia, the central government in New Zealand implemented several rules regulating town planning, for example, the Municipal Corporations Ordinance of 1842, the New Zealand Waste Lands Act of 1858, and the Plans of Towns Regulation Act of 1875. However, these only applied to new Crown settlements (New Zealand Productivity Commission 2015).

Glen Innes has experienced similar historical development to the wider Tāmaki area. In relation to the mechanisms of form production, the development of Glen Innes can be categorised into four distinct morphological periods: embryo development period (pre-1949), early post-war development (1950–1969), repletion and consolidation (1970–1999), and transformation and regeneration (post-2000).

5.2 Changing Spatial Characteristics in Glen Innes

5.2.1 Embryo Development (Pre-1949): From Māori Land to Private Estate

In pre-European times, Glen Innes was a fortified Māori settlement. By the early 1840s, the area was made up of scrub-covered hills and valleys. Before roads were built, access to the area was by tracks running along ridges extending through Newmarket and Remuera, or by boat along the Purewa Creek.

After the signing of the Treaty of Waitangi, William Innes Taylor acquired the original Glen Innes estate, which he owned from 1843 to 1862. This estate was bounded to the north by a line extending almost to Riddell Road, by an imaginary line going through Sierra Street and then along Line Road, to the south-west by Taniwha Street, and to the east by the Tāmaki River and Omaru Creek, encompassing about 760 acres in total (Fig. 5.1). The owner named his estate 'Glen Innes' after himself and his mother, whose family name was 'Innes'. The suburb now called Glen Innes occupies half of the original Taylor estate. The northern part of this estate now forms part of the suburb of Glendowie (Jackson 1978). At the beginning of the twentieth century, the Taylor family gradually started to sell off their land. Around 1945, the family sold the last remaining piece to the government, which used most of the area to provide state housing for returning soldiers after World War II (Jackson 1978).

West Tāmaki Road, Line Road, and Point England Road were the earliest roads in Glen Innes and already existed in the 1840s. West Tamaki Road and Point England Road stretch from east to west, while Line Road extends from north to south. In 1910, a street whose name is uncertain was built parallel to Point England Road, between Line Road and the coastline. Taylor Street was built in the 1920s, connecting the current Line Road and West Tamaki Road. It was curve-shaped, one segment running from north to south, and the other from east to west. By 1930, the current road network was largely formed (Fig. 5.1). In the 1930s, a railway station was built next to the Glen Innes town centre. This morphological frame formed the foundation for the future development of Glen Innes. The expansion of the road network reflected Glen Innes' gradual engagement in the trend towards suburbanisation in Auckland, which emerged from the 1920s.

5.2.2 Post-War Development (1950–1969): Building the Kiwi Dream

Development during the period spanning the 1940s to the 1960s was significantly influenced by a major central government policy and local government decision-making, both related to suburbanisation (Auckland Council 2019). The government's state-housing programme began with the aim of constructing single-unit suburban homes for relief workers in the mid-1930s. The government continued to build public housing through the 1950s and also provided loans to encourage the setting up of housing firms. In the 1950s, Auckland itself was committed to building its transport system on motorways rather than developing a comprehensive public transport system. This policy encouraged the use of private motor vehicles, allowing people to live in detached houses on large plots in the suburbs. The development of Glen Innes in this period corresponded to Auckland's urban expansion in the 1950s and 1960s (Arbury 2005; Auckland Council 2019).

Extensive development took place in this period. Subdivision of large tracts of land and parcellation were the main trends. Farmland was quickly divided into parcels and

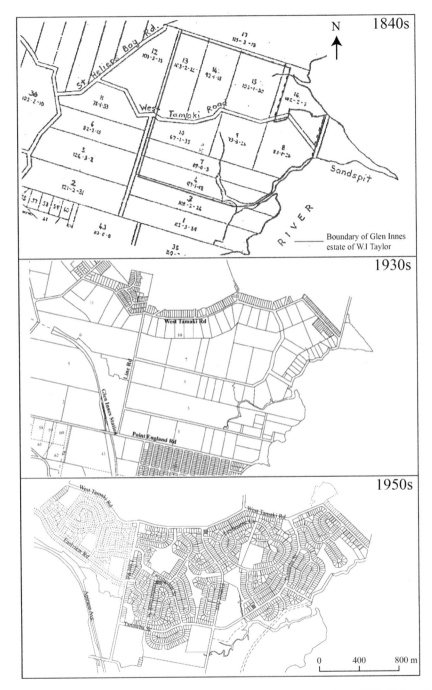

Fig. 5.1 Glen Innes in the 1840s, 1930s and 1950s (*Source* Based on Jackson 1978, Whitcombe and Tombs 1930 and Auckland City Council 1952)

sold to the government and private owners. Within two decades, plots were occupied by spacious single-family houses (Fig. 5.1). Houses were generally rectangular in plan and contained between two and five bedrooms. Elevations were plain without decoration (Elkink and Pringle 2011). The style of the early 1960s house was akin to those of the 1950s, but with more variation in plan forms (Elkink and Pringle 2011). Garages became more common during the early 1960s. A low roof pitch, more glazing (often floor to ceiling), and multiple direct access points to the outdoors were considered typical features of a modern house (Fig. 5.2).

Designated as a main area for state housing, the whole Tāmaki area including Glen Innes subsequently experienced rapid growth. The land east of Line Road was developed first, while the subdivision plan for the west of Line Road was not implemented until later. Overall, construction during this period formed the morphological structure of Glen Innes. Even later construction during the repletion and consolidation period (the 1970s–2000) was based on the plan made in this period. Hundreds of state houses were built for a large number of immigrants from the Pacific Islands, who were encouraged to move to New Zealand to fill the gap in unskilled labour. Most of the residents were therefore 'blue collar' workers (Friesen 2009, p. 60). Some of these low-income families did not have a family vehicle, which stimulated the development of shops and a thriving town centre.

In August 1955, the Auckland City Council designed a town centre in Glen Innes to serve residents living in the eastern suburbs. It was the first comprehensively planned town centre of its size in Auckland. By 1960, 20 shops had opened for

Fig. 5.2 Post-war state houses in Glen Innes (*Source* Auckland Libraries 2022a. Reproduced with permission)

business and a further 16 were under construction (Glen Innes Business Association 2016). Public facilities such as underground power, telephone lines, the Glen Taylor School, the community library, a council owned car park with 118 parking spaces, and a vehicle testing station were also built during this period. Glen Innes became a thriving village with women and men's fashion and footwear outlets, jewellers, tearooms, and dairies (Fig. 5.3).

The street system was expanded and changed during this period. The road between Point England Road and the former Taylor Street was removed. The direction of the eastern segment of Taylor Street was altered and became the current Taniwha Street. More streets and roads were built with the construction of state houses, with most designed as curvilinear. The main roads including West Tamaki Road, Line Road, Taniwha Street, and others formed a morphological frame for neighbourhood construction that remained a persistent influence on subsequent developments.

The main roads can be characterised as early built and less curved and interconnected. Functioning as the skeleton of Glen Innes, their construction significantly influenced the direction of housing expansion, land values, and the distribution of different ownership, including state and private houses. For example, the earliest buildings were located at the intersection of West Tamaki Road and Line Road.

Fig. 5.3 Glen Innes town centre in 1961 (*Source* Auckland Libraries 2022b. Reproduced with permission)

The community through streets, mainly distributed within the residential areas and commercial areas, connects different housing areas and shops. They still make up the largest proportion of the street network in Glen Innes, shaping the street blocks in neighbourhoods. Community cul-de-sacs are also common in this area. Cul-de-sacs are used to maximise the use of land and normally end in the shape of a round. They are widely distributed within the street blocks in Glen Innes. Lanes are designed to provide shortcuts between large street blocks; they are paved but designed for pedestrians only.

The plot pattern and building types in the different blocks demonstrate continuity and homogeneity in this residential area. Approximately, rectangular plots with short sides facing the street and a back-to-back plot arrangement were the dominant plot pattern. One-storey detached houses with front and back gardens invariably lined the curving streets. Almost all of the street blocks were characterised by curving streets and back-to-back plot grouping. A street block constitutes a group of plots bounded by street lines (Conzen 1960). Figure 5.4 shows five super-street blocks bounded by axial streets and a number of sub-street blocks bounded by through streets.

Almost all buildings in Glen Innes were built after 1900 (Fig. 5.5). The largest proportion of houses were built during the 1950s and the 1960s, while the 1970s witnessed little house construction. Houses built after 2000 show different floor coverage and plot patterns. The year 2000 represents a milestone when major redevelopment projects began to be implemented. The distribution of building types thus provides simple clues to the historical development of Glen Innes.

The characteristics and quality of the state houses built in this period were strongly influenced by New Zealand's economic status after World War II. Due to the war, building materials including copper, steel, zinc, and electrical cable were in short supply, which in turn led to a big housing shortage in the post-war period (Elkink and Pringle 2011). To address this issue, the government began to actively build state

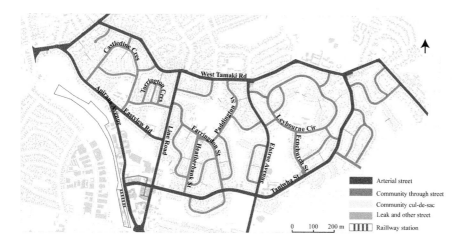

Fig. 5.4 Street blocks in Glen Innes (*Source* Based on Auckland Council 2020)

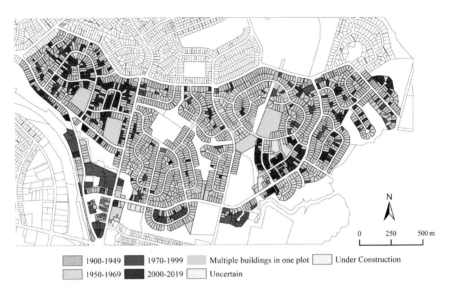

1900-1949   1970-1999   Multiple buildings in one plot   Under Construction
1950-1969   2000-2019   Uncertain

Fig. 5.5 Building types in Glen Innes (*Sources* Based on Corelogic 2020 and authors' fieldwork, April 2020)

houses from the 1940s to the 1960s. In the 1940s, government-funded state houses made up about 28% of new domestic construction. By the end of the 1950s, the figure had fallen to 20% as the gap between housing supply and demand reduced. In the 1960s, this figure decreased to 10% (Elkink and Pringle 2011). A large number of state houses significantly impacted the building type for private houses from the 1940s to 1960s, creating the 'state house style' that typifies the houses built during this period.

Due to the social and economic conditions, state houses and most private houses were built in the most cost-effective way. Most had a practical layout and were structurally very sound. Their simple design was usually a square or rectangle with one roof line. Most state houses were located in the suburbs, with shops, amenities, and greenspace. They largely took the form of back-to-back detached houses with a small front yard and back yard, as seen in the Glen Innes, Point England, and Panmure areas in Tāmaki. Some were designed as multi-units set out in a star shape, as in Talbot Park in the area now known as Point England and Freemans Park (Philip Block) in Freemans Bay.

After 1949 when the National Party came into office, the new government encouraged private ownership by providing low-cost finance for new building construction, particularly when the new construction followed the state house designs. The government also initiated legislation that allowed state house tenants to buy their state houses. These two approaches encouraged the development of private ownership during the period from the mid-1950s to the early 1960s. Meanwhile, due to the conditions placed on government financial support, many private housings built during the 1940s and 1950s were similar to state houses in appearance (Elkink and Pringle 2011). Designated as a main area for state housing, around 50% of the houses built in the Tāmaki area during this period were state houses. The 'state housing style' was a significant feature of the physical fabric in Glen Innes, as shown by the homogenous housing type before redevelopment.

5.2.3 Repletion and Consolidation (1970–1999): Declining Economy and Rundown Neighbourhoods

The construction of residential buildings, the town centre, and the street system in the 1950s and 1960s formed the physical layout of Glen Innes. Development during the repletion and consolidation period (1970s–1999) was mostly confined within the plan made in the previous post-war period. However, during the 1970s and 1980s, Glen Innes gradually lost economic ground due to the development of the Pakuranga Plaza shopping mall and the St. Johns Centre. The stock market crash of 1987 hit the manufacturing sector in New Zealand, resulting in high unemployment in Glen Innes. Some researchers further argue that the decision to encourage highly liberalised international trade and tight restrictions on shop-trading hours may also have reduced the competitiveness of local manufacturers, which indirectly affected workers living in Glen Innes (Glen Innes Business Association 2016). By the early 1990s, the unemployment rate in the area had increased to 27%, one of the highest in Auckland. Glen Innes came to be recognised as a socioeconomically deprived area with high levels of crime and alcohol and drug abuse.

The morphological period from 1970 to 1999 was thus a period of repletion and consolidation. There were about 183 houses were built in this period. Density, plot pattern, and the street network remained largely unchanged until the late 1990s. However, major change subsequently took place in the post-2000 period of transformation and regeneration when intensification and redevelopment became the keywords in Auckland's strategies for development.

5.2.4 Transformation and Regeneration (After 2000): Intensification and Mixed Building Type

In the past 20 years, changes in zoning ordinances have impacted Glen Innes. The main trends have been increasing density and intensity and diverse housing forms. When state houses were built, the lot sizes varied from $600\,m^2$ to $1,000\,m^2$ and most of the houses were one-storey (Jackson 1965). However, sites have become increasingly smaller and higher building heights now apply. At the same time, apartments, terrace houses, and attached houses have been introduced to Glen Innes. As shown in Table 5.1, the intensity of development has increased in recent years.

Table 5.1 Zoning codes and ordinances for Glen Innes in the past 20 years

Plans	Year	Zones	Site area	Floor area	Building height	Density
Auckland Isthmus District Plan	1999	Residential 5	500 m^2	None	Up to 2 storeys, max. 8 m	Low
		Residential 6a	375 m^2	Studio units: 35 m^2 1-bedroom units 45 m^2 2-bedroom units: 70 m^2 3 bedrooms: 90 m^2	Up to 2 storeys, max. 8 m	Medium
		Residential 6b	300 m^2	Studio units: 35 m^2 1-bedroom units 45 m^2 2-bedroom units: 70 m^2 3 bedrooms: 90 m^2	Up to 3 storeys, max. 10 m	Medium
Auckland Isthmus District Plan (Plan Change 58, 61)	2004	Residential 8a	Up to 1 unit per 150 m^2	Max. 70% of net site area	Up to 3 storeys, max. 11 m	Medium–high
		Residential 8b	Up to 1 unit per 100 m^2	Max. 80% of net site area	Up to 4 storeys, max. 14 m	Medium–high
Unitary Plan	2016	Mixed Housing Suburban Zone	None	Min. 30 m^2 for studio dwellings; Min. 45 m^2 for 1 or more-bedroom dwellings	Up to 2 storeys, max. 8 m	Medium
		Mixed Housing Urban Zone	None	Min. 30 m^2 for studio dwellings; Min. 45 m^2 for 1 or more-bedroom dwellings	Up to 3 storeys, max. 11 m	Reasonably high
		Terrace Housing and Apartment Building Zone	None	Min. 30 m^2 for studio dwellings; Min. 45 m^2 for 1 or more-bedroom dwellings	Up to 5, 6, or 7 storeys, max. 16 m	High

In the Auckland Council District Plan Isthmus Section released in 1999, most of Glen Innes was zoned Residential 6, which allows for less spacious units, often more diverse in form, than traditional residential units. The Residential 6 zone was further divided into two sub-zones, Residential 6a and 6b, with different rules for density and height. The Residential 6a zone allowed for sites 75 m^2 bigger than in the Residential 6b zone, with a density of one residential unit for every 375 m^2 of site area. Height limits in these two sub-zones also varied. In the Residential 6a zone, intended for one or two-storey development, a height limit of 8 m is applied. An increased height limit of 10 m and a more intense development style applied to sites in the Residential 6a zone. This zone was intended to accommodate up to three storeys of development.

In 2000, Glen Innes was selected as an area suitable for intensification due to its convenient location and great potential for growth in accordance with the liveable communities strategy, part of the Auckland City Growth Management Strategy. As defined by the Ministry for the Environment, a liveable urban environment is 'a place that is good to live, work and play—a place that meets the needs and expectations of the people who live there' (Ministry for the Environment 2002, p. 2). The core of the liveable community concept is an intensive mix of different activities, including businesses, shops, entertainment, and housing located close to public transport (Ministry for the Environment 2002).

In 2004, Glen Innes was duly rezoned to Residential 8 in plan change number 58 to allow higher density. Residential 8 is characterised as medium to high density, with a mix of activities, high-frequency transport, and concentrated population. It includes three subsets with specific standards for height allowance and density. Residential 8a, which generally applies to residential areas within walking distance of the town centre, allows a maximum of three storeys and a density of up to one unit per 150 m^2. Adjacent to the town centre and consistent with existing town centre commercial buildings, Residential 8b permits a maximum of four storeys with a density of up to one unit per 100 m^2. Residential 8c applies within 2 km of the town-centre area and allows up to five storeys, with density controlled by height and maximum site coverage of 60%. The Residential 8, as originally defined in plan change 58, was seen as the main means of achieving Auckland Council's liveable communities strategy and a more compact urban form (Auckland City Council 2004).

In Glen Innes, Residential 8 was initially introduced in Talbot Park, a state-housing area. The rezoning was introduced in tandem with the Talbot Park Community Renewal Project, which was launched by Housing New Zealand Corporation (HNZC) in 2002 to develop a medium-density housing area. Talbot Park was subsequently rezoned to Residential 8b, permitting one unit per 100 m^2 and up to four storeys (maximum 14 m). In the course of this project, residential density increased from 33.4 units per hectare to 43.8 units per hectare, with 111 new houses built and 108 refurbished. In 2005, plan change 61 was applied to wider Glen Innes, covering approximately 481 private properties and 684 state houses (Ministry for the Environment 2008).

The Unitary Plan released in 2016 further refined site sizes, height limits, and housing forms. Residential areas in Glen Innes were zoned as either Terrace Housing and Apartment Buildings, Mixed Housing Urban, or Mixed Housing Suburban, enabling increasing density and intensification. The Terrace Housing and Apartment Buildings Zone in Glen Innes is located around the town centre and train station. This zone is designed to support the highest level of intensification. Buildings can be up to five, six, or seven storeys, typically up to 16 m in height. In the areas of Glen Innes now zoned Mixed Housing Urban, higher density and intensity of development are now permitted than previously allowed on the same sites, with flexibility in terms of dwelling sizes and forms, which include detached dwellings, terrace housing, and low-rise apartments up to three storeys and not exceeding 11 m. In the Mixed Housing Suburban Zone, much of the building form is characterised as mainly one or two-storey standalone buildings set back from site boundaries with landscaped gardens. Buildings in this zone must not exceed 8 m in height. The zone supports both intensified development and the retention of the suburban built character.

Launched in 2018, the Auckland Plan 2050 takes a quality compact approach as the basis for its development strategy over the next 30 years. The strategy incorporates significant redevelopment and intensification of areas already under development, and the establishment of new neighbourhoods in future urban areas. In the plan, Glen Innes and Tāmaki are among 18 development areas prioritised for targeted investment and housing and business growth. Glen Innes is specially identified as a hotspot for redevelopment and regeneration between 2018 and 2020. The goal of the Glen Innes redevelopment is to achieve 3,600 extra dwellings over the period 2018 to 2048.

The community renewal and regeneration activities have changed the ground plan of Glen Innes, especially in the redevelopment sites in Northern Glen Innes, Wai O Taki Bay, and Fenchurch. The most fundamental change is the modification of plots. Many plots have been amalgamated and then re-subdivided alongside the demolition of old buildings and construction of new buildings. Meanwhile, plot boundaries in this area are being rearranged. The subdivision plots are less concentrated and normally distributed in different street blocks. The subdivisions have kept the old plot boundaries and, in some cases, the old buildings. Plots in these areas have experienced changes over the past 20 years, especially the plots owned by Creating Community and the Tāmaki Regeneration Company (TRC), which have seen a significant increase in building density. As a flow-on effect of the state-housing regeneration programmes and an increase in land values, some privately owned plots have also been subdivided since the 1980s.

Based on plot information obtained from Auckland Council, Property Guru, and development plans prepared by the Tāmaki Regeneration Company, the pattern of plot transformation in Glen Innes can be divided into three categories—orthomorphic, hypometamorphic, and metamorphic, according to the extent and type of changes (Conzen 1962; Whitehand et al. 2016). In the case of Glen Innes, metamorphic plots are those fundamentally changed by amalgamation, re-division, truncation, and redevelopment of plots. Hypometamorphic plots are those slightly changed by a subdivision, while orthomorphic plots are still in their original 1950s state, with no changes. Plots in the areas affected by social housing redevelopment programmes such as Northern Glen Innes, Fenchurch, Rowena Crescent, and Wai O Taki Bay have experienced metamorphic transformation. Almost all these plots are or were owned by Housing New Zealand or the Tāmaki Regeneration Company and have experienced major changes to plot structure and building coverage as a result of large-scale redevelopment. In this process, the original old houses were demolished and modern buildings such as detached houses or apartments were built. The new plots are much smaller and new streets have been built, generating new blocks.

Hypometamorphic plots are mainly privately owned or on less intensively developed land owned by the Tāmaki Regeneration Company, where large-scale redevelopment is not allowed. Different from metamorphic plots, hypometamorphic plots are normally the result of the subdivision of single plots, which increases house density but with little impact on the physical layout of Glen Innes. They can be found in the areas along West Tamaki Road and Apirana Avenue. Orthomorphic plots represent survival and are distributed within the Leybourne Crescent area and north of Heatherbank Street. However, most of the plots in these two areas belong to the Tāmaki Regeneration Company, and they are scheduled for a large-scale redevelopment within the next ten years. Some orthomorphic plots in other neighbourhood areas are intermingled with plots that have undergone changes.

Three types of plot metamorphosis have occurred in Glen Innes in the process of transformation (Figs. 5.6 and 5.7). The first type is plots still in their original state where the parent plot and original building are retained in their original form. Type 2 has plots derived from a parent plot that has been divided within the parent plot's original boundaries. Two sub-types are recognised in Type 2. In Type 2.1, the original building is retained in one part of the plot, with a new building in the other part, normally behind the original building. In Type 2.2, the parent plot has been divided into three or more plots. Here, the original building is demolished to free up the land for new buildings. Type 3 involves the amalgamation of plots. In Glen Innes, this type occurs in small-scale redevelopment areas. Often, the backyards of two plots are amalgamated and a new building built on the resulting site (Type 3.1). Alternatively, two or more plots have been amalgamated, and the new site is then divided into smaller plots (Type 3.2). Type 3.3 emerges in medium or large-scale redevelopment sites in the form of a series of parallel plots. Type 3.4 happens in large-scale redevelopment sites such as Fenchurch when a large number of plots or an entire block is involved in the redevelopment.

Building type has shown most obvious changes, particularly in the transformation from garden suburb to medium-density modern communities (Table 5.2). One-storey detached houses have been replaced by modern buildings in the form of two-storey single houses or townhouses on a smaller plot. Like other suburbs built after World War II, Glen Innes was typified by single houses with big back and front yards to provide a high degree of privacy and a lifestyle close to nature. However, new dwellings built after 2000 have limited private green space, mostly in the form of small courtyards.

In the large regeneration sites such as Fenchurch and Torrington Crescent in northern Glen Innes, the community street network has changed in the process of amalgamation, subdivision, and building construction. As shown in Fig. 5.8, Skippy Patuwai Lane in north Glen Innes and Aveline Place and Marsics Street in Fenchurch

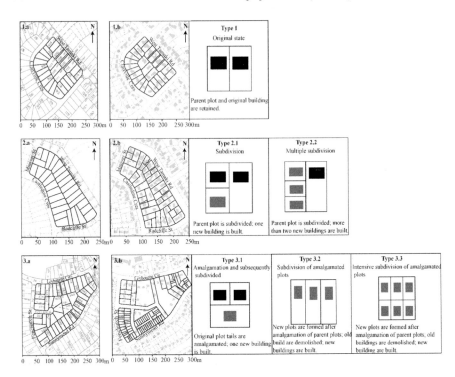

Fig. 5.6 Examples of types of metamorphic, hypometamorphic, and orthomorphic plots (*Source* Based on Auckland Council 2020 and authors' fieldwork, April 2020)

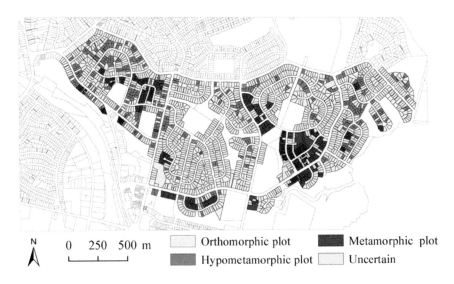

Fig. 5.7 The distribution of orthomorphic, hypometamorphic, and metamorphic plots in Glen Innes (*Source* Based on Auckland Council 2020 and authors' fieldwork, April 2020)

Table 5.2   Basic building types in Glen Innes

Building type	
	Conventional single-family single-storey detached house with large open space around the house in a large plot
	Newly built single-family house with small open space in a medium-sized plot
	Terraced house or newly built single-family house in a narrow plot
	Semi-detached duplexes
	Courtyard terraced houses; two rows of terraced houses surrounding a common space

Source Authors' photographs (2020)

have been added. These new roads act as community through streets in the street system. The redevelopment projects have generally occurred internally within street blocks without changing the pattern of super-blocks. However, the ground plan within the street block has experienced major change. The previous blocks filled with two rows of back-to-back plots have been replaced by four rows of plots divided by alleys.

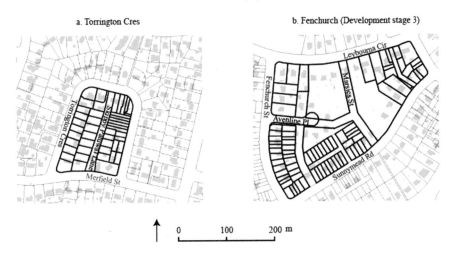

Fig. 5.8 The development of new streets in Glen Innes (*Source* Based on Auckland Council 2020)

5.3   Plan Units, Spatial Diversification, and Uneven Geographical Development

The (social) inculcation of injustice into our geographies (and histories) arises from the inequalities that are produced by the uneven geographical effects of every individual action and all social processes (Soja 2010). As discussed by Soja in relation to geographically uneven development and spatial justice, social processes never occur uniformly over space and they always bring unevenness to the space in which they occur. Further, through creating or maintaining individual and social inequalities, this geographical unevenness can be considered a contributing factor in social and spatial injustice (Soja 2010). Rather than occurring randomly, uneven development is a result of capitalist development. Although often unconsciously, individuals and social groups in capitalist society classify each geographical location in terms of its value. It is through this process that capital accumulation and circulation are enabled (Walker 1978).

Spatial differentiation and capital mobility are recognised as two main sources of uneven development (Harvey 1978). Spatial differentiation is a process by which social divisions are translated into spatial divisions due to the desire of individual and social actors to use space to their advantage. This phenomenon is closely associated with urbanisation and urban development (Smith 1982). More recently, it is also exemplified in the process of urban regeneration and renewal programmes. In relation to urban neighbourhoods that have undergone redevelopment or regeneration, a comparison of their morphological characteristics contributes to identifying how the value of the location is maximised through land-use policies, with implications for understanding how spatial difference is produced within neighbourhoods.

Smith (1979, 1987) points out that a plot of land is given actual capitalised ground rent based on its current use and potential 'higher and better' use. It is this gap that motivates regeneration and gentrification in a given neighbourhood, leading to social, physical, and economic changes. In the context of Glen Innes, the rapid growth of land values drove the changes in the built environment. The patterns of spatial changes can correspondingly help to develop a concrete understanding in relation to how capital mobilises within the neighbourhood. With a focus on the changes of each plot, plan analysis extends the analysis of spatial differentiation to the single 'plan unit' scale by providing an approach that enables a description of the characteristics and evolution of actual and tangible building types and urban form (King 1984; Kropf 2011).

In the preceding analysis of building form, plot subdivision and amalgamation, block pattern, street systems, ownership distribution, and the regeneration process, the morphological characteristics of these individual components are made explicit in relation to their formative period and evolutionary stages. This lays the foundation for examining the morphogenetic types of plan units and corresponding geographical landscape structure.

Six major types of plan units can be identified in Glen Innes in relation to building age, early post-war development area, the late twentieth-century development area, redeveloped residential area mainly from the 2000s, redeveloped residential area from the 2010s, town-centre unit, and green space unit (Fig. 5.9).

Plan Unit 1: Early post-war development area. The first and oldest plan unit is the post-war residential area with typical state-housing characteristics formed in the 1950s and the 1960s. It is most widely distributed in Glen Innes, especially in Paddington St, and in the areas north, south, and east of Leybourne Circle. Within this unit, two sub-types are evident: traditional plot series with post-war houses,

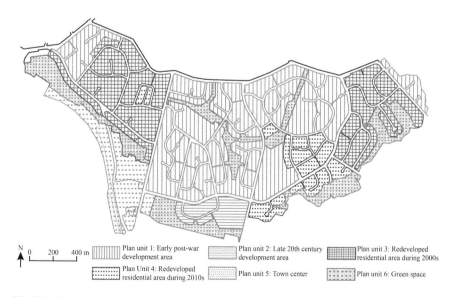

Fig. 5.9 Plan units in Glen Innes

exemplified by the Leybourne Circle area; and the original post-war plots with recent houses, such as those along the west side of West Tamaki Road.

Plan Unit 2: The late twentieth-century development area. Of the six types of plan unit, areas falling into Plan Unit 2 have the largest concentration of buildings built between 1970 and 1999. They are characterised by terrace houses and semi-detached houses, as found in Rowena Crescent.

Plan Unit 3: Redeveloped residential area mainly from the 2000s. This plan unit comprises two sub-types: (1) subdivided traditional plot series with two-level single houses on varying shapes and sizes of plot found west and north of Torrington Crescent in northern Glen Innes; and (2) newly subdivided plots series with two-level semi-detached or terrace houses, as in Lyndhurst Street in the Wai O Taki Bay area. Both sub-types appeared during redevelopment between 2001 and 2009 by Creating Community. With the exception of the area surrounded by Torrington Crescent, the redevelopment predominantly took place on a small scale by subdividing single plots and amalgamating adjacent plots.

The rent gap of each plot of land varies according to their location relative to community facilities and amenities. Northern Glen Innes and Wai O Taki Bay were the first to be slated for redevelopment. The main reason, according to the theory of uneven geographical development, is that land ground rent in these two areas had the potential to bring maximum profit to investors and developers. Under advanced capitalism, every plot of land has uneven location in terms of use-value in space (Smith 1982; Walker 1978). Northern Glen Innes is close to Glen Innes town centre and stretches alongside the West Tamaki Road. The Wai O Taki Bay area faces the sea and is close to the Point England Reserve. Both areas are close to the middle-class neighbourhoods of St Heliers and Glendowie, which makes new houses more attractive to potential buyers. These factors led to them being the main redevelopment areas in the first stage of large-scale regeneration.

Plan Unit 4: Redeveloped residential area from the 2010s. The redevelopment occurring in the 2010s produced the most complex morphological changes. This unit is characterised by medium-density and highly mixed building forms. Single-family detached houses, terraced houses, and semi-detached houses predominate in this unit.

Plan Unit 5: Town centre. The plan type areas discussed so far are residential areas and thus are categorised based on ownership, building type, and plot and block pattern. The last two units are introduced according to their built form and land use. The town centre unit is located right at the bottom of Glen Innes and its shape is triangular. It is surrounded by three arterial streets: Apirana Avenue, Eastview Road, and Line Road. As one of the main roads connecting the town centre and residential areas, Taniwha Street stretches across the middle of the town centre. The town centre area extends along the railway, which provides the most straightforward route connecting Glen Innes to Auckland's CBD.

Plan Unit 6: Green space unit. Glen Innes has large areas of green space. Apirana Reserve, Maybury Reserve, Point England Reserve, Wai O Taiki Nature Reserve, Tahuna Torea Reserve, and Tahuna Torea form a ring surrounding the built-up area of Glen Innes from north-west to north-east. Inside Glen Innes, there are three main green spaces: the first is located between Weybridge Crescent and Paddington Street; Glen Brae Reserve sits across the Leybourne Circle; and a third greenspace is bordered by Taniwha Street, Paddington Street, Elstree Avenue, and Sloane Street.

5.4 Spatial Distribution of Social Housing

Change in housing ownership is another important outcome of the regeneration of state-housing areas. Of the existing housing stock, about 1,140 of 3,297 dwellings are owned by the Tāmaki Redevelopment Company, with the rest either owned by other companies or private owners. Figure 5.10 shows a decrease in the proportion of social housing in northern Glen Innes, Fenchurch, and Wai O Taiki Bay over the past 20 years. The changes in property ownership as a result of regeneration can be divided by type and characteristics. First, the houses or land owned by the Tāmaki Redevelopment Company have tended to be sold to private or company owners. The process of privatisation has mainly occurred in neighbourhoods that have undergone community regeneration.

The construction of mixed-tenure communities in Tāmaki has been accompanied by the demolition of state houses and subsequent displacement of tenants. Figure 5.11 shows the distribution of various types of property ownership in Glen Innes in 2019. The transfer of ownership is a complex process, involving transfer between companies, private owners, and institutions. Several main types of ownership transactions are evident. First, there has been ownership transfer from Housing New Zealand or Tāmaki Regeneration Company to private owners in the regeneration process. The second type of transfer is from Housing New Zealand or Tāmaki Regeneration Company to private companies, such as Creating Community and Mike Greer Homes South Auckland Limited. These transactions have mainly occurred in northern Glen Innes and Wai O Taiki Bay. The third type is ownership transfer from companies, such as RPV Rawa Limited, Mike Greer Homes South Auckland Limited, Classic Developments Fenchurch 3A Limited, and New Zealand Housing Foundation to private owners, as apparent in the development of Fenchurch. Both the second and third types involve third-party partners in the process of regeneration. These developers have taken responsibility for social housing redevelopment and delivery in Glen Innes. According to data from Property Guru, around 344 houses from the existing housing stock have been transferred to private owners. This number is forecast to increase with the implementation of future regeneration projects. Finally, the Crown has also played an important role in this process, with some properties transferred from the Crown to private ownership.

0   200   400 m   Housing held by Housing New Zealand

Houses held by Tāmaki Regeneration Company

Fig. 5.10 The distribution of social houses in 2001 (a) and 2018 (b) (*Source* Based on Housing New Zealand 2001; Auckland Council 2020)

5.5   Physical Planning and Design

The physical form of Fenchurch and part of Wai O Taki Bay has obviously been influenced by new urbanism (Fig. 5.12). Based on a single neighbourhood, the *Fenchurch Neighbourhood Plan* aims to create 'mixed communities—developing a range of housing types and tenures (ownership) to attract different types of people to each

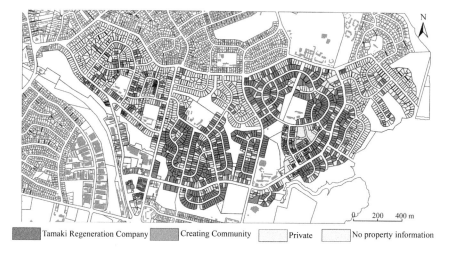

Tamaki Regeneration Company   Creating Community   Private   No property information

Fig. 5.11 Distribution of various types of property ownership in Glen Innes (*Source* Based on Corelogic 2020)

neighbourhood creating diverse communities' (Tāmaki Redevelopment Company 2014, p. 7).

'Perhaps more ideology than theory' (Fainstein 2000), new urbanism began with practitioners applying design methods to create vibrant urban spheres. The resulting set of design principles, such as mixing land uses, creating safe and walkable streets, and providing a range of commercial and communal activities within walking distance, then received a theoretical envelope. Under new urbanism, the urban environment is designed to enhance social life, provide fair access to opportunities, minimise spatial gaps, and be socially and environmentally sustainable. The claim that new urbanism safeguards the public's interest and promotes social justice is, however, contested.

Some researchers see new urbanism as dealing mainly with questions of urban design as a subset of planning and oriented towards practitioners rather than planning. As such, it is remote from the issues of social justice and ecological sustainability that form the core of urban planning (Gunder 2011). Others argue that new urbanism seeks the greatest happiness for the greatest number of people, making it closer to utilitarianism than the pursuit of justice (Fainstein 2005; Grant 2006). Still others claim that the physical aspect of planning is inseparable from the social, hence theories of the built environment inevitably reflect this interpretation. Moreover, enhanced social integration has been reported for those living in new urbanist communities (Podobnik 2011).

Talen (2002), among others, claims that new urbanism is oriented towards social equity. From this point of view, compact, mixed, and lively urban development is the most just built environment, particularly because it enables equal access for all, in contrast to suburban areas as well as low-density vehicle-oriented cities. According to Talen (2002), 'the ideal of equal access is roughly synonymous with the notion

Fig. 5.12 An aerial view of Fenchurch in 2022 (*Source* Authors' photograph, February 2022)

of spatial equity: that everyone should have to travel a similar distance to benefit from a public resource' (p. 180). Her work analysing the New Urbanism Charter reveals that eight of its 27 principles deal directly with social equity, in addition to 19 explicitly relating to the promotion of the common good (Alfasi and Fenster 2014). New urbanism appears to be outcome-oriented urban coding that is concerned with the structuring of a city. The structure of decision-making, which is part of spatial thinking, complements new urbanism in promoting a just city.

5.6 Summary

Morphological analysis provides a basis for interpreting and reflecting on the formation and production of physical space. The character of Glen Innes is defined by its site, ground plan, building forms, and land and building utilisation. The development outcomes in Glen Innes during different morphological periods are the result of government policies, legislation, and planning decisions and have followed a top-down planning model. Due to the need to build homes for workers post-World War II, Glen Innes was designated as a state-housing area in the 1950s and 1960s. The strong government intervention in state housing stimulated its rapid growth.

The development that took place in the 1950s and 1960s formed the physical characteristics of Glen Innes, including large plots with private open space, and comfortable and spacious indoor space. Deeply involved in the development of Glen Innes, the government aimed to make a garden suburb that reflected an ideal image of suburban working-class life. People living in Glen Innes at the time had a strong sense of community. The morphological frame generated in the 1950s and 1960s is still evident. Despite the subdivision of plots beginning in the 1980s, the dominant building type is still single-family houses with large gardens. From 2000, government housing policy together with the privatisation process that followed the passing of the 1992 Housing Restructuring Act has catalysed the transformation of Glen Innes and further altered ownership, density, and other morphological characteristics in this area.

Recent morphological changes in Glen Innes represent a typical process of urban intensification through medium-density development. Building demolition and replacement have resulted in a diverse array of physical building characteristics. These morphological processes have taken place within the morphological frame of the street blocks created in the 1950s and 1960s. Even large-scale redevelopment sites created through intensive amalgamation and division have followed the former street-block boundaries. In general, both the social housing redevelopment and subdivision of private plots have followed the morphological frame shaped by the existing street system and street-block pattern. Social housing redevelopment has generally occurred through a combination of major changes to plots by amalgamation, re-subdivision and truncation, and reconstruction of houses. The ground plan, which contributes to the community's character at the higher level, has undergone only limited changes. However, the building forms, which contribute to community character mainly at the medium level, have changed significantly. Significant public green space, on the other hand, has been preserved over the past two decades. The analysis further revealed that intensification and gentrification in the form of increasing building coverage and changes in plot pattern are particularly evident after 2000.

Morphological understanding of the existing urban form and its characteristics is derived from reconstructing the process of urban development. The morphological complexes of Glen Innes arising from the dynamics of ownership transactions have been analysed using a detailed plot-by-plot survey, historical records, and data from a GIS database and property database. Due to Glen Innes' short history and homogenous land utilisation, changing characteristics between different morphological periods are mainly expressed in relation to density, building fabric, and ownership.

References

Alfasi N, Fenster T (2014) Between socio-spatial and urban justice: Rawls' principles of justice in the 2011 Israeli protest movement. Plan Theory 13(4):407–427

Arbury J (2005) From urban sprawl to compact city: an analysis of urban growth management in Auckland. Dissertation, University of Auckland

Auckland City Council (1952) Auckland city council planning map. NZ Map 3519, Sir George Grey Special Collections. Auckland Libraries, Auckland

Auckland City Council (2004) Glen Innes into the future. Auckland City Council, Auckland

Auckland Council (2019) A brief history of Auckland's urban form. https://knowledgeauckland.org.nz/media/1419/a-brief-history-of-aucklands-urban-form-2019-web.pdf. Accessed 25 October 2022

Auckland Council (2020) GeoMaps. https://geomapspublic.aucklandcouncil.govt.nz/viewer/index.html. Accessed 25 Oct 2022

Auckland Libraries (2022a) Auckland libraries heritage collections 895-A62532, State housing, Kestrel Place, Glen Innes 1960, photographer Gregor Riethmaier. Copyright: Archives New Zealand Te Rua Mahara o te Kāwanatanga

Auckland Libraries (2022b) Auckland libraries heritage collections 580-ALB22-184, Glen Innes shopping centre 1961, photographer Whites Aviation. Whites Aviation number WA-55659-F. https://natlib.govt.nz/records/23221626. Accessed 25 Oct 2022b

Barry-Martin DE (1956) The development of town planning legislation in New Zealand. Technical Books, Wellington, New Zealand

Conzen MRG (1960) Alnwick, Northumberland: a study in town-plan analysis. Institute of British Geographers, London

Conzen MRG (1962) The plan analysis of an English city centre. In: Norborg K (ed) Proceedings of the IGU symposium in urban geography, Lund, 1960. Gleerup, Lund, Sweden, pp 383–414

CoreLogic (2020) CoreLogic New Zealand. https://www.corelogic.co.nz/. Accessed 26 October 2022

Elkink A, Pringle T (2011) Renovate: 1940–1960. Branz, Porirua, New Zealand

Fainstein S (2000) New directions in planning theory. Urban Affairs Review 35(4):451–478

Fainstein SS (2005) Planning theory and the city. J Plan Educ Res 25(2):121–130

Friesen W (2009) The demographic transformation of inner-city Auckland. New Zealand Population Review 35(1):55–74

Glen Innes Business Association (2016) Glen Innes village: looking back 60 years 1956–2016. https://www.gleninnesvillage.co.nz/pdf/GI-jubilee-booklet.pdf. Accessed 25 Oct 2022

Grant J (2006) Planning the good community: new urbanism in theory and practice. Routledge, London

Gunder M (2011) Is urban design still urban planning? An exploration and response. J Plan Educ Res 31(2):184–195

Harvey D (1978) The urban process under capitalism: a framework for analysis. Int J Urban Reg Res 2(1–3):101–131

Housing New Zealand (2001) Development planning analysis report, current Housing New Zealand landholdings Glen Innes/Panmure. Housing New Zealand, Wellington

Jackson E (1978) Delving into the past of Auckland's eastern suburbs. Premier Print Services, Auckland

Jackson R (1965) State housing in Auckland. Dissertation, University of Auckland

King AD (1984) The social production of building form: theory and research. Environ Plan D Soc Space 2(4):429–446

Kropf K (2011) Urbanism, politics and language: the role of urban morphology. Urban Morphol 15(2):157–161

Ministry for the Environment (2002) Creating great places to live+work+play: livable urban environments: process, strategy, action. https://www.mfe.govt.nz/sites/default/files/publications/rma/live-work-play-jun02/section-1-2-jun02.pdf. Accessed 25 Oct 2022

Ministry for the Environment (2008) Community renewal: Housing New Zealand Corporation, Talbot Park, Auckland. http://www.mfe.govt.nz/publications/towns-and-cities/urban-design-case-studies-local-government/community-renewal-%E2%80%93-housing. Accessed 25 Oct 2022

New Zealand Productivity Commission (2015) Better urban planning. https://www.productivity.govt.nz/assets/Documents/0a784a22e2/Final-report.pdf. Accessed 25 October 2022

Podobnik B (2011) Assessing the social and environmental achievements of new urbanism: evidence from Portland, Oregon. J Urban Int Res Placemaking Urban Sustain 4(2):105–126

Smith N (1979) Toward a theory of gentrification a back to the city movement by capital, not people. J Am Plann Assoc 45(4):538–548

Smith N (1982) Gentrification and uneven development. Econ Geogr 58(2):139–155

Smith N (1987) Gentrification and the rent gap. Ann Am Assoc Geogr 77(3):462–465

Soja EW (2000) Postmetropolis: critical studies of cities and regions. Blackwell, Oxford

Soja EW (2010) Seeking spatial justice. University of Minnesota Press, Minneapolis

Talen E (2002) The social goals of new urbanism. Hous Policy Debate 13(1):165–188

Tamaki Redevelopment Company (2014) Fenchurch neighbourhood plan. https://www.tamakiregeneration.co.nz/sites/default/files/site-files/2014-02-05_TAMAKI_FIRST_HOUSING_-_FENCHURCH_Report_v1.2_-_150dpi.pdf. Accessed 20 Oct 2022

Walker RA (1978) Two sources of uneven development under advanced capitalism: spatial differentiation and capital mobility. Review of Radical Political Economics 10(3):28–38

Whitcombe and Tombs (1930) Whitcombe's map of Auckland City and suburbs. NZ Map 6140, Sir George Grey Special Collections, Auckland Libraries

Whitehand JWR, Conzen MP, Gu K (2016) Plan analysis of historical cities: a Sino-European comparison. Urban Morphology 20(2):139–158

Chapter 6
Changing Social Housing Policy in the Context of Neoliberalism

Abstract This chapter explores the impact of ideological shifts on the public housing policies and planning documents that have guided the development and regeneration of social housing areas in New Zealand. Rather than seeking to evaluate urban planning and housing policies, the aim is to develop an understanding of the ideologies behind these policies and planning practices, and their effects on social housing redevelopment. To achieve these aims, a political-economic approach to critical discourse analysis is applied. The descriptive analysis investigates historical and current policy and planning documents and news reports about the study area collected from newspapers including *The New Zealand Herald* and the *East and Bays Courier*. This helps track how public housing areas have been defined in different historical periods. Following Soja's ideas about the production of unjust geography and the political production of space, the reflective analysis examines the process by which injustice becomes infused in the political dimension. This phase of the research seeks to uncover underlying political and economic structures hidden behind the public housing (re)development programmes through exploring the representations of ideology, strategy, language, and practice in planning processes.

Keywords Social housing policy · Neoliberal planning · Social housing redevelopment · Tāmaki · Glen Innes

As argued by Soja (2010), spatial justice is not just an abstract concept; it is closely connected to the political and practical objectives of national policies, local urban planning, and community-based organisations and their activities, making it relevant to urban regeneration at the community level. Therefore, examining the ways in which social housing and planning policies have produced and reproduced Glen Innes from the perspective of spatial justice is crucial to reflecting on and understanding the processes of decision-making and implementation. Urban intensification and regeneration have become an important topic in Auckland, as in many cities in the UK, the USA, Canada, and other countries (Couch 2003; Fainstein 2009; Lees 2014). Despite urban regeneration in these countries being concerned, generally, with spatially contextualised resource (re)distribution, they present different structuring principles for relevant policies and different subjects of policy action (Ferrari 2012).

© The Author(s), under exclusive license to Springer Nature Switzerland AG 2023   111
S. Wang and K. Gu, *Spatial Justice and Planning*, The Urban Book Series,
https://doi.org/10.1007/978-3-031-38070-9_6

In public and social discourse during different periods of development, Glen Innes has variously been portrayed as good for workers' and soldiers' welfare, a marginalised area for low-income people, and an ideal place for affordable housing.

6.1 Changing Social Housing Policy Under Neoliberalism

The year 1984 is regarded as a watershed between two contrasting economic and political patterns in New Zealand. After their election in July 1984, as with First Labour Government in the 1930s, the Fourth Labour Government revolutionised the mechanisms used to govern the economic sector and public administration in New Zealand, with wide-ranging reforms named 'Rogernomics' after the then Minister of Finance Roger Douglas who initiated the reforms (Evans et al. 1996; Goldfinch 1998).

Prior to this reform, New Zealand was facing unsustainable fiscal and current account deficits, runaway inflation, and a foreign exchange crisis (Stillman et al. 2010). Aiming to restore market mechanisms and reduce government intervention, the economic reforms introduced by Roger Douglas covered agriculture, industry, the financial sector, transport and distribution, competition policy, the labour market, tax reform, and welfare changes (Easton 1994; James 2015; Schick 1996).

With regard to management of the public sector, the reforms moved some responsibilities from government departments into government-owned corporations. The reforms also adjusted the structure of government administration by introducing market principles to encourage competition and efficiency (Scott 1996). As a result, New Zealand was transformed from a highly regulated economy to one of the least regulated among OECD countries (the Organisation for Economic Co-operation and Development) (Britton 1991; Britton et al. 1992; Murphy and Kearns 1994). The rationale behind the reforms was that 'efficiency could be improved by approximating a private sector model' (Duncan and Bollard 1992, pp. 14–15). Thus, competition and efficiency became both aims and themes in policymaking.

It was during this period that the Building Act 1991 and Resource Management Act (RMA) 1991 were enacted to transform the housing construction sector and planning system. The Building Act 1991 reduced the regulatory restrictions on consumer choices and promoted the utilisation of new housing materials and techniques, while the RMA brought in a new environmental effect-based planning system (Murphy 2014). It shifted the New Zealand planning system from a basis in land-use planning to a system that provided a new approach to environmental issues alongside other related legislation (Perkins et al. 1993). The core purpose of the RMA was to promote the sustainable management of natural and physical resources in relation to urban planning activities and land use (The New Zealand Productivity Commission 2015). The reforms in housing construction and planning were the result of the government's strong commitment to deregulation.

Much has been written to unpack the neoliberalist ideology behind the reforms, including the words and phrases that feature in the language of liberalism, such as free market, free trade, liberalisation, and freedom. These terms constructed a language system that normalised free-market ideas, which had not previously been part of the nation's governance processes. As a result, business terms like competition, commodities, profit, profitability, productivity, the discipline of the market, privatising, enterprise, and innovation are featured extensively in government documents (Cooke 2010). To achieve the goals illustrated by these terms, the corporatisation of a wide range of government agencies and departments became the norm.

It is argued that neoliberalism is only interested in private benefits rather than the public interest. The drive to maximise profit has led to a high degree of competition between different parties in the market. However, the power between contracting parties is not always equal and monopoly situations are common in the free market, requiring state intervention (Rosenberg 1993). Apart from the unequal power between different parties, the issue of inequalities in the distribution of income and wealth and gender inequality have also been raised in relation to neoliberalism. As Roper (2005) notes, the income gap between the wealthy and the poor has widened. Increasing unemployment and welfare dependency have also contributed to growing inequality. Some commentators, therefore, argue that New Zealand's neoliberal reforms have brought more benefits to private enterprise, which has advantaged high-income groups (Marcetic 2017; Rosenberg 1993; Roper 2005).

6.1.1 Phase 1: Corporatisation, Privatisation, and Residualisation of the State-Housing Sector

Based on the welfare system built under the Keynesian model of economics, homeownership and the provision of subsidised state rental housing constituted the two strands of housing policy in New Zealand up until the 1980s. The central government promoted homeownership through government-backed mortgage schemes and indirect aid to the construction industry (Thorns 1988). At the same time, the government was engaged in providing state housing for workers and returning soldiers from the 1930s onwards (Murphy 2009).

However, neoliberal housing policy reform in the 1980s dramatically turned its back on these twin pillars of housing policy. The policy shift was described as the 'most fundamental redirection in housing policy since the 1930s' (Luxton 1991, p. iv) and 'a radical retreat from a long-held commitment to social rented housing' (Murphy and Kearns 1994, p. 634). As a result of the neoliberal reforms, government intervention in housing provision was profoundly curtailed while the effect of the market was strongly emphasised according to the principles of fairness, self-reliance, efficiency, and personal choice. These housing reforms changed both the administration of housing and the nature of housing support (Thorns 2006).

In 1991, the then Minister for Housing, John Luxton, argued that the existing housing system failed to 'encourage fairness, self-reliance, efficiency or personal choice' (p. 120). As part of the government's efforts to apply these four principles in the social sector, the market was introduced to the state-housing sector. The government enacted the Housing Restructuring Act in 1992, which established Housing New Zealand Ltd (HNZ, frequently referred to simply as Housing New Zealand) to replace the Housing Corporation of New Zealand (HCNZ). The state's involvement in housing provision was duly transferred from the Housing Corporation of New Zealand to Housing New Zealand, in line with government policies towards corporatisation and privatisation (Murphy and Kearns 1994). In contrast to the Housing Corporation of New Zealand, which was a state-run organisation, Housing New Zealand was a state-owned but commercially driven company (Murphy and Kearns 1994). It was expected to operate 'primarily as a business rather than a social delivery agency' (Kelsey 1993, p. 31).

The housing mortgages previously managed by the Housing Corporation of New Zealand, were sold for NZ$511.7 million in 1992 (Massey 1995). As a result, the mortgage market was now dominated by banks rather than the government. Housing New Zealand then adopted the 'reconfiguration programme' to sell existing state housing stock in high amenity areas, which subsequently led to state-housing tenants becoming concentrated in areas where Housing New Zealand is the dominant housing provider. At the same time, about 20% of state house sales took place in Auckland, which has the highest average house prices and rents, and so the most severe housing affordability issues (Murphy 2006).

The income-related rent subsidy was viewed by the government as distorting the market (King 2019) because it privileged state-housing tenants over tenants in the private market, as well as encouraging 'dependency' on state-housing tenure (Schrader 2005) and limiting state tenants' choices in the rental market (Murphy 2004). With the aim of encouraging efficiency and competition between the private and state rental sectors, the rents for state houses were tagged to market rents rather than tenants' income. The market rent strategy meant locational premiums were added to state house rents, making them unaffordable for their existing tenants. It also placed greater pressure on tenants moving into state houses. During the period from 1992 to 1999, Housing New Zealand rents increased by 106%, while rents in the private sector rose by 23% (Cheer et al. 2002).

The government also introduced the accommodation supplement in 1993, which replaced all other housing benefits (King 2019). The accommodation supplement paid up to 70% of the above-entry threshold housing costs. Although the accommodation supplement was intended for low-income households, tenants received less assistance than they had with income-related rents. A study carried out by the Department of Social Welfare reported that the over 30,000 households receiving the accommodation supplement were paying 50% of their income in rent (Department of Social Welfare 1999).

This housing reform received much criticism and protest from tenants and welfare advocacy groups such as the Salvation Army and other people working with the poor. It was seen as promoting the residualisation of the state-housing sector in New Zealand, described as '…the process whereby public housing moves towards a position in which it provides only a "safety net" for those who for reasons of poverty, age or infirmity cannot obtain suitable accommodation in the private sector. It almost certainly involves lowering the status and increasing the stigma attached to public housing' (Malpass and Murie 1982, p. 174).

The housing policy reforms in general were criticised as 'ill-conceived, risking fiscal blowout for the state, and [...] likely to increase the marginalisation and poverty of tenants' (Murphy and Kearns 1994, p. 634). As a result, there was high tenant turnover and mobility in the state sector in the 1990s and state-housing areas experienced increased stigmatisation.

6.1.2 Phase 2: 'Third-Way' Housing Policy Under a Labour-Led Government—Stepping Back from the Market

As discussed in the previous section, the state-housing policy reforms in the 1990s resulted in many housing problems. In 1999, a Labour Government was elected. In 2000, the government enacted the Housing Restructuring (Income Related Rents) Amendment Act, signalling their intention to modify the neoliberal housing reforms (Murphy 2004, 2020). The new government reintroduced income-related rent into the state-housing sector, while retaining the option of charging market rent if a tenant's income exceeded a given threshold. A new housing entity, Housing New Zealand Corporation (HNZC), was set up in 2001. Housing New Zealand Corporation was formed by amalgamating Housing New Zealand Ltd. and Community Housing Ltd. This new corporation, identified as a Crown entity, had four roles: provide and manage state houses; provide help, services, and advice to people on low or modest incomes; engage with housing renewal and land renewal; and provide advice to the government. These functions meant the Housing New Zealand Corporation would be deeply involved in the process of social housing redevelopment.

The new housing policies were regarded as a retreat from the neoliberal housing reforms of the 1990s. Re-emphasising the importance of direct government intervention in housing, the policies stepped-back from a 'market model' solution to housing problems (Murphy 2004). However, they did not completely change the neoliberal nature of the housing market. Falling somewhere between housing policy in the time of the welfare state and the neoliberal housing reforms, the new housing strategy promoted both wider government interventions in the housing market and commod-ified forms of housing provision. The accommodation supplement, a central element of neoliberal housing policy, was retained but was only allocated to tenants in the private sector. The government also committed to engaging with stakeholders such as housebuilders, local authorities, social agencies, government departments, and tenants.

These combined new approaches, identified as 'third-way' housing policy, were nevertheless still embedded in neoliberal parameters. As Murphy (2009) pointed out, 'at a broader level, the new housing policies represent a form of 'soft' neoliberalism that differs from the extremes of the 1990s but continues to be market-oriented' (p. 212). Although it was a return to the spirit of the earlier state-housing approach, state housing continued to be treated as a resource for those in greatest need.

6.1.3   Phase 3: Social Housing Reform Under National-Led Coalition Government

In 2008, a national-led coalition government came into office and again readjusted housing policy. The housing policies implemented by this central-right government significantly influenced housing provision and planning practice over the following decade. While keeping existing housing policies, such as the accommodation supplement, and renewing existing social rental housing, the new government was more focused on market mechanisms. It reintroduced the tenant purchase scheme that allowed non-strategic, freehold, standalone state houses to be sold to tenants (Olssen et al. 2010). The government claimed the proceeds from the sales would be reinvested in state housing in high-demand areas. The government also reduced restrictions on planning practice in relation to housing supply and retained support measures for small-scale private landlords (Murphy 2020).

6.1.3.1   From State Housing to Social Housing

In 2013, the passage of the Social Housing Reform Bill marked the beginning of a new era by introducing a suite of changes to the social housing system in New Zealand. In April 2014, when the Social Housing Reform (Housing Restructuring and Tenancy Matters Amendment) Act 2013 (SHRA) came into force, Minister for Housing Dr Nick Smith explained that 'the fundamental change in this bill is shifting from state housing to social housing. Governments for 75 years have believed that only the state can meet the housing needs of disadvantaged families. These reforms will encourage the growth of a more diverse range of new social housing providers' (Smith 2013).

Traditionally, state/public housing in New Zealand has been owned and managed by the government, local territorial authorities, and not-for-profit organisations (Johnson 2017). The Social Housing Reform Act created a new framework of housing provision that included private for-profit companies along with the traditional players. In 2003, NZ$64 million was spent on state-housing demonstration projects to encourage initiatives from alternative social housing providers, including iwi, third-sector housing providers, and local government (Housing New Zealand Corporation 2005). The term 'social housing' has since crept into the language of New Zealand housing policy (Johnson 2017). The new nomenclature reflects a commitment to provide housing to people who really need it (King 2019).

Since 2008, the 'third sector' has become an important player in the provision of social housing. Third-sector or community housing providers have been encouraged to become involved in housing. The third sector is defined as 'organisations established by people on a voluntary basis to pursue social or community goals' (Corry 2010, p. 13). More specifically, community housing providers make below market rents possible by using capitalised or recurrent subsidies from the state or local government, and/or dedicating private assets at zero or sub-market rates of return, and/or the provision of volunteer effort.

The term third sector is often used to distinguish this grouping from the public sector (government) and the private sector (market). Organisations in the third sector are non-governmental and not-for-profit. Encouraging third-sector involvement signalled the state's intention to step back from its role in social housing provision and transfer the responsibility to such organisations (Conradson 2008; Crampton et al. 2001; Gordon 2015; Warrington 1995). Although the government remains involved in regulating the operations of these organisations, its role is limited to management (Gordon 2015; Kearns and Joseph 2000).

The social housing reform of 2013 diversified social housing provision and formed the basis of the current social housing system. This system incorporates different models with different types of ownership and subsidies. The traditional state/public model is state-owned housing funded by public subsidies. In the second model, state housing is privately owned but operated by a state agency such as Housing New Zealand Corporation. While Housing New Zealand has traditionally owned and managed the state-housing stock, it does not own all the rental housing it operates; it leases between 2,000 and 3,000 units from private owners on long-term contract. In the third model, the social housing stock is publicly owned but operated by a private entity or a joint venture involving a private entity (Johnson 2017).

Another model, often referred to as community housing (Ministry of Social Development 2018), relies on private owners registered as community housing providers who are responsible for providing access to rental accommodation in the local community on a small-scale. To get funding from the government, Community Housing Providers need to register and be monitored by the Community Housing Regulatory Authority. They are non-government social housing providers in the form of not-for profit organisations, such as Māori trusts, not-for-profit companies, charitable trusts, and incorporated societies (The Auckland Community Housing Providers Network 2019). The government allocates tenants to the Community Housing Providers and pays them the income-related rent subsidy (IRRS) (Table 6.1).

The separation of funders and providers in social housing provision aligns with general social service reforms impacted by the neoliberal turn, which reflected a broad international trend (Barnett et al. 1998; Kearns 1998). The government participates in social housing provision by initiating contracts with Community Housing Providers. This new type of arrangement is talked about in terms of partnership and 'contracting out', signifying that the Community Housing Providers and other organisations are functioning as semi-government organisations. Such organisations are referred to collectively as the 'shadow state' (Beaumont 2008; Czischke et al. 2012; Mullins et al. 2012).

Table 6.1 New Zealand models of social housing provision

	Public ownership	Private ownership
Public operation	Public, state, or council rental housing—one public agency owns and provides social housing	Housing stock leased from private owners and provided by the public agency
Private operation	Provision of rental housing contracted out to a private agency	Social housing provided by private agencies through subsidies and contracts with the state

Source Based on Johnson (2017)

6.1.3.2 Reviewable Tenancies

As in the UK and Australia, the Social Housing Reform Act 2013 dismantled guaranteed security of tenure in social housing and set out a new regime based on reviewable tenancies. This change has been described as a shift from providing a 'permanent "safety net" to a (temporary) "ambulance service"' (Fitzpatrick and Pawson 2014, p. 597). The Act enabled the Ministry of Social Development (MSD) to review all social housing tenants' eligibility every three years. Social housing tenants included all Housing New Zealand Cooperation tenants who became tenants after July 2011 and tenants of registered community housing providers who are paying an Income Related Rent (IRR) (Ministry of Social Development 2013). A notification sent to Housing New Zealand Cooperation tenants at the time stated: 'The main change for you is that in future, your tenancy will be reviewed on a regular basis. Tenancy reviews won't come into effect until next year and will be introduced in stages. Tenancy reviews have already been announced for people who become Housing New Zealand tenants after 1 July 2013' (Ministry of Social Development 2013, p. 3).

The rationale behind this policy was that social housing is for people with the highest need, but people's circumstances can change, thus regular reviews are a logical mechanism for the allocation of a scarce resource. The reviewable tenancies policy constructed social housing as a transition to renting in the private sector rather than an alternative to the private sector. However, concerns were raised about the possibility of creating a poverty trap due to the implication that tenants were liable to lose their rental houses once their economic circumstances improved. Tenants could, therefore, be encouraged to remain in need if they wanted to keep their security of tenure (Murphy 2020).

6.1.3.3 Stock Transfer and the Changing Role of Housing New Zealand Cooperation

As part of its wider programme of reform, the Social Housing Reform (Housing Restructuring and Tenancy Matters Amendment) Act 2013 also redefined the role of the Housing New Zealand Cooperation. The responsibility for assessing and allocating tenants to available Housing New Zealand Corporation houses was moved from Housing New Zealand Corporation to the Ministry of Social Development. Following the reform, Housing New Zealand Corporation functioned as just one of many social housing providers in the market. The Ministry of Social Development took on the role of managing social housing and purchasing houses. It also had the responsibility of forecasting demand and setting purchasing intentions to indicate its long-term requirements in advance to the market. This achieved a separation of the provider role from the demand management role in social housing provision: Housing New Zealand Corporation was identified as a public housing provider and landlord involved in public housing supply, while the Ministry of Social Development was the government agency managing the demand side.

This reform also enabled the government to transfer state-housing stock from Housing New Zealand Corporation to community housing providers (Bennett 2016), with 1,500 state houses and tenancies in Tauranga and Invercargill marked for transfer to Registered Community Housing Providers (Adams 2017). Finally, in 2017, a total of 1,140 houses were transferred to Accessible Properties, a community housing provider. In Auckland, around 2,800 state houses were transferred to the Tāmaki Redevelopment Company in 2016 as part of urban regeneration and social housing redevelopment programmes in Tāmaki. The stock transfer programme was ended by the incoming Labour-led government in 2017.

The changing role of Housing New Zealand Corporation and stock transfer gave effect to the National government's commitment to reducing the role of the state as landlord and encouraging the growth of the third sector (Murphy 2020). It also strengthened the trend towards the marketisation of social housing in New Zealand, which was presented as a rational and effective means to solve housing problems. On the one hand, this policy supported the growth of multiple housing providers and added a private asset base to social housing provision. The government also claimed the transfer would provide benefits to tenants if the transfer of housing stock itself was well executed. On the other hand, this transfer potentially put housing stock at financial risk (Pawson and Gilmour 2010; Murphy 2020).

A new regulatory regime was subsequently created by the incoming Labour Government to take charge of housing and urban development. In 2018, the government announced the formation of a new Ministry, the Ministry of Housing Urban Development (MHUD), consisting of sections of the Ministry of Business and Innovation (MBIE), the Treasury, and the Ministry of Social Development. Then in October 2019, Housing New Zealand Corporation, combining KiwiBuild and the HNZC development subsidiary Homes, Land, Community (HLC), established a new centralised housing and urban development authority, Kāinga Ora—Homes and Communities. Kāinga Ora acts as the public housing landlord and is also responsible for leading urban development projects of all sizes in New Zealand. As Table 6.2 shows, Kāinga Ora, the Ministry of Social Development, and the Ministry of Housing Urban Development play different roles in New Zealand housing and urban development.

Table 6.2 The roles of housing agencies

Kāinga Ora—Homes and Communities	The Ministry of Social Development	The Ministry of Housing and Urban Development
Kāinga Ora manages and maintains around 65,000 public houses. It also places people from the housing register into homes. It is charged with delivering more public, transitional, and affordable housing to help meet supply and leading and coordinating urban development projects	The Ministry of Social Development works with people who need housing, income, and employment support. The Ministry of Social Development assesses eligibility for and manages applications on the public housing register and calculates income-related rentals for public housing tenants. The Ministry of Social Development also provides financial assistance to help people access and sustain long-term accommodation, and administers the emergency housing special needs grant to help individuals and whanau meet the cost of short-term, emergency accommodation	The Ministry of Housing and Urban Development is responsible for the strategy, policy, funding, monitoring, and regulation of New Zealand's housing and urban development system. It works to deliver more public housing, transitional housing, and services to tackle homelessness in New Zealand. The Ministry of Housing and Urban Development also monitors community housing providers

Source Based on Kāinga Ora Homes and Communities (2020)

The period of National government from 2008 to 2017 was marked by a series of housing reforms involving initiatives for affordable housing underpinned by a neoliberal logic that resulted in the transformation of the nature and character of social housing provision in New Zealand. Both small- and large-scale agents were encouraged to get involved in the process of social housing provision. Neoliberal ideas such as 'market efficiency' and 'consumer choice' appeared in the language of policy and plan making, with brownfield intensification and greenfield development promoted in 'major urban centres' such as Auckland, Hamilton, Tauranga, Wellington, Christchurch, and Queenstown (Ministry for the Environment 2019).

These neoliberal housing policies altered the organisational character of social housing and further changed housing provision practices at the community level. The Social Housing Reform (Housing Restructuring and Tenancy Matters Amendment) Act 2013 restructured the administration and monitoring of housing needs and changed the process of social housing management through the complementary roles of Housing New Zealand Corporation and the Ministry of Social Development. The Act allocated funding to community housing providers, thus changing the financial basis of social housing provision and having a significant impact on the social housing sector. The implementation of reviewable tenancies challenged the principle of secure tenancy for state tenants.

After the 1990s reforms, the state-housing sector was still under the control of the central government. However, a series of housing policies implemented post-2008 has changed social housing and the nature of the social rental housing sector by marketising it (Murphy 2020). All these changes to social housing provision have profoundly shaped the institutional context of social housing redevelopment and community regeneration practices in Glen Innes, and in turn changed the physical landscape and residents' life experiences. These impacts and how they are manifesting will be explored in the following sections.

6.2 Delivering Mixed Housing Types in the Discourse of Regeneration Policy

Mixed-tenure housing has become a go-to approach for restructuring post-war public housing across the world (August 2016). This approach is normally seen in low socioeconomic areas where the aim is to replace the existing state housing with a mix of private and social housing (Sautkina et al. 2012). Given the effects of housing tenure on health, employment, crime, welfare, wealth, and education (Waldegrave and Urbanová 2016; Tunstall 2002), mixed-tenure housing is widely regarded as having a positive impact on surrounding communities. Firstly, it increases the diversity of housing within a certain neighbourhood and thus contributes to maintaining the stability of the population and allowing the estate to adapt to people's dynamic housing preferences over time (Casey et al. 2007). Secondly, through observation and social interactions, the higher-income owner-occupiers are seen as role models for social housing tenants in terms of behaviour and aspirations, thereby building a better reputation for the community and reducing social exclusion (Kleinhans 2004). Thirdly, the role that mixed-tenure housing can play in promoting diversification and reducing concentrated deprivation and spatial inequalities is one of the main justifications for government urban renewal policies. Mixed-tenure housing is seen as contributing to the sustainability of housing estates by reducing the concentration of disadvantaged households (Casey et al. 2007; Atkinson and Kintrea 1998).

Recently, mixed housing has become the predominant housing policy approach in relation to urban regeneration in Auckland. Alongside the social housing redevelopment projects, housing diversification has been introduced to Glen Innes and other areas with high levels of state rental housing. The argument underlying the mixed housing strategy is that it will alleviate upward pressure on house prices and allow land to be utilised more effectively. Building with greater density provides a greater variety of housing types and mixed land use in neighbourhoods previously dominated by low-density, single-family homes (Aurand 2010). It is expected that the mixed housing policy will contribute to erasing the past stigma attached to state-housing areas, often portrayed as dysfunctional sites with high levels of crime, unemployment, alcohol and drug misuse, and poor education (Arthurson 2012; Morris et al. 2012; Randolph et al. 2004).

The plan *Glen Innes into the Future* 2004 emphasises the need to 'provide a variety of housing types', focusing on choice in housing size. It claims that 'as the population of Glen Innes grows, there is a need to provide a variety of housing types to cater for the population's changing accommodation and lifestyle needs. Not everyone wishes to, or can afford to live in, a detached house on its own section' (p. 18).

The Tāmaki Regeneration Company *Strategic Framework* (2013) further states that the new homes built should provide a range of housing types and tenures to meet the needs of current and future residents. In the framework, the Tāmaki Redevelopment Company commits to providing fully supported rental, assisted rental, and affordable assisted ownership, market affordable, and market housing options to cater to all types of people and households. Importantly, a proportion of homes will be retained as social housing for those in the highest need. This may include the provision of housing for mental health patients and people coming out of the justice system, with support linked to other services in line with their needs (Tāmaki Redevelopment Company 2013, p. 38).

Creating mixed-tenure neighbourhoods is emphasised in various plans and strategies produced by the Tāmaki Redevelopment Company. The *Tāmaki Reference Plan* (2016a, vision 0.17) states that through its shareholders, the Tāmaki Redevelopment Company has been mandated to replace 2,500 social houses with a minimum of 7,500 mixed-tenure houses over a period of 15 years. The Tāmaki Redevelopment Company will achieve this by: (1) engaging with a consortium comprising a large-scale development partner and a long-term owner of the redeveloped social housing; and (2) maintaining the momentum of catalyst projects over the next three to five years to deliver approximately 800 new homes. These developments will be an opportunity to test, refine and benchmark the outcome expected of large-scale development (Tāmaki Regeneration Company 2016a, p. 33).

Alongside the *Tāmaki Reference Plan* (2016b, vision 0.17), the *Design Framework*, launched on 7 December 2016, provides detailed information to guide house design. The document specifies: 'Where the Tāmaki Redevelopment Company is involved in development of other land uses, for example where retail may form part of a mixed-use development on land under the Tāmaki Redevelopment Company control, the higher-level Design principles will form an important consideration in any design review process' (Tāmaki Regeneration Company 2016b, p. 33).

In the *Design Framework*, mixed housing is defined as including mixed tenure, typologies, affordability, and uses. The Design Framework proposes 'providing a mixture of housing key outcome and contributes to a wider range of strategic objectivities. The Tāmaki Redevelopment Company seeks housing choices for different stages of life, varying incomes, and preferences, supports extended family, and avoids stigmatising low-income groups' (Tāmaki Regeneration Company 2016b, p. 33).

The guidelines require that design should: (1) be mixed tenure; (2) be 'tenure-blind'; (3) be appropriate to the context; (4) include mix housing types within a neighbourhood, street, block, and site as much as possible, including attached houses, detached houses and apartments; (5) incorporate building forms that vary according to site context and attributes, to create spacious outdoor relationships; (6) mix the sizes of homes within neighbourhoods, providing different numbers of bedrooms even within similar forms; (7) target a varied market with regard to family typology, including young families, older families, couples, single person households, owner-occupiers, and rental investors; and (8) provide a variety of parking locations and types within each block or street to allow flexibility and optimise space. In addition, delivering Papakainga to accommodate a communal intergenerational form of living relevant to Māori and Pasifika culture is encouraged (Tāmaki Regeneration Company 2016b).

The recently launched *Tāmaki Precinct Masterplan* also emphasises meeting diverse housing needs: 'Tāmaki needs a variety of housing options so people from all walks of life can live within the area'. Consideration is given to addressing 'cultural responsiveness, affordability, communal models of living, mixed use, vertical mixed use, accessibility, and adaptive design'. Different types of housing are proposed including the 'small house, shell house, DIY interior, dual key, mortgage buster, big house, apartment, terrace house, standalone co-housing/papakainga: multiple units with communal facilities, culturally and age responsive house, social house, market house, for future in-fill, affordable building design for future mixed use' (Tāmaki Regeneration Company 2019a, p. 31).

In policy, plans, strategies, and design documents relating to the Tāmaki Regeneration Programme, mixed housing is frequently mentioned and explained as both an approach and an outcome. In mixed-tenure neighbourhoods, 'state housing tenants will live within a diverse community of private renters, new homeowners (through affordable housing products), and more established families, leaving behind the stigma of living in a state house' (Tāmaki Regeneration Company 2019b, p. 7). Diversity in neighbourhoods will be encouraged through providing 'a range of housing types and tenures (ownership) that attract different types of people to each neighbourhood' (Tāmaki Redevelopment Company 2013, p. 7).

As evidenced previously, definitions of 'mixed' and 'diversity' relate to both tenure and physical forms in relation to housing needs. The mixed housing policy being implemented in Glen Innes aims to improve the housing stock and optimise land use through providing diverse housing choices for different levels of income and introducing higher-income earners and homeowners into Glen Innes. With regeneration, the fabric of physical forms and structure of housing tenure change dramatically, thereby impacting the socioeconomic and demographic characteristics of local residents in terms of income, educational background, age, ethnicity, household type, and gender (Atkinson and Jacobs 2008; Kleit and Carnegie 2011).

However, whether increasing diversity in physical housing form and social groups will naturally and necessarily lead to 'inclusive' communities is questioned by many researchers and the public (Kleit and Carnegie 2011; Morris et al. 2012; Randolph et al. 2004). According to the extensive existing research, the degree of success is highly reliant on the quality of urban planning and urban design in the renewed area (Allen et al. 2005; Casey et al. 2007). In the Tāmaki regeneration programmes, although a lot of attention has been paid to building diverse housing types that suit the different needs of different social groups and creating a strong and inclusive community, the question of how to facilitate community cohesiveness through planning and design has not been addressed.

The question of whether mixed housing can create an 'inclusive' and strong community remains open in the context of Glen Innes. Historically, Glen Innes has been characterised by high levels of ethnic diversity, income diversity, and strong networks (Cole 2015; Gordon et al. 2017; Hancock et al. 2007), where the mixing of cultures is widely acknowledged. Mixed housing policy is believed to increase diversity with regard to income level (Lupton and Tunstall 2008). However, in terms of community cohesion, the level of social interaction and contact between residents from different housing tenures in Glen Innes is not clear. The interventions towards constructing a mixed-tenure community have come at the cost of demolishing previous state housing and the displacement of tenants, thus making the objective of 'creating an inclusive community' more complicated to achieve.

6.3   The Rationales for Different Regeneration Projects

Impacted by the corporatisation and privatisation of the state-housing sector, Glen Innes became a 'residualised' area intended to house the poor and 'special needs' groups. Government and public discourse characterised Glen Innes as a problem area made up of problem neighbourhoods, and thus it became the target for a series of redevelopment programmes after 2000 (Table 6.3).

The assumptions underlying intensification and renewal firstly focus on the place itself, with the upgrading of the neighbourhood regarded as the main concern. For housing renewal initiatives, 'problem areas' are generally seen as being those with high concentrations of sub-standard housing. Accordingly, the solution involves the improvement or removal of that housing stock, while 'success' is measured in terms of the physical characteristics of the housing stock. 'Problem neighbourhoods' are

Table 6.3 Brief outline of social housing redevelopment programmes in Glen Innes

Programme	Main development sites	Start date and status
Community Renewal Programme	Talbot Park	2001, now completed
The Glen Innes Liveable Community Plan	All land within a 10-min walk of Glen Innes town centre	2004, now completed
Tāmaki Transformation Programmes Phase 1 (led by Creating Communities)	Northern Glen Innes	2007, now nearly completed
	Wai O Taiki Bay	2007, now nearly completed
Tāmaki Regeneration Programme	Fenchurch	2013, ongoing
	Farringdon Street	Ongoing
	Line/Epping	Ongoing
	Overlea	Ongoing

also associated with high levels of unemployment, poverty, poor health, poor educational attainment, and crime. These are the underpinning assumptions of the Community Renewal Programme, the Glen Innes Liveable Community Plan, and Northern Glen Innes Redevelopment Project, implemented mainly to upgrade the physical environment, especially the post-war state housing.

6.3.1   Social Inclusion and Strong Sustainable Communities

The Community Renewal Programme—Talbot Park Renewal Project—is one of six community renewal projects initiated by Housing New Zealand Corporation in 2001 to 'address social exclusion and foster strong sustainable communities' (Ministry for the Environment 2008, para. 21). While part of the suburb of Glen Innes when the project began, Talbot Park is now identified as Point England. It is a five-hectare triangular block of land (four hectares of housing neighbourhoods and one hectare of existing public reserve) bounded by Pilkington Road, Point England Road, and Apirana Avenue. The justification behind the Talbot Park Renewal Project was the deprivation, social exclusion, and long history of ongoing security and social problems associated with the high concentration of HNZC properties and privately owned low-income rental housing.

Prior to the Talbot Park Renewal Project, the area was predominantly state housing, with 167 of the original 180 properties owned by Housing New Zealand Corporation (Fig. 6.1). More than half of the state housing had been built in the early 1960s (Fig. 6.2). A wide range of ethnicities were represented in Talbot Park, with around 50% Pacific peoples, 20% Māori, 20% Asian and 10% other (including Iraqi, Iranian, Fijian Indian, and European) (Ministry for the Environment 2008). The area included nine three-storey 'star flat' blocks (containing 108 units) and 59 two-storey 'duplex flats' (Boffa Miskell Ltd. 2009).

By the completion of the programme, 111 new and 108 refurbished units had replaced the 167 state houses, increasing the density from 1 unit/240m^2 to 1 unit/180m^2. The original site layout had also been replaced by a new urbanist-inspired master plan. The multi-size housing units range from single bedroom or 2-bedroom apartments, to 3-bedroom terrace houses, and up to large 4–8 bedroom family homes (Bracey 2007). Apart from the housing redevelopment, this programmes also incorporated various sustainability measures. Two new parks were built to provide shade and a children's playground. A low-impact urban design was deployed, with rainwater recycling and greywater systems, solar water heating, and a retention tank system. Other features included improved design and layout of roads and ease of pedestrian access (Ford 2011; Ministry for the Environment 2008).

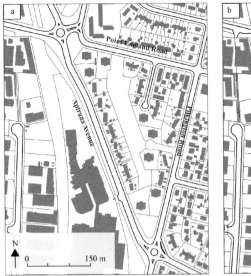
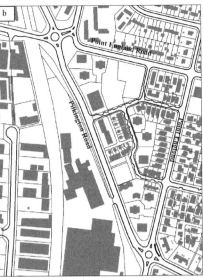

Fig. 6.1 Ground plans of Talbot Park before and after housing renewal in the early 2000s. **a** Before renewal; **b** After renewal

Duplex flats (before renewal)   Star flats (before renewal)

Apartments (after renewal)

Fig. 6.2 Residential buildings in Talbot Park before and after housing renewal in the early 2000s (*Source* Authors' photographs)

6.3.2 Liveability, Urban Growth, and Diversity of Activities

The Glen Innes Liveable Community Plan forms part of Auckland City's Growth Management Strategy, which seeks to 'improve the physical environment and attract business investment, stimulate development, and encourage a diversity of activities to bring about life and vibrancy to an area of change' (Auckland City Council 2004, p. 6). It is also a component of Auckland City's Liveable Communities 2050 Strategy, which aims to build 'safe, attractive places that encourage walking and cycling, offer a choice of lifestyle and a choice of transport, have mixed use at their core and are able to create a sense of belonging' (Scott et al. 2006, p. 5). Following a four-year mandatory period for community consultation, the Glen Innes Liveable Community Plan (*Glen Innes into the Future*) was released in 2004. To maximise the potential of the railway station and encourage more people to use trains, the Glen Innes train station is the focal point of the design. All land within a 10-min walk of Glen Innes town centre, totalling around 1 hectare or more, is designated an area of change in the plan (Auckland City Council 2004).

Auckland Council believes the intensification and urban renewal programmes will create a more liveable and safer community. Selected areas of Glen Innes have, therefore, been rezoned Residential 8a and Residential 8b to support the provision of medium-density housing, such as town houses, terrace housing, and low-rise apartments. The plan also incorporates landscaping, private open space, energy efficiency, and neighbourhood character. The rezoning indicates the Council's intention to promote urban growth by increasing housing density. The building of amenity and infrastructure is expected to create liveability by improving the physical environment. However, critics claim that liveability is being used as a strategy to reduce crime and polish the image of Glen Innes rather than solve the problems of poverty, as limited attention has been paid to social issues such as social inequality and social justice (Scott et al. 2006).

6.3.3 Healthier and Safer Community

In 2007, the Tāmaki Transformation Programme was set up to address social issues and take advantage of opportunities in Tāmaki (Laing et al. 2010). The programme has since been working to redevelop the Tāmaki area over the next 15–20 years and make it a thriving and prosperous place to live. This programme is the first and largest community-based regeneration programme in New Zealand (The Treasury 2013).

From 2007 and 2012, the redevelopment was facilitated by Housing New Zealand working with a private company, Creating Communities. Headed by developer Murdoch Dryden, Creating Communities is a partnership between Arrow International Group Limited, Hopper Developments, and Southside Group Management. Creating Communities was contracted by Housing New Zealand to transform the

156 state rental properties in northwestern Glen Innes and Wai O Taiki Bay into 260 new homes (Dey 2013; Arrow International 2020; Arcus Property Limited 2015).

Overall, the project has built more than 350 mixed-tenure homes. However, only 78 homes remain owned by Housing New Zealand, with about 39 others owned by other social housing providers in Glen Innes. The project involved the relocation of 142 households (Arrow International 2020; Arcus Property Limited 2015). The remaining 148 homes were sold to private owners. As a result, the number of state houses was reduced by 40.

The developer claims their social housing designs for small and individual sites provide higher quality, more modern homes. However, the decrease in social housing raises questions regarding for whom the 'healthier and safer community' was built. Another issue is the relocation of existing tenants. Some had to move to areas outside Glen Innes or the wider Tāmaki area. This relocation thus affected the whole community. Those who had to move away felt they were losing their home. 'I don't want to move. To me, this is my home', Tere Tarapu told a Television New Zealand Pacific correspondent (Barton 2014). For those left behind, the sense of community was weakened. Based on a survey sent out to the community of 16,000 members, Peter Fa'afiu, chief of communications for the Tāmaki Redevelopment Company noted the prevailing sentiment in the 1,100 responses received was 'Less hui (meetings), more doey' (Barton 2014). At the time of writing, Creating Communities had completed its redevelopment of state housing in Northern Glen Innes.

6.3.4 Cultural Density, Community Cohesion, and Community Approach

In 2012, the Tāmaki Redevelopment Company (TRC), co-owned by the government (59%) and Auckland Council (41%), was established to 'continue the transformation of Tāmaki (the suburbs of Glen Innes, Pt England, and Panmure) that was started through the Tāmaki Transformation Programme' (Tāmaki Redevelopment Company 2013, p. 7). The Tāmaki Transformation Programme was renamed the Tāmaki Regeneration Programme, with a scope incorporating 880 ha across Glen Innes, Point England, and Panmure and 10 development sites. Among them, the Northern Glen Innes, Wai O Taiki Bay, Fenchurch, Overlea, and Line/Epping developments are all located in Glen Innes. On March 31, 2016, all the Housing New Zealand Corporation properties in Tāmaki were transferred to the Tāmaki Redevelopment Company. The value of the assets transferred was $1.6 billion (Tāmaki Regeneration Company 2017). However, it was not until 2014 that the Tāmaki Redevelopment Company began to directly engage in the redevelopment. The first plan involved the demolition or removal of 144 Housing New Zealand Corporation homes in the Fenchurch and Overlea neighbourhoods, and their replacement by 550 mixed-tenure houses. By 2020, the regeneration activities in Fenchurch, Wai O Taiki Bay, and Northern Glen Innes were nearly completed.

Valuing cultural diversity and the 'Tāmaki way of working' have been identified as important strategies for inclusive redevelopment. For example, the 2013 *Tāmaki Strategic Framework* identifies Tāmaki as 'a place where cultural diversity, social inclusiveness, creativity and heritage are celebrated' (p. 18). It also says, 'The community has developed the "Tāmaki way of working" – an approach to engagement that respects the unique cultural identity and expectations of the people of Tāmaki. This includes a grass roots approach that is reflected in the commitment the Tāmaki Redevelopment Company has to involve the Tāmaki community in shaping the physical, social and economic regeneration of the area' (p. 15).

The 2018 Tāmaki masterplan summary presents a vision of an 'inclusive Tāmaki, a place where everyone can flourish and prosper in an inclusive, affordable and vibrant community'. As Lees (2008) argues, 'diversity is figured alternatively as an obstacle to, the means for, and even the objective of urban regeneration' (p. 615). Celebrating ethno-cultural diversity is highly valued in plans and frameworks describing and envisioning Glen Innes, not only in the Tāmaki Regeneration Programme, but also in previous programmes. The documents analysed use phrases such as 'cultural diversity of the community', 'unique identity and ethnic diversity of Glen Innes', and 'rich cultural heritage and young, diverse, multi-cultural population' to portray the community's characteristics. However, plans and frameworks pay more attention to the cultural arts, events, and experience as selling points and increasing heterogeneity regarding income in relation to the diversity identified as an outcome of community regeneration.

6.4 Discourse of Partnership: Towards a Hybrid Approach to Social Housing Provision

As in cities in the UK, the USA, Australia, and Europe, the community-based social housing redevelopment programmes in Glen Innes have been increasingly influenced by the inter-sector hybrid approach since 2000 (Atkinson 1999; Blessing 2012). The biggest regeneration programme in New Zealand, the Tāmaki Transformation Programme, reflects a hybrid approach that connects 'more than one sector – public, private and third' (Bratt 2012, p. 439). An institutional hierarchy consisting of central government agencies, local government, place-based joint-ownership organisations, private companies, and third-sector housing providers has been formed. As shown in Table 6.4, these agents have played different roles with regard to the development and redevelopment of Glen Innes. Both the formation and operation of this partnership are a result of New Zealand social housing reform.

As discussed in the previous section, during the period from 2000 and 2008, the state-housing sector was still under the control of central government and state housing in Glen Innes was managed by Housing New Zealand Corporation. The current redevelopment is based on a contract between Housing New Zealand Corporation and Creating Community. The new partnership was enabled by the Social

Table 6.4 Partnerships in regeneration programmes

Programme	Partnership
Community Renewal Programme	Housing New Zealand Corporation, Auckland City Council, and the Glen Innes Community
The Glen Innes Liveable Community Plan	Auckland City Council with the community and key stakeholders
Tāmaki Transformation Programmes	Housing New Zealand Corporation and Creating Communities
Tāmaki Regeneration Programmes	Tāmaki Regeneration Company, Community, Kāinga Ora—Homes and Communities, mana whenua, Auckland Council, and the private sector

Housing Reform (Housing Restructuring and Tenancy Matters Amendment) Act 2013, which allocated more responsibility for social housing services and redevelopment to local government and community housing providers. The establishment in 2012 of the Tāmaki Redevelopment Company, co-owned by the government (59%) and Auckland Council (41%), exemplifies this trend (The Treasury 2013). The company took an active role in redeveloping the community. Apart from taking charge of approximately 2,800 Housing New Zealand Corporation properties in Glen Innes, Panmure, and Point England from the year 2015, it was also provided with a $NZ200 million Crown loan to support the regeneration (The Treasury 2013). The Tāmaki Redevelopment Company established the Tāmaki Housing Association (THA), which is responsible for managing social housing tenancies, thus acting as a community housing provider. The Tāmaki Housing Association delivers these services for the Tāmaki Redevelopment Company's existing portfolio of around 2,800 social houses. It is a registered community housing provider and a wholly owned subsidiary of Tāmaki Redevelopment Company.

The Tāmaki Redevelopment Company published the *Tāmaki Reference Plan* in 2016 and in 2018 refreshed the masterplan for Tāmaki in partnership with Kāinga Ora—Homes and Communities, Auckland Council, and Auckland Transport (Tāmaki Regeneration Company 2020). The *Tāmaki Reference Plan* outlines four areas of activity: social transformation, economic development, placemaking, and housing resources. At this stage, the main activities of the Tāmaki Redevelopment Company revolve around social housing redevelopment. As outlined in the reference plan, the regeneration in Tāmaki is housing-led. In accordance with zoning ordinances for house building, 'significantly intensified redevelopment' and 'mixed-tenure neighbourhood' are characteristic of the social housing redevelopment occurring there.

While the city level plans formulated by Auckland Council provide guidelines for land use and housing building standards, the community level plans have mainly been proposed by the Tāmaki Regeneration Company and specify sites for development and the design of development. The plan drawn up by the Tāmaki Regeneration Company specifically targets social housing in Glen Innes for redevelopment.

The *Tāmaki Reference Plan* was the main guiding document between 2016 and 2019. In 2019, the Tāmaki Redevelopment Company launched the *Tāmaki Precinct Masterplan*, which outlines a bold vision for the future of Tāmaki regeneration. Apart from these two main documents, the Tāmaki Regeneration Company has released a Tāmaki strategic framework, Tāmaki design framework, the Fenchurch Neighbourhood Plan, the Tāmaki Redevelopment Company Annual Report 2019, and Tāmaki Regeneration Statement of Performance Expectations 2020–2021. As instruments or expressions of planning ordinances, all these documents have significantly affected social housing redevelopment in Tāmaki.

6.4.1 Reducing the Role of Central Government in Social Housing Provision

As part of the National government's wider programme of reform, the Social Housing Reform (Housing Restructuring and Tenancy Matters Amendment) Act 2013 redefined the role of Housing New Zealand Corporation. The responsibilities for assessing and allocating tenants to available houses were shifted from Housing New Zealand Corporation to the Ministry of Social Development. Since the reform, Housing New Zealand Corporation has functioned as one of many social housing providers in the market. The Ministry of Social Development has taken over the role of managing social housing and purchasing social housing properties. The Ministry of Social Development also has responsibility for forecasting demand, and setting purchasing intentions to indicate its long-term requirements to the market in advance. Through transforming the roles of Housing New Zealand and the Ministry of Social Development, the National government separated the provider and demand management functions in housing provision, with Housing New Zealand Corporation now identified as a public housing provider and landlord in charge of public housing supply, and the Ministry of Social Development as the government agency managing the demand side.

In relation to the Tāmaki Regeneration Programme, Homes, Land, Community, as a subsidiary company of the former Housing New Zealand, and a team from Kāinga Ora formed a partnership with the Tāmaki Regeneration Company in 2018. Homes, Land, Community now acts as the master developer in regeneration projects and is responsible for delivering new houses in Tāmaki through working with the Tāmaki Regeneration Company on urban design and placemaking. The objective is to 'drive the supply of diverse housing stock to the Auckland market through the housing redevelopment programme, including the delivery of state, affordable, KiwiBuild, and private market homes' (Tāmaki Regeneration Company 2020, p. 15). At the same time, the task of monitoring the Tāmaki Regeneration Company has been shifted from Treasury to MHUD (Tāmaki Regeneration Company 2019a).

6.4.2   Planning for Housing Affordability: The Support from Auckland Council

Plans and strategies initiated by local government are important. They provide guidance for community-based regeneration and there is increasing emphasis on facilitating the provision of social and affordable housing through the planning system (Austin et al. 2014). The Auckland Council has played an important role in transforming Glen Innes through planning control and zoning ordinance.

A sharp increase in house prices occurred during the 2000s (The New Zealand Productivity Commission 2012). House prices increased by 80% in the period 2002–2008 (Department of The Prime Minister and Cabinet 2008). Meanwhile, the rate of home ownership fell by 4% in the period 1996–2006 and was projected to decrease by a further 5 or 6% by 2016 because of younger people being unable to afford to purchase a first home (Austin et al. 2014). In response to the affordability issue, in 2008 the Labour Government implemented the Affordable Housing: Enabling Territorial Authorities Act, which enabled 'local councils to adopt an affordable housing policy requiring developers to make an affordable housing contribution' (Austin et al. 2014). Although this Act did not work well due to its complex, costly, and risky requirements, and the lack of a government subsidy, it was an attempt by the government to facilitate housing affordability in New Zealand. After 2008, the National government restructured the Affordable Housing: Enabling Territorial Authorities Act, and housing affordability has remained one of the main themes of housing policy ever since.

The 2012 New Zealand Productivity Commission report reviewing housing affordability identified that the existing urban planning approach in New Zealand was constraining the release of new residential land and thus creating scarcity, limited housing choice, and increased house prices (The New Zealand Productivity Commission 2012). The report further suggested that land supply should be increased in both brownfields and greenfields. It also called on councils to 'review regulatory processes with the aim of providing simplified, speedier and less costly consenting processes and formalities' (The New Zealand Productivity Commission 2012, p. 268). The arguments made with respect to freeing up land supply and reducing constraints on housing development had a strong impact on planning practices in the following years.

In response to the Productivity Commission report, the Housing Accords and Special Housing Area Act (HASHAA) was passed in 2013 to 'enhance housing affordability by facilitating an increase in land and housing supply in certain regions or districts, listed in Schedule 1, identified as having housing supply and affordability issues' (Ministry of Housing and Urban Development 2013, p. 6). A housing accord is an 'agreement between the Minister and a territorial authority to work together to address housing supply and affordability issues in the district of the territorial authority' (Ministry of Housing and Urban Development 2013, p. 10).

Following the passing of the Act, the Auckland Housing Accord was signed by Housing Minister Dr. Nick Smith and Auckland Mayor Len Brown. The accord aimed to increase housing supply and affordability by fast-tracking planning permission for new housing in Special Housing Areas before the Auckland Unitary Plan become operative and the government's Resource Management Act reforms for planning processes took effect. The accord was a 3-year agreement, which expired 22 May 2017 (Ministry of Housing and Urban Development 2013, 2018).

Special Housing Areas are defined as 'geographic locations in a scheduled area, which are identified and then jointly approved by Council and the government, and have the potential to deliver increased land and housing supply' (Ministry of Housing and Urban Development 2013). They are established in greenfield and brownfield areas inside the Rural Urban Boundary and are directly subject to the qualifying development criteria pursued under an operative plan (Doyle 2013). Under the Housing Accord Act, only Auckland Council could exercise power over the planning process and grant resource consents with regard to housing in these areas, while the government committed to not using its power under the RMA to override Council's power. Developers were required to make 10% of the houses built affordable, whereby the house price would not exceed 70% of the median house price for Auckland, or to build 5% affordable housing, defined as housing costs not exceeding 30% of Auckland's median gross household income (Cole 2017). By the end of 2016, a total of 10 tranches of Special Housing Areas had been established, including 154 Special Housing Areas (Auckland Council 2016).

The Housing Accords and Special Housing Area Act was an attempt to increase land supply through changing local urban planning procedures and practices. In Auckland, the Council significantly promoted urban intensification and greenfield development to address housing unaffordability issues. As 'a fast policy' circuit, the Act helped speed up intensification and development activities in the period between 2013 and 2017. Responding to the New Zealand Productivity Commission's (2012) call, the Auckland Plan (2012) proposed building a compact city and providing affordable housing (Murphy 2016). The Draft Unitary Plan confirmed the Council's commitment to set out 'additional tools for enabling affordable neighbourhood'. The inclusionary housing regime or inclusionary zoning policies are set out in the Addendum to the draft Unitary Plan (Murphy and Rehm 2013).

To increase affordable housing, Auckland Council increased the supply of land for housing in Auckland in relation to the Special Housing Areas Act. This goal was also embedded in the Auckland Unitary Plan after the Act expired. Inclusionary zoning has been the main tool deployed by Auckland Council to encourage the development of affordable housing for lower-income groups. Private developers are included in the provision of affordable housing through requirements or incentives.

Table 6.5 shows how Glen Innes was defined in a series of plans as an area in need of 'revitalisation' and suitable for 'medium' or 'high' density housing. The zoning ordinances in the District Plan and Unitary Plan, along with the spatial strategy outlined in the Auckland Plan, have provided regulatory support allowing the redevelopment in Glen Innes to occur. Since 1999, five main plans launched by Auckland Council have directly impacted the development of physical form in Glen Innes. The development of spatial planning and design guidance within these plans has provided the basis for the evolution from low-density to medium- and high-density residential areas in Glen Innes through various standards for site size, building height, and housing form.

6.5   Māori Housing Policy

National housing policies in response to issues experienced by Māori have changed over time. In the 1910s Māori had lower incomes relative to European New Zealanders in the settler economy and in the decades following frequently lived in 'deplorable' housing conditions, with most Māori people unable to afford their own homes (Krivan 1990). Between 1920 and 1939, there were a small number of Māori people living in Auckland. Of the around 805 Māori living there in 1929, many were living in the central city district. Their housing conditions were poor, with nearly one-third living in huts, whares, or camps. New Zealand health officials at the time believed the poor housing conditions significantly contributed to high rates of tuberculosis among Māori (Krivan 1990).

Māori housing policies were separate from general housing policies, especially with regard to funding, scope, and access. The Department of Māori Affairs (DMA) housing programme was established in the 1930s under the Māori Housing Act (1935) and the Māori Housing Amendment Act (1938). Māori had been able to apply for construction loans from the Special Māori Housing Fund since the Māori Land Settlement Scheme 1929 and the Native Housing Act 1935 were put in place. However, the proportion spent on Māori housing was smaller than expenditure on general state housing because few Māori met the application criteria. Contributing factors were the discriminatory practices occurring within the State Advances Corporation (SAC), and the fact that organisations charged with allocations and funding mainly focused on rural land (The Ministry of Health 2019).

During World War II, many young Māori moved from rural areas to cities for employment. Approximately 10,000 Māori were living in Auckland in 1943 when New Zealand's Māori population was 96,457 (Wanhalla 2006). Both central and local governments were unprepared for the rapid increase in urban migrants, which increased pressure on accommodation. At the same time, the number of Māori who living in urban slums and in desperate need of housing increased. A survey conducted by the Native Affairs Department found that 46% of 369 Māori houses assessed had no windows and 59% were overcrowded.

The Māori Hostel Movement was one of a range of responses to Māori Housing. The aim of Māori hostels was to provide healthier living conditions for young Māori men and women (Campbell 2020). Massive state-housing developments were another response, beginning in Glen Innes in 1946 and Orakei in 1947. Different policies have been implemented by successive governments. In general, Labour governments have attempted to increase state rental housing stock with the National preferring to support home ownership by selling state homes to tenants.

Table 6.5 Plans initiated by Auckland City Council and Auckland Council

Plan	Responsibility	Year	How Glen Innes is described	Objective
Auckland Isthmus District Plan	Auckland City Council	1999	Area zoned for medium-intensity development;	Enable residential development to occur that is distinctly different to the higher densities able to be achieved in the Residential 7 zones and the low-intensity character that the Residential 5 zone will maintain
Auckland Isthmus District Plan (Plan Change 58, 61)	Auckland City Council	2004	Area needs revitalisation; A Priority 1 'area of change'; Suitable locations for quality higher density housing;	Build urban living communities; Develop a liveable community plan; Making Glen Innes an attractive place to live, work, and invest
The Auckland Plan 2050	Auckland Council	2018		Anticipated household growth during 2018–2048: 3,590; Anticipated population growth during 2018–2048: 10,210; Enabled housing capacity (does not include centre and mixed-use zones): 23,560
Unitary Plan	Auckland Council	2016	High, reasonably high, and medium-intensity residential area	Enables intensification

Māori have faced challenges in accessing state rentals and loans. As noted by the Waitangi Tribunal, although Māori theoretically had access to State Advances Corporation (SAC) and Housing Division resources, in reality they were effectively excluded from mainstream housing assistance until the 1950s. In 1944, the government built a separate pool of state rentals for Māori, but only 97 houses were placed in this pool between 1948 and 1954 for the whole country. In 1948, the government incorporated Māori into the wider state-housing rental scheme. In the same year, the 'pepper-potting' policy, which intended to place Māori in Pākēha neighbourhoods, began in Tamaki. This policy originated in the fear that concentrations of Māori would contribute to accusations of ghettoisation (Orange 1977; Ferguson 1995).

In the 1950s, the Department of Māori Affairs increased the number of houses being built for Māori. More Māori entered the state rental housing sector and secure tenure, then described as a 'house for life'. In terms of property ownership, few Māori became homeowners, with many becoming reliant on state housing for life. As pointed out by Claudia Orange (1977), home ownership by Māori did not receive enough support from the First Labour Government among their other reforms.

In 1961, the Department of Māori Affairs argued that housing was central to ensuring social and economic equality and sufficient access to resources for Māori. While state houses began to be sold to the public in 1950, Māori state tenants were only able to purchase the state houses they lived in from 1961. In that period, housing stock in New Zealand increased at the highest rate in the country's history. About 2,160 houses were being built each year, peaking at 3,440 in 1975 (Rout et al. 2020). This construction boom was supported by state supplied deposits and low mortgage rates. Over 10,000 state houses were built between 1960 and 1971. The *Report of the Commission of Inquiry: Housing in New Zealand* 1971 criticised the Department of Māori Affairs on the grounds that their housing intervention had led to the ethnic concentration of Māori in Otara, Mangere, and Porirua. The Department of Māori Affairs shifted its attention to kaumatua flats, youth hostels, and rural housing improvements from the 1970s (Woods 2002).

Owning to the high level of support in the form of cheap loans and the chance to buy state houses, 52% of Māori owned their own home in 1976. By the end of the 1970s, it was believed the housing crisis facing Māori had been overcome. Cooperation between the Department of Māori Affairs and State Advances Corporation contributed to this achievement. The Department of Māori Affairs referred all qualified applicants to the State Advances Corporation for home loans, and it also developed schemes for those who did not currently qualify (Moteane 1984). Māori housing support reached its peak in Auckland in 1986, when 86% of finance for Māori mortgages came from the state.

J. Cornwall (1982 as cited in Rout et al. 2020) argued there was little evidence of 'special Māori housing needs' beyond those experienced by Pākeha of similar socioeconomic status. The main concern identified in relation to Māori housing was communal ownership of Māori land. Disagreeing with these conclusions, The New Zealand Māori Council commissioned an investigation led by Professor Whatarangi Winiata. The resulting report argued that a special housing programme was needed for Māori because of cultural differences, the lower average socioeconomic status of Māori, and overt racism in the housing market (Winiata 1983).

In 1986, the Residential Tenancies Act was launched. This Act provides legal protection for tenants and landlords, but it does not address the issue of secure occupancy. The Act marked a shift in the houses for life policy by giving landlords the power to move tenants out after giving adequate notice.

A rapid decline in home ownership and a housing crisis among Māori took place in the 1990s. Since the early 1990s, the focus had been creating a seamless rental market in which the cost of renting in both the public and private sectors would be set by market forces (Murphy 1997, p. 272). The number of state houses decreased and full market rents were introduced for state housing. Similar to the central government, Auckland Council also sought to reduce its involvement in housing provision during the 1990s by selling its residential properties. All these policies significantly reduced Māori homeownership.

Māori have experienced a growing housing crisis in Auckland as housing prices have soared. Concerns about homelessness, housing insecurity, and unhealthy housing have grown. According to a 2015 report: (1) a total of 11,730 Māori experienced severe housing deprivation; (2) an estimated 1,290 Māori were homeless, 235 were in emergency accommodation, and 1,056 lived in commercial accommodation or on Marae, and 9,149 lived in severely overcrowded private homes; and (3) a further 22,184 Māori (34.5% of all recipients) received an income-related rent subsidy as Housing New Zealand Corporation clients (Māori Housing Network Investment Strategy 2015, p. 6).

Housing policies implemented by successive governments have withdrawn direct government responsibility for Māori housing. While the introduction of the third sector to provide community housing showed some support for Māori. However, it has limited capacity to solve the general housing crisis arising from large structural problems. Meanwhile, a number of tailored schemes mainly target rural Māori land, such as papakāinga housing—a group of three or more houses built on whenua Māori (Māori land) as a 'community' that may include broader support and occupant involvement (The Māori Housing Network 2017, p. 3). The Ministry of Māori Development (The Te Puni Kōkiri) has produced a series of policy documents to support the development of small-scale papakāinga (generally 3–10 houses) on whenua Māori.

6.6 Summary

This chapter has examined the influence of shifts in ideology on the evolution of state-housing policy and the process of Glen Innes's regeneration, including the justification for mixing housing neighbourhoods, the rationale behind the development programmes, and the principle of partnership. Economic and political trends in New Zealand have followed ideological shifts in wider Western society from Keynesianism to neoliberalism, the dominant ideology behind globalisation and contemporary reforms in various countries (Peck and Tickell 2002). This change is reflected particularly in the role of central government and governance rules, including those for social housing and planning practice, and how they have influenced the built environment in an era of transformation.

Urban regeneration, by its nature, is an interventionist activity. Following the political and economic reforms of 1991 in New Zealand, the economic characteristics and features of neoliberalism have been reflected in the role of urban regeneration, and the way it operates (Roberts and Sykes 2000). Based on the principles of equality of opportunity, social housing policy had previously been oriented towards creating social equity in the New Zealand context.

Looking back at the history of Glen Innes, as well as the related historical political-economic context, it is clear that Glen Innes has been shaped by the political and economic ideologies that were or currently are dominant in New Zealand. Glen Innes benefitted from the birth of the welfare state and the ensuing wave of housing construction during the period from the 1940s to the 1960s. The construction of both state houses and private houses in wider Auckland and the Tāmaki area proceeded quickly. Between 1945 and 1948, 2,500 to 3,000 new private houses were being built in Auckland each year, along with 800 state houses. In the Tāmaki area, 3,000 units were built in these three years. With new residents moving in, the Glen Innes town centre was the first planned town centre in Auckland. Glen Innes gradually became a mature community. This process of rapid construction significantly transformed the landscape from a rural area to an urban suburb, with the Crown playing an important role in the development of state houses. The development of market gardens into private subdivisions was already taking place as early as 1927 when most of the land in Tāmaki was privately owned. The Crown, therefore, had to negotiate with landowners in order to buy the land for state houses (Jackson 1965).

The historical processes occurring in Glen Innes have contributed to its unique character. Prior to 1840, it was the site of Māori settlements. It then became famous for its fertile rural land under the Liberals, before being developed as a garden suburb in the process of building a welfare state under Keynesian ideology. Finally, under neoliberalism, it became a run-down area viewed as in need of redevelopment. Ideologies from different historical periods have thus defined and contextualised Glen Innes. The discourse of Glen Innes has shifted from a suburban garden utopia for workers, to a run-down suburb beset by poverty and crime, to the best choice for first-home buyers. Glen Innes has always been viewed as having a distinct character, with particular features magnified and used to justify the development and redevelopment activities.

The introduction of the market promoted the regeneration and privatisation of state housing in Glen Innes. Due to the rapid growth of the Auckland population, and increasing pressure on housing, state housing occupying valuable land in urban and suburban areas has experienced redevelopment activity. In Glen Innes, state housing has been sold, and market rentals introduced for state tenants.

The institutional structure affecting the development of housing and the built environment of state housing in Glen Innes has also been shaped by neoliberal governance mechanisms. The withdrawal of Housing New Zealand Corporation and the introduction of the Tāmaki Regeneration Company have resulted in a new partnership structure consisting of the central government, local council, Housing New Zealand Corporation, and the Tāmaki Regeneration Company. All play different roles in the process of regeneration: central government is responsible for social housing policy; Auckland Council is responsible for spatial development strategies and the zoning ordinances used to manage the density and intensity of land use; and the Tāmaki Regeneration Company is the agent putting policies and plans into practice.

Housing density and intensity of land use in Glen Innes have gradually increased with the support of changing policies and plans. The mixed housing strategy implemented in the process of housing renewal has significantly changed the physical form and social-economic characteristics of Glen Innes and is expected to lessen the stigma attached to the Glen Innes area and restore its reputation. However, mixed housing does not naturally and necessarily lead to community cohesion, and the question of how to promote social cohesiveness in the process of mixing tenure and housing types has been ignored. In the following chapter, this thesis explores the physical characteristics of housing renewal and the impact of housing renewal on local residents.

References

Adams A (2017) New landlord for 1140 Tauranga Housing New Zealand tenants. Minister of Social Housing. https://www.beehive.govt.nz/release/new-landlord-1140-tauranga-hnz-tenants. Accessed 20 October 2022

Allen C, Camina M, Casey R et al (2005) Mixed tenure, twenty years on: nothing out of the ordinary. Joseph Rowntree Foundation, York. https://urbanrim.org.uk/cache/Allen-et-al_twenty-years-on.pdf. Accessed 20 October 2022

Arthurson K (2012) Social mix and the city: challenging the mixed communities consensus in housing and urban planning policies. CSIRO, Melbourne, Australia

Atkinson R (1999) Discourses of partnership and empowerment in contemporary British urban regeneration. Urban Stud 36(1):59–72

Atkinson R, Jacobs K (2008) Public housing in Australia: stigma, home and opportunity. Housing and Community Research Unit, Hobart, Australia

Atkinson R, Kintrea K (1998) Reconnecting excluded communities: the neighbourhood impacts of owner occupation. Scottish Homes, Edinburgh

Arcus Property Limited (2015) Glen Innes redevelopment project update. http://www.arcusdevelopments.co.nz/blog/new-glen-innes-redevelopment-starts/. Accessed 20 October 2022

Arrow International (2020) Glen Innes residential development: creating communities in Auckland's housing shortage. https://arrowinternational.co.nz/portfoliopage/glen-innes-residential-development/. Accessed 20 October 2022

Auckland City Council (2004) Glen Innes into the future: Auckland urban living. Auckland City Council, Auckland, New Zealand

Auckland Council (2012) The Auckland plan 2012. https://www.aucklandcouncil.govt.nz/plans-projects-policies-reports-bylaws/our-plans-strategies/Documents/auckland-plan-2012-full-document.pdf. Accessed 20 October 2022

Auckland Council (2016) Housing supply and special housing areas. https://www.aucklandcouncil.govt.nz/grants-community-support-housing/Pages/housing-supply-special-housing-areas.aspx. Accessed 20 October 2022

August M (2016) Revitalisation gone wrong: mixed-income public housing redevelopment in Toronto's Don Mount Court. Urban Stud 53(16):3405–3422

Aurand A (2010) Density, housing types and mixed land use: smart tools for affordable housing? Urban Stud 47(5):1015–1036

Austin PM, Gurran N, Whitehead CME (2014) Planning and affordable housing in Australia, New Zealand and England: common culture; different mechanisms. J Housing Built Environ 29(3):455–472

Barton C (2014) The battle of Glen Innes. https://www.metromag.co.nz/city-life/city-life-property/the-battle-of-glen-innes. Accessed 20 October 2022

Barnett JR, Barnett P, Kearns RA (1998) Declining professional dominance? trends in the proletarianisation of primary care in New Zealand. Soc Sci Med 46(2):193–207

Beaumont J (2008) Introduction: faith-based organisations and urban social issues. Urban Stud 45(10):2011–2017

Bennett P (2016) Social housing reform bill passed into law. https://www.beehive.govt.nz/release/social-housing-reformbill-passed-law-0. Accessed 20 October 2022

Blessing A (2012) Magical or monstrous? hybridity in social housing governance. Hous Stud 27(2):189–207

Boffa Miskell Ltd. (2009) Case studies of intensive urban residential development projects. https://www.parliament.nz/resource/0000119091. Accessed 20 October 2022

Bracey S (2007) Making Talbot Park a better place to live. https://www.buildmagazine.org.nz/assets/PDF/B100-41-TalbotPark.pdf. Accessed 20 October 2022

Bratt RG (2012) The quadruple bottom line and non-profit housing organizations in the United States. Hous Stud 27(4):438–456

Britton S (1991) Recent trends in the internationalisation of the New Zealand economy. Aust Geogr Stud 29(1):3–25

Britton SG, Le. Heron R, Pawson E (1992) Changing places in New Zealand: a geography of restructuring. New Zealand Geographical Society, miscellaneous series, no 10

Campbell E (2020) The māori hostel movement. Māori Home Front. https://www.maorihomefront.nz/en/whanau-stories/maori-hostels/. Accessed 26 October 2022

Casey R, Coward S, Allen C, Powell R (2007) On the planned environment and neighbourhood life: evidence from mixed-tenure housing developments twenty years on. Town Plann Rev 78(3):311–334

Cheer T, Kearns R, Murphy L (2002) Housing policy, poverty, and culture: 'discounting' decisions among Pacific peoples in Auckland, New Zealand. Eviron Plann C Gov Policy 20(4):497–516

Cole V (2015) 'We shall not be moved': community displacement and dissensus in Glen Innes, Tāmaki Makaurau, Dissertation, University of Auckland

Cole V (2017) Why landlords and investors love the Auckland unitary plan, and why you shouldn't. Economic and Social Research Aotearoa. https://www.google.com/search?client=safari&rls=en&q=Why+landlords+and+investors+love+the+auckland+unitary+plan,+and+why+you+shouldn%27t&ie=UTF-8&oe=UTF-8. Accessed 27 October 2022

Conradson D (2008) Expressions of charity and action towards justice: faith-based welfare provision in urban New Zealand. Urban Stud 45(10):2117–2141

Cooke D (2010) Corporate colonizing. In: Cooke D, Hill C, Baskett P, Irwin R (eds) Beyond the free market: rebuilding a just society in New Zealand. Dunmore, Auckland, New Zealand, pp 37–41

Corry O (2010) Defining and theorizing the third sector. In: Taylor R (ed) Third sector research. Springer, New York, pp 11–20

Couch C (2003) City of change and challenge, urban planning and regeneration in Liverpool. Ashgate, Aldershot, UK

Crampton P, Dowell A, Woodward A (2001) Third sector primary care for vulnerable populations. Soc Sci Med 53(11):1491–1502

Czischke D, Gruis V, Mullins D (2012) Conceptualising social enterprise in housing organisations. Hous Stud 27(4):418–437

Department of Social Welfare (1999) Social environment scan. https://www.msd.govt.nz/docume nts/about-msd-and-our-work/publications-resources/archive/1999-socialenvironmentscan.pdf. Accessed 27 October 2022

Department of the Prime Minister and Cabinet (2008) Final report of the house prices unit: house price increases and housing in New Zealand. https://dpmc.govt.nz/sites/default/files/2017-03/ hpr.pdf. Accessed 27 October 2022

Dey B (2013) New Glen Innes redevelopment starts. https://www.propbd.co.nz/new-glen-innes-red evelopment-starts/. Accessed 27 October 2022

Doyle J (2013) Regulatory impact statement. https://www.treasury.govt.nz/sites/default/files/2013-05/ris-mbie-cspa-may13.pdf. Accessed 14 July 2023

Duncan I, Bollard A (1992) Corporatization and privatization: lessons from New Zealand. Oxford University Press, Oxford

Easton B (1994) Economic and other ideas behind the New Zealand reforms. Oxf Rev Econ Policy 10(3):78–94

Evans L, Grimes A, Wilkinson B, Teece D (1996) Economic reform in New Zealand 1984–95: the pursuit of efficiency. J Econ Lit 34(4):1856–1902

Fainstein S (2009) Spatial justice and planning. Justice Spatiale/Spatial Justice. https://www.jssj. org/wp-content/uploads/2012/12/JSSJ1-5en1.pdf. Accessed 27 October 2022

Ferguson (1995) Background report for the Wai 60 Claim. https://forms.justice.govt.nz/search/Doc uments/WT/wt_DOC_94029549/Wai%2060%2C%20A002.pdf. Accessed 26 October 2022

Ferrari E (2012) Competing ideas of social justice and space: locating critiques of housing renewal in theory and in practice. Int J Hous Policy 12(3):263–280

Fitzpatrick S, Pawson H (2014) Ending security of tenure for social renters: transitioning to 'ambulance service' social housing? Hous Stud 29(5):597–615

Ford M (2011) Auckland and sustainable neighbourhoods. Dissertation, Massey University

Goldfinch S (1998) Evaluating public sector reform in New Zealand: have the benefits been oversold? Asian J Pub Adm 20(2):203–232

Gordon R (2015) State-led gentrification and impacts on residents and community in Glen Innes, Auckland. Dissertation, University of Auckland

Gordon R, Collins FL, Kearns R (2017) 'It is the people that have made Glen Innes': state-led gentrification and the reconfiguration of urban life in Auckland. Int J Urban Reg Res 41(5):767–785

Hancock F, Chilcott J, Epston D (2007) Glen Innes visioning project: documenting a tacit community vision. In: Chile L (ed) Community development practice in New Zealand: exploring good practice. AUT University, Auckland, New Zealand, pp 117–142

Jackson R (1965) State housing in Auckland. Dissertation, University of Auckland, Auckland, New Zealand

James C (2015) New territory: the transformation of New Zealand, 1984–92. https://www-fulcrum-org.ezproxy.auckland.ac.nz/concern/monographs/k0698767n. Accessed 27 October 2022

Johnson A (2017) Taking stock: the demand for social housing in New Zealand. https://www.sal vationarmy.org.nz/sites/default/files/uploads/20170814spputakingstockreport.pdf. Accessed 27 October 2022

Housing New Zealand Corporation (2005) Annual report 2004/05. Housing New Zealand Corporation, Wellington

Kāinga Ora Homes and Communities (2020). https://kaingaora.govt.nz/. Accessed 27 October 2022

Kearns R (1998) Third sector stories-taking community seriously. Health Soc Care Community 6(4):221–223

Kelsey J (1993) Rolling back the state: privatisation of power in Aotearoa/New Zealand. Williams Books, Wellington, New Zealand

Kearns R, Joseph A (2000) Contracting opportunities: interpreting post-asylum geographies of mental health care in Auckland, New Zealand. Health Place 6(3):159–169

Kleinhans R (2004) Social implications of housing diversification in urban renewal: a review of recent literature. J Housing Built Environ 19(4):367–390

Kleit RG, Carnegie NB (2011) Integrated or isolated? the impact of public housing redevelopment on social network homophily. Soc Netw 33(2):152–165

King J (2019) National's social policy legacy in social housing. NZ Sociol 34(2):227

Krivan M (1990) The department of Māori affairs housing programme, 1935-1967. Dissertation, Massey University

Laing P, O'Reilly J, Ou C, Perese L, Scott K, Soa-Lafoa'I M, Smith L (2010) Tamaki transformation programme: outcomes framework for the evaluation. https://thehub.swa.govt.nz/assets/docume nts/Tamaki%20Transformation%20Programme,%20Outcomes%20framework%20report% 20May%202010.pdf. Accessed 27 October 2022

Lees L (2008) Gentrification and social mixing: towards an inclusive urban renaissance? Urban Stud 45(12):2449–2470

Lees L (2014) The urban injustices of new Labour's 'new urban renewal': the case of the Aylesbury Estate in London. Antipode 46(4):921–947

Lupton R, Tunstall R (2008) Neighbourhood regeneration through mixed communities: a 'social justice dilemma'? J Educ Policy 23(2):105–117

Luxton J (1991) Housing and accommodation: accommodation assistance. Government Printers, Wellington, New Zealand

Malpass P, Murie A (1982) Housing policy and practice. Macmillan, London, UK

Māori Housing Network Investment Strategy (2015) https://www.tpk.govt.nz/en/o-matou-moh iotanga/housing/maori-housing-network-investment-strategy-2015-201. Accessed 27 October 2022

Marcetic B (2017) New Zealand's neoliberal drift. Jacobin. https://www.jacobinmag.com/. Accessed 27 October 2022

Massey P (1995) New Zealand: market liberalisation in a developed economy. Macmillan, London, UK

Ministry for the Environment (2008) Community renewal: Housing New Zealand Corporation, Talbot Park, Auckland. http://www.mfe.govt.nz/publications/towns-and-cities/urban-des ign-case-studies-local-government/community-renewal-%E2%80%93-housing. Accessed 27 October 2022

Ministry for the Environment (2019) Planning for successful cities: a discussion document on a proposed National Policy Statement on Urban Development. https://www.mfe.govt.nz/pub lications/towns-and-cities/planning-successful-cities-discussion-document-proposed-national. Accessed 27 October 2022

Ministry of Housing and Urban Development (2013) Auckland housing accord—signed version October 2013. https://www.hud.govt.nz/assets/Residential-Housing/Housing-Affordability/ Housing-Accord-and-Special-Housing-Areas/Auckland-Housing-Accord/9b554e8cd1/auc kland-housing-accord.pdf. Accessed 27 October 2022

Ministry of Housing and Urban Development (2018) Regulatory impact statement establishing special housing areas in Auckland under the housing accords and special housing areas act (2013). http://www.mbie.govt.nz/info-services/housing-property/housing-affordability/doc ument-image-library/signed-housing-accords/ris-wellington-tauranga-tranche-4.pdf. Accessed 27 October 2022

Ministry of Social Development (2013) Joint Ministers' meeting: reviewable tenancies. https:// www.msd.govt.nz/documents/about-msd-and-our-work/work-programmes/social-housing/bac kground-documents-shrp/2013/report-joint-ministers-meeting-reviewable-tenancies-dated-11- december-2013.pdf. Accessed 20 June 2017

Ministry of Social Development (2018) Public housing plan. https://www.hud.govt.nz/assets/Com munity-and-Public-Housing/Increasing-Public-Housing/Public-Housing-Plan/dd7ef6758d/ Public-Housing-Plan-2018-2022.pdf. Accessed 20 June 2017

Mullins DC, Van Bortel G (2012) Exploring the meaning of hybridity and social enterprise in housing organisations. Hous Stud 27(4):405–417

Morris A, Jamieson M, Patulny R (2012) Is social mixing of tenures a solution for public housing estates. Evid Base: J Evid Rev Key Policy Areas 1:1–21

Moteane MN (1984) Māori housing programme in New Zealand: its history, services currently offered and issues of major concern. Dissertation, Victoria University of Wellington

Murphy L (1997) New Zealand's housing reforms and accommodation supplement experience. Urban Policy and Research 15(4):269-278

Murphy L (2004) To the market and back: housing policy and state housing in New Zealand. GeoJournal 59(2):119–126

Murphy L (2006) Counting the costs: reflections on the impacts of the privatisation of state housing in New Zealand. Hous Works 4:22–24

Murphy L (2009) Market rules: neoliberal housing policy in New Zealand. In: Glynn S (ed) Where the other half lives: lower income housing in a neoliberal world. Pluto Press, London, UK

Murphy L (2014) 'Houston, we've got a problem': the political construction of a housing affordability metric in New Zealand. Hous Stud 29(7):893–909

Murphy L (2016) The politics of land supply and affordable housing: Auckland's housing accord and special housing areas. Urban Stud 53(2):2530–2547

Murphy L (2020) Neoliberal social housing policies, market logics and social rented housing reforms in New Zealand. Int J Hous Policy 20(2):229–251

Murphy L, Kearns RA (1994) Housing New Zealand Ltd: privatisation by stealth. Environ Plan A: Econ Space 26(4):623–637

Murphy L, Rehm M (2013) Inclusionary zoning and brownfield residential development: a feasibility study. https://www.aucklandcouncil.govt.nz/plans-projects-policies-reports-bylaws/our-plans-strategies/unitary-plan/history-unitary-plan/docs321affordablehousing/Appendix-3.21.3.pdf. Accessed 20 October 2022

Olssen A, McDonald H, Grimes A, Stillman S (2010) A state housing database: 1993–2009. Motu Economic and Public Policy Research, New Zealand. http://motu-www.motu.org.nz/wpapers/10_13.pdf. Accessed 20 October 2022

Orange C (1977) A kind of equality: Labour and the Maori people, 1935-1949. Dissertation, University of Auckland

Pawson H, Gilmour T (2010) Transforming Australia's social housing: pointers from the British stock transfer experience. Urban Policy Res 28(3):241–260

Peck J, Tickell A (2002) Neoliberalizing space. Antipode 34:380–404

Perkins HC, Memon PA, Swaffield SR, Gelfand L (1993) The urban environment. In: Memon PA, Perkins HC (eds) Environmental planning in New Zealand. Dunmore Press, Palmerston North, New Zealand

Randolph B, Wood M, Holloway D, Buck B (2004) The benefits of tenure diversification. https://www.ahuri.edu.au/data/assets/pdf_file/0005/2030/AHURI_Final_Report_No60_Benefits_of_tenure_diversification.pdf. Accessed 20 October 2022

Roberts P, Sykes H (eds) (2000) Urban regeneration: a handbook. Sage, London, UK

Rosenberg W (1993) New Zealand can be different and better: why deregulation does not work. New Zealand Monthly Review Society, Christchurch, New Zealand

Roper B (2005) Prosperity for all? economic, social and political change in New Zealand since 1935. Thompson, Southbank Victoria, Australia

Rout M, Reid J, Whitehead J, Walker G (2020) The impact of housing policy on māori in Tāmaki Makaurau. Contemporary research division, Indigenous social, economic & political development series. Ngāi Tahu Research Centre, Christchurch

Sautkina E, Bond L, Kearns A (2012) Mixed evidence on mixed tenure effects: findings from a systematic review of UK studies, 1995–2009. Hous Stud 27(6):748–782

Schick A (1996) The spirit of reform: managing the New Zealand state sector in a time of change. https://ssc.govt.nz/resources/spirit-of-reform?e138=action_viewall. Accessed 20 October 2022

Schrader B (2005) We call it home: a history of state housing in New Zealand. Reed, Auckland, New Zealand

Scott K, Shaw A, Bava C (2006) Liveable communities, healthy environments or 'slumification' in Glen Innes, Auckland, New Zealand. http://citeseerx.ist.psu.edu/viewdoc/download?doi=10.1.1.527.2560&rep=rep1&type=pdf. Accessed 20 October 2022

Scott MGC (1996) Government reform in New Zealand, No 140. International Monetary Fund, Washington

Soja EW (2010) Seeking spatial justice. University of Minnesota Press, Minneapolis

Smith N (2013) New era for social housing after bill passes. New Zealand Government. https://www. beehive.govt.nz/release/new-era-social-housing-after-bill-passes. Accessed 20 October 2022

Stillman S, Velamuri M, Aitken A (2010) The long-run impact of New Zealand's structural reform on local communities. J Comp Econ 38(4):432–448

The Auckland Community Housing Providers Network (2019) Home. https://www.communityhou sing.org.nz/. Accessed 20 October 2022

The Māori Housing Network (2017) A guide to papakāinga housing. The Māori Housing Network, Wellington

The New Zealand Productivity Commission (2012) Housing affordability. https://www.productiv ity.govt.nz/assets/Documents/9c8ef07dc3/Final-report-Housing-affordability.pdf Accessed 20 October 2022

The New Zealand Productivity Commission (2015) Using land for housing. https://www.pro ductivity.govt.nz/assets/Documents/6a110935ad/using-land-for-housing-final-report-v2.pdf. Accessed 20 October 2022

The Treasury (2013) Briefing to the incoming Minister of Housing: monitoring housing New Zealand Corporation and Tāmaki Redevelopment Company. http://purl.oclc.org/nzt/big-1530. Accessed 20 October 2022

Tāmaki Redevelopment Company (2013) Strategic framework August 2013: Tāmaki regeneration, making it happen. https://tamakiregeneration.co.nz/assets/Key-Documents/Strategic_Framew ork.pdf. Accessed 20 October 2022

Tāmaki Regeneration Company (2016a) Tamaki reference plan. https://www.tamakiregenerat ion.co.nz/sites/default/files/site-files/TRC%20Reference%20Plan%20resized.pdf. Accessed 20 October 2022

Tāmaki Regeneration Company (2016b) Design framework. https://www.tamakiregeneration.co. nz/sites/default/files/site-files/TRC%20Design%20Framework.pdf. Accessed 20 October 2022

Tāmaki Regeneration Company (2017) Briefing to incoming ministers. https://www.tamakiregene ration.co.nz/sites/default/files/site-files/T%C4%81maki%20Redevelopment%20Company_Bri efing%20to%20Incoming%20Ministers.pdf. Accessed 20 October 2022

Tāmaki Regeneration Company (2019a) Tāmaki precinct masterplan. https://www.tamakiregenerat ion.co.nz/regeneration-programme/t%C4%81maki-masterplan. Accessed 20 October 2022

Tāmaki Regeneration Company (2019b) Statement of performance expectations 2019-2020. https:/ /www.tamakiregeneration.co.nz/sites/default/files/site-files/TRC%20SPE%202019-2020.pdf. Accessed 20 October 2022

Tamaki Regeneration Company (2020) Statement of performance expectations 2020–2021. https:/ /www.tamakiregeneration.co.nz/sites/default/files/site-files/TRC%20SPE%202020-2021_F INAL.pdf. Accessed 20 October 2022

Tamaki Regeneration Company (2022) Tāmaki is where Auckland's story began. https://tamakireg eneration.co.nz/. Accessed 20 October 2022

Thorns DC (1988) New solutions to old problems: housing affordability and access within Australia and New Zealand. Environ Plan A: Econ Space 20(1):71–82

Thorns DC (2006) The remaking of housing policy: the New Zealand housing strategy for the 21st century. Hous Financ Int 20(4):20

Tunstall R (2002) Housing density: what do residents think? The East Thames Housing Group and The National Housing Federation London Branch, London, England

Wanhalla A (2006) Housing un/healthy bodies: native housing surveys and Maori health in New Zealand 1930-45. Health and History 8(1): 100–120

Waldegrave C, Urbanová M (2016) A report for the New Zealand housing foun- dation. http://familycentre.org.nz/wp-content/uploads/2019/04/Socialand_Economic_Impacts_ of_Housing_Tenure-1.pdf. Accessed 20 October 2022

Warrington M (1995) Welfare pluralism or shadow state? the provision of social housing in the 1990s. Environ Plan A: Econ Space 27(9):1341–1360

Winiata W (1983) Housing submissions. New Zealand Māori Council, Wellington

Chapter 7
People, Place, and Policy

Abstract In relation to the conception of geographies of the body, this chapter seeks embodied knowledge for planning through examining the impact of changing public housing policies and physical environments on residents' lived experiences. Embodied research reflects on the processes and outcomes of urban planning and housing policies as a system of power that affects and shapes bodies, as well as identifying people's needs and demands. It also contributes to enriching current professional knowledge by allowing the voices of marginalised groups to be heard and their agency and capability incorporated into the process of decision-making and implementation. Residents interviewed for and quoted in this chapter include long-term social housing tenants and new commercial housing residents. Exploring their lives, social encounters, and community is expected to reveal the dynamics of public housing communities within the process of community regeneration.

Keywords Embodiment research · Body of power · Experiencing body · Embodied encounter · Planning · Tāmaki

Participant observation and semi-structured interviews were used to obtain data for a study of lived space in spatial justice. Among the 17 residents interviewed, 12 were long-time residents and five were newcomers. All interviews were conducted in places the interviewees lived or socialised. A reflective and extended case study method is employed in this chapter to structure the research information (Burawoy 1998) and interpret the complex interactions between people, place, and policy. This model emphasises the interactions between the researchers and participants who have situational knowledge, and the mutual influences of the social processes within the locale of the study and political-economic forces beyond the study area.

7.1 Planning for Social Housing Redevelopment and Community Resistance

Before the establishment of the Tāmaki Regeneration Company, Housing New Zealand Corporation was in charge of neighbourhood redevelopment in the area and the relocation of state tenants. Criticisms still linger over its poor communication with residents. In 2011, Housing New Zealand Corporation sent a letter to its tenants notifying them of the social housing redevelopment and informing them they would be required to relocate within 90 days. This letter was called a 90-day eviction notice. Because of the established tradition of state houses as 'houses for life', this letter caused major anxiety and stress. Since July 2011, all state residents in areas marked for redevelopment have been put on a fixed-term tenancy agreement, clearly signalling that a state house is no longer 'a house for life'.

Tenants felt they were being pushed out of their community and their homes were being destroyed. The government was criticised for 'effectively kicking out old and poor people and making room for the rich'. 'They talk about social housing and affordable housing. We can't buy a home on our incomes and they won't want us. This is the Government wiping its hands of its social obligations' (New Zealand Herald 2013, 2017). Their concerns were also expressed in banners proclaiming, 'GI state houses are not a goldmine for property developers', 'Stolen from GI', 'This home is occupied', 'Housing is a right not a privilege', 'Tāmaki is a community not a company', and 'GI is not for sale'. These slogans expressed a strong and clear resistance to social housing redevelopment that corresponded with residents' feelings and experiences. The policy changes were seen as providing security for the people able to afford new houses.

The Tāmaki Housing Group was established in 2011 after social housing tenants received a letter from Housing New Zealand informing them of the Northern Glen Innes redevelopment (Cole 2015). Led by long-term social housing tenants and their supporters, the group's aim was to resist social housing redevelopment, in both the Tāmaki area and at a national level (Gordon 2015). They claimed, 'The Tāmaki Regeneration Company have silenced the voices of community members who are concerned with their future' (Online News Team 2015, para. 3). In addition to the organisation of marches, the Tāmaki Housing Group initiated many other activities to make their voices heard. For example, a large number of supporters staged a sit-in to protest the eviction of a state-housing tenant (Gihousing 2017, para. 2).

When Niki, a key member of the Tāmaki Housing Group, received a 90-day eviction notice on 9 May 2014, she and her group started a campaign based on the slogan—'This Home is Occupied'. Starting from 18 May 2014, members and supporters stood alongside Niki outside her house at peak commute times (Fig. 7.1). Their activities attracted the attention of motorists passing by on Taniwha Avenue. 'We intend to put our bodies on the line to stop this eviction', one activist said (New Zealand Herald 2017).

Other protests have taken place at other former state-housing sites. On one occasion, six activists locked themselves in two trucks being used to move a house.

Fig. 7.1 This home is occupied (*Source* Authors' photograph, May 2014)

A family member of one of the protesters had lived in one of the houses for 25 years prior to the eviction. He later said, 'After a stand off with the police, the decision was made to postpone the removal of the house' (Bagge 2014, para. 5).

> I think the problem for protestors, especially the biggest one is a misunderstanding. To be honest, no one knew Tāmaki Regeneration Company was coming. Maybe the high income, maybe they knew, but residents we didn't know. We didn't know about the changes. And we didn't know Housing New Zealand was no longer here. Some families still think I need to call Housing New Zealand to fix my window. They still think it is Housing New Zealand. No one knows Tāmaki Regeneration Company. And if they do know, it is not a good thing. They see people get to move out of their houses. They just see the bad side. They see people now having to change the history of lifestyle … you can say some families knew, but for me, a lot of island families did not know the change was happening. So when I worked in Tāmaki Housing, I was getting a lot of questions from my parents, friends, aunties and uncles…A lot of them are really comfortable with Housing New Zealand because this system works for them. So I think some people just are uncomfortable with the change.

Arguments for protecting state housing and human rights have been used by public housing tenants to resist changes. Their resistance has produced impactful results in the process of community regeneration. However, the primary focus on material outcomes neglects residents' experiences of empowerment. In many cases, broadening access to the planning processes is yet to be fully realised. The current practice is invariably devoid of time and place and deemed to be non-spatial.

7.2 Lived Experience of Poverty and Individual Agency and Claims

Lefebvre (1991) notes that 'a body as conceived, as produced and as the production of space, is immediately subject to the determinants of that space: symmetries, interactions and reciprocal actions, axes and planes, centres and peripheries, and concrete (spatiotemporal) oppositions. The materiality of this body is attributable neither to a consolidation of parts of space into an apparatus, nor to a nature unaffected by space, which is yet somehow able to distribute itself through space and so occupy it. Rather, the spatial body's material character derives from space, from the energy that is deployed and put to use there' (p. 195).

A large majority of the research participants who were living in Glen Innes before the regeneration acknowledged that Glen Innes is a low-income suburb where cycles of poverty exist. They appeared to think state assistance was required in terms of education and employment resources. A young woman who quit high school and became a teenage mother said,

> The conditions and the way of you live, where you live don't have to determine your future. But a lot of the case, a lot of time, it does. Because it is a cycle. Those parents were born up in poverty. That's all they knew. Therefore, their kids were brought up in poverty and the cycle carries on.

> I suppose very few people here really make over \$40,000 a year. If you make over \$40,000, you are considered rich to us in Glen Innes. But I suppose the criminal activities are around because some are purely lazy, to be honest, some don't want to work. Some of those are lack of knowledge, lack of understanding, and lack of education. And others just lack resources. Everyone here commits a specific crime for certain reasons. I think for me the biggest reason why we have so much violence here is a misunderstanding. Misunderstanding is definitely the lack of understanding, the lack of education and the lack of accumulating knowledge.

Both long-time residents and newcomers residing in Fenchurch and Wai O Taki Bay mentioned concerns over social problems, such as drugs, unhealthy food, alcohol abuse, and safety issues. One resident stated, there are '…too many alcohol sources in Glen Innes. Alcohol makes a lot of families unhappy… too many take away'.

A new resident commented,

> …the liquor store has a lot of visits on Friday and Saturday nights. I've never had any issues, but I know from the stories in the past, there's been issues there. I can understand when some people go through, I can understand how sometimes that place would have seen trouble. This one like, it's harmless. I don't think this is trouble. I haven't seen, and then you do see the school kids coming around here like smoking weed sometimes, but then of course I haven't seen anyone causing trouble. They are just teenagers smoking late. You know it's not like they're trying to do anything, but you know that those things do happen a little bit as well.

However, an older woman whose family had been living in Glen Innes for over 30 years felt differently:

> I feel unsafe. People kick off the doors to get inside the building. They don't push the buttons. I cannot safely come home with grocery shopping because everybody knows I have a shopping bag. So you know, they want something, get a food bank thing like that.

Health and hygiene were other issues discussed.

> People dump the rubbish in several sections along Point England Road where the houses have already been taken away and there's no fencing around it and its just grass. But the dumping of the black rubbish bags starts to appear. The rubbish, people think as one can dump there, then another wouldn't think over about the shame.

One resident further expanded on this, saying,

> Eastern Auckland is a quarter of the size of south Auckland, but yes we have the highest suicide rate. We are like a corner of south Auckland. But in the last ten years, Glen Innes has had the most suicide, and has the most diabetes.

The need to upgrade the old houses in Glen Innes was emphasised by several residents. One new resident stated,

> …there's a lot of state housing that needs upgrades. I think in the old part of Glen Innes, there, I think some of those houses are very old and I can't imagine they're very nice to live in. Yeah I don't know how many of those of private and how many of those state houses. But there are a lot of old houses in this area and I know what old New Zealand houses are like: they are damn, they are cold. They are not very nice.

A life-long social house tenant living in Glen Innes confirmed this impression:

> …we used to live in a house down the road, which has a better condition than the one now. We moved into the new home, which is an old house. My kids suddenly get sick. They get sick but not often. Within six months, my son developed rheumatic fever…because we are in an old house, they are not willing to spend as much on repairs. I completely understand. Mine and my kid's health and safety should be the priority. My son has heart damage now, I blame the conditions of the houses. It is damp, cold in winter. It is crazy. We only have one wall heater to heat the entire house.

As well as the houses, the commercial buildings in the town centre were described as very old and run down by both newcomers and longer-term residents. When asked about the infrastructure, both groups mentioned the lack of parking spots, but there were differing opinions regarding playgrounds. Most social housing tenants interviewed said they needed a bigger playground, while newcomers had a different opinion. A newcomer who had been living in Wai O Taki Bay for six months said, 'There is a huge playground…that looks relatively new actually…it got a variety of activities for different ages'.

Furthermore, while most of the newcomers believed that residents and the community are well served by the existing facilities, they noted a lack of opportunities for consumption and leisure time activities. As one resident mentioned, 'I think there could be some cafés, there are not really many in this area, but that is a private business decision'.

Local residents expressed a desire for changes they believed would bring more hope to their community. However, they recognised the importance of ensuring any ongoing changes and future changes met their needs, and were good for their community. Some comments were:

...it is still a poor place. The houses are still the same, no good; they are cold for the children; they will get sick; they are mouldy. It takes a long to get the TRC to fix a house if there are problems.

Educate people on budgeting and wellbeing. Focus on budgeting and wellbeing. Money issues and wellbeing. People should learn how to invest money to earn money. People need to know what to do with their money, and earn the best interest for their future. ...Yeah teach people how to manage. People need to be given the tools to learn how to manage and be effective in their life. Management of money is the key to poverty. It is also to be an effective lifestyle.

The desires of long-time tenants, highly connected with Glen Innes, extended beyond the materialities of physical space, such as warm houses, to a wish for more social support and access to opportunities for education or training to reduce poverty. They felt education was needed to improve the ability of some tenants to manage their money, time, and life, and this was seen as crucial to solving social problems, like drugs, unhealthy diets, alcohol abuse, and safety issues.

Although the aim of the redevelopment programmes in Glen Innes has been to build a mix of housing to create a mixed community, it seems that long-time residents and newcomers are not building strong community connections. When newcomers were asked, 'Do you know some of the people who are living in the old houses in Glen Innes?', most answered, 'No, I don't know anyone who lives in this area'. A private house owner said, 'I don't know my neighbours. They seem to be always busy...I have been thinking about probably we should have a street party or something like that, so a street barbecue or something like that, make the time people can meet. Otherwise, you know, everybody is busy'.

This resident was involved in the Tāmaki Transformation Programme launched in early 2016. Based on her experience, she pointed out, 'I think that the Tāmaki Transformation Programme was supposed to be sort of looking at more also the community building, but also give people the sense of how to build community rather than not doing it at all'.

A resident who was a social housing tenant now living in a new state house in Fenchurch commented,

And the other thing is you need to be proactive and still keep in touch with whatever is going on in your community just because one thing is falling over and that's not the reason why our community is falling apart.

Another long-term state tenant said,

I think it hasn't really changed. Like, the people who are buying houses in this area on the private market, you know, new homes, I don't think they hang out in Glen Innes. You know, it has always been a poverty-stricken community. If you think about it, it is still a poverty-stricken community, you know, everyone still considers poor.

In response to questions concerning whether the regeneration programmes were making the Glen Innes area more 'pleasant', 'affordable', and 'liveable' for newcomers or potential buyers, but ignoring the needs and desires of the existing long-time residents, one responded:

Yeah absolutely if I talk to my friends or anyone who grows up in Auckland, Glen Innes is a rough area, I don't want to live there. Because they know the old Glen Innes, but when we've bought into this development you take a risk, because you don't know if this still going to be the people, you know, stealing your car, breaking into houses or is it still a rough area. There's been a few incidents with people's cars, not my car. But a few people on the street said that they've had some issues, but I have not encountered anything. So for me it's been perfectly fine I can walk to the train station, and I've never sort of felt unsafe or felt like there were any issues. And I think eventually too, as more of these new houses go into the area, new shops will start to develop and that will improve the shopping area as well and so that would just lift the whole suburb.

7.3 Gentrification and Direct and Indirect Displacement

The implementation of new social housing policies and redevelopment programmes has disrupted the sense of community and belonging promoted by previous state-housing policies, no longer offering the security of tenure (Murphy 2004; Morrison 1995). 'Moving people involuntarily from their homes or neighbourhoods is wrong. Regardless of whether it results from government or private market action, forced displacement is characteristically a case of people without the economic and political power to resist being pushed out by people with greater resources and power, who think they have a 'better' use for a certain building, piece of land, or neighbourhood. The pushers benefit. The pushed do not' (Hartman et al. 1982, pp. 4–5).

In the urban gentrification and regeneration literature, the most widely accepted definition of displacement describes out-migration from the originating neighbourhood. Researchers have naturally linked displacement to the loss experienced by those having to physically move out of gentrifying neighbourhoods. In this section, another feeling of displacement will be discussed in relation to long-time tenants. This model of displacement addresses the sense of loss of place experienced by remaining residents, even though they have managed to stay in their original neighbourhoods (Davidson 2009; Lees et al. 2010; Hackworth 2002).

In Lefebvre and Soja's understanding of space/place, displacement experienced as the sense of loss of place is not necessarily equal to the dislocation of forced eviction, but is nevertheless a factor for residents who remain in the neighbourhood (Davidson 2009). These long-time residents witness visible changes to the physical environment, with the social relations around them also changing dramatically in the process of regeneration and redevelopment. The amenities and space they have used daily disappear, new streets are built, and friends are leaving the neighbourhood. Faced with new streets, new public buildings, regenerated neighbourhood, and social connections, the residents who remain are gradually defamiliarised. They inevitably experience a strong sense of loss, insecurity, discomfort, unease, and subordination (Marcuse 1986). Both direct displacement and indirect displacement have occurred in Glen Innes.

Long-term state house tenants in Glen Innes have fought continuously against the intensification projects. They argue that these programmes have been forced upon them, moving them from their homes and breaking longstanding bonds of family and community (Bradford 2015).

This eviction and displacement process had a significant effect on the elderly and disabled. There were reports of some elderly tenants having passed away shortly after being relocated from life-long homes (Collins 2013). One of the greatest impacts on local residents has been the community changes as old communities were split up and new communities formed. For these social housing tenants, the social connections they relied on for assistance in daily life have been broken. Family members and friends have had to move to other areas such as Māngere.

Many social housing tenants had a lot of family living in the Tāmaki area, with family members and friends taking care of each other because 'we don't have that much money'. The displacement of some tenants broke support networks, leaving people feeling uncertain and insecure (Gordon 2015), as reflected in the following comments:

> Most of the people I know are living in bad conditions with children. I don't know, they have not been fixed. But the good thing, yeah community, we got a good community here. You walked out in the evening; you chat with people all the time. Young people greet young people.

> My mother grew up here; she passed away a couple of years ago; my father always drinks in the pub here. You know the people in the community; you know their last names. You know the doctor, a Pākehā, and their children.

As reported in *The New Zealand Herald*, Shannon, whose family was living in one of two Housing New Zealand houses still in use in 2012, said, 'Half of me loves it here but half of me is insecure. We could get told tomorrow we are moving out. It could mean a change of school, a change of jobs, anything. Nobody knows what's happening to the empty houses and empty lots. Housing New Zealand does not tell you anything unless you are behind in your rent' (Collins 2014). Before moving to their current house, Shannon and her family were living in a run-down state house in Glen Innes in which one of her boys had developed asthma and skin problems.

The longstanding residents had a strong sense of losing social connection with the people they would go to for support and assistance. As noted by one resident, 'What do I think about it? I don't like it. I mean because lots of my friends that I grew up with had moved away, and been pushed out of their houses. I'm in between'.

The Tāmaki redevelopment programmes led to a lot of insecurity and uncertainty, generating protest activities in Glen Innes by some local residents concerned and worried about the effects of social housing redevelopment. Another reason for the resistance was some local residents felt they are being forced out without any consultation or opportunity to voice their opinions, leaving them with a strong sense of powerlessness.

> I think they feel like, a long time ago, Freemans Bay was like Glen Innes. I think it is what they feel like. Freemans Bay, you know, is a nice suburb, for high-income people. And I think it is what they are doing here because a lot of houses are been sold on the private market and a lot of houses have been sold to private buyers.

The redevelopment in Glen Innes reminded local people of the gentrification of Freemans Bay because they felt similarly pushed out of their community. Many of the longstanding residents claimed strong, 'lifelong' ties to the area, with one saying, 'I have been living here since I was a child'. As pointed out by other researchers, such 'autochthonous claims' are the last resort of those feeling powerless (Goossens et al. 2020). This sense of powerlessness was the basis of insecurity and uncertainty for both social housing tenants and private housing owners. As described by a private owner, 'You know, whether it is a balcony or you sort of have the way you look out on, but over here, you don't know what your neighbour going to do with housing intensification'.

7.4   Perception of Changes: Social Housing Residents and Newcomers

Physical changes in the built environment always imply social changes. Newcomers, generally young professional couples, bring new lifestyles, dress codes, and habits. For long-time residents, the changes happening around them create a new place with a different atmosphere and characteristics, making them feel they and the social groups they belong to are now excluded (Atkinson 2015).

Some new residents also implied that the new communities of Fenchurch and Wai O Taki Bay are seen as separate from old Glen Innes. A newcomer living in Wai O Taki Bay was asked if she thought of Wai O Taki Bay as part of Glen Innes or whether they were separate areas in terms of belonging to a community, and if so, which community did she feel she belonged to. She answered,

> I think of it as a different suburb. But I think it is very close when I describe where I live to people, I say Glen Innes…In terms of we are a young professional couple; we would say that we are more like Wai O Taki Bay and Glendowie than Glen Innes. In terms of the local shops that we go to, where other friends live, my friends are our neighbours now, we are Glen Innes still the same, still a further way. I walk my dogs twice a day, and I always walk out around Glendowie. So I don't know, in my heart, I feel more like that community.

Long-term residents welcomed new residents because they bring new knowledge and skills to the community, but problems were identified in the lack of connection between newcomers and existing residents. The newcomers are mostly young couples, or young singles, working full-time in private companies or government agencies. The new dwellings built in Fenchurch, for example, are intended as affordable housing for first-home buyers, so that new communities of young people are forming in Fenchurch and Wai O Taki Bay. As a newcomer living in Fenchurch stated,

> I don't know everyone but quite a few people because most people here are first-home buyers so everyone's kind of young. And because we all moved in at the same time. It feels like, it's kind of like a new sense of community. As I guess if you moved into an old house or you know into a year that's already developed, you might not necessarily have the same sense of community.

Changes in the physical and social environment have always been understood as at the root of the process of defamiliarisation and a sense of loss of place. Residents identified the physical and social characteristics of Glen Innes before and after regeneration, mentioning both positive and negative aspects. As can be seen in Table 7.1, there are differences between the perceptions of social housing tenants and newcomers. People who had been living in Glen Innes for a long time pointed out more positive than negative aspects when asked to describe the characteristics of Glen Innes before regeneration, whereas newcomers identified more negatives. Both groups agreed that the residential housing and town-centre area was run down and needed to be upgraded.

Long-time residents emphasised Glenn Innes as a close-knit community, with family connections, interactions among residents, and a sense of community as its most valuable characteristics. For them, the regeneration programmes have not only changed the physical characteristics of Glen Innes, but also its identity.

Table 7.1 The characteristics of Glen Innes before and after community regeneration

| | Before regeneration | | After regeneration | |
	Positive	Negative	Positive	Negative
Social housing long-time residents	Great Community	Bad housing conditions	Warm houses	Lost the community spirit and space
	Creative People	Dodgy	Modern life	Not many kids are out on the road anymore
	Friendly, nice, and welcoming people	Too many alcohol sources	New demographic and diverse	Lost the sense of what the community used to be like
	Caring, family-orientated	Too many take aways		Houses are not for the elderly or those who have back, or leg problems
	Quiet	Poverty		No big yards
	Looking after each other's kids	Rough around the edges		
	International and diverse			
Newcomers	People are friendly	A rough area; high crime rate; not feeling safe and comfortable Old and rundown Low socio-economic area	Lifting the quality of the community Enables those who have lived in the area to lift their behaviour maybe People are nice and people are friendly	Gentrification

The strong contrasts in the physical environment created by the regeneration emerged as an important factor in the sense of loss of place. The redeveloped areas showed different characteristics in terms of building type, materials, and decoration, with the new houses characterised as warm and modern by long-time state tenants. Taking Fenchurch as an example, almost all the people previously living there had moved out and the old houses had been demolished. Warm and modern houses had been built and new residents who were wealthier and well-dressed moved in. This transformation made people still living in old social housing feel disconnected from the new built neighbourhood where their friends or family used to live.

7.5 The Tāmaki Regeneration Company and Community

The claimed partnership between residents and the Tāmaki Regeneration Company proved not to be a reality (Collins 2013). As the organisation directly interacting with local residents during the change, its activities have significantly impacted local residents' experience of the redevelopment. As a lifelong state house tenant said, 'I do think they (the Tāmaki Regeneration Company) are doing some good things, but there could be a better way around them'. The lack of communication between the Tāmaki Regeneration Company and local residents appeared to have created unnecessary stress and anxiety in the neighbourhood.

A resident working in the Tāmaki Regeneration Company said,

> They are not only just building houses, but they also do community engagement stuff as well, so they reach out, they support like local scaphoids, community, things trust and they have neighbourhoods advance going on, we bring the family along against tests, you know, some sausages grilled on the BBQ, and jumping food for the kids. I think they are trying to do things differently not just sitting in their offices working and distancing themselves away from the community. They actually stepped out of their offices and stepped into the community to make the community and do these things.

The Tāmaki Regeneration Company has organised workshops and events to engage and build a community around social housing redevelopment. However, these activities have been criticised as failing to effectively connect different parts of the community and respond to the most important problems in Glen Innes. As one resident pointed out,

> ...the events you are hosting do not bring our community together. Do you realise that? The ones do come out, and other ones have been heard, but it is not all of the community. They all like maybe about ten percent. The event they putting on the wrong kind of events types. There is a lot of suicide going on around here. They need a target you know, events based around certain things just blow up castle, not just a free barbecue something about that. Sometimes as people just want somebody to talk to them...They do have the work area down there. It is doing well for some but I haven't really seen evidence out there of it giving our children a sense of purpose. I think it is more of getting a job, making money and getting out, but not giving people the sense of purpose like going somewhere knowing that skills you have can make difference somewhere.

Criticisms were also raised about their tenant management, as evidenced by the following question and these responses. When asked, 'How does the Tāmaki Regeneration Company deal with and respond to complaints or comments raised by tenants', people said:

> Oh, they suck, they so suck. The communication around that, I had a complaint about my house might begin in May, and it wasn't dealt with straight away but a few months later. Most of them, it's usually tenant managers, and not all of them execute that well.

And,

> No proof of good to say. When I go to the office, they are good people. Some of them are, I don't know, I ask them questions, and what they do is go through the book and read up about it. They should just know their jobs. And it takes ages to fix a house, so I stopped, and one of my aunties ran into them in the face and took them to court, and then they came down and sold the house. They were shocked. Her house literally was falling into bits. And my baby, the hospital said that she needs to stay in a warm house. But we don't have a good place; I lost my baby.

The relationship between tenancy managers and tenants was criticised in terms of a lack of consistency and deep engagement.

> Other than these big festivals, I didn't see one to one, you know, I didn't see relationships. For me it is important. For someone to know their tenancy manger. I reckon it is very important, you know your tenancy manager the same way you would know, anyone in your life, like your banker. For me I knew my banking man since I was in University, you know, because he knew my money, he knew everything about my financial patterns, and he knew how to advise me. I reckon these things are important that we should know the Tāmaki Regeneration Company and tenancy management in the same way. But I don't say we didn't. Some of these tenancy mangers have really good relationships with their tenants, but it is not consistent. You know, the lack of consistent engagement unless it is a big festival. But I think for me, the one to one relationship is more important than doesn't really have.

> I wouldn't say so. I think it's a couple of months ago. Someone came to our home, and they did a survey on behave the Tāmaki Regeneration Company, but that was it. There was no outcome. There was no follow-up. There was no informing us of the decision. So I think that there is less follow-up. So they engage, or they kind of engage, and then they just disappear.

In terms of the activities of the Tāmaki Regeneration Company, interviewees commented that more work needs to be done on infrastructure.

> When you look at what's been developed, and intensified, it is my bit to the Tāmaki Regeneration Company, still no answer from them is that nothing is being done in infrastructure. Because they want to do these big things on Point England which is one way in and one way out. But you can imagine the stress on that piece of road. A lot of roads in Tāmaki aren't wide enough to accommodate the extra needs for transport as well. Because with more people intensification, you need more buses, and you look around, there are not many buses going down the narrow streets. But in some areas, I think that the Council needs to remember if you are going to allow this much development in this area, I mean, it is goanna be stress on storm water, water itself but also stress on the people that live in this area as well. So it is not, you can just intensify, you got to be smarter with how you intensify.

7.6 Summary

This chapter has explored the needs and desires of local residents in Glen Innes from the perspective of lived experience. First, the lived experience of the established population, specifically longstanding tenants, longstanding owners, and also newcomers reveals the most pressing needs in the area. Residents expressed their concerns and desires towards improving the physical and social environment in Glen Innes. The main problems identified include: (1) run-down houses that are cold and damp, with poor living conditions resulting in many health problems; (2) drug and alcohol abuse, crime and safety issues, and stereotypes concerning lazy beneficiaries; (3) a firm belief among some residents that lack education and knowledge and skills for time and money management are the main reasons underlying social problems. They called for more social support for improving education and access to other social resources.

Secondly, as discussed above, displacement in Glen Innes is not just about the replacement of longstanding state tenants by new, wealthier incomers; it is also established residents feeling alienated by the physical, social, economic, and cultural transition occurring around them. The regeneration programme has led to a loss of sense of community and security among long-term state tenants. Further, relationships between long-term residents and newcomers have not developed as expected in policies and plans. While people are physically mixed, there is still a long way to go to achieve the goal of a socially mixed community.

Finally, residents' agency emerged as a strong theme in the interviews and news items. They exercised agency in the process of protesting against privatisation and gentrification, and actively appealed for the opportunity to engage in the process of decision-making and neighbourhood regeneration. Despite their demands not being fully met, residents have made their voices heard and obtained support from wider society.

The findings reported in this chapter resonate with the findings from previous chapters. Compact, mixed tenure, and sustainable urban development is regarded as a just built environment that enables equable accessibility for all. However, there are contradictions between the imagined spatiality of justice and individuals' socialised sensory space. Protecting community character and their human rights has motivated social housing tenants to resist changes, impacting the early stages of community renewal. The primary focus on material outcomes as a barometer of success neglects the myriad experiences of resident disempowerment. While the forces that limit tenant resistance are considerable, tenants who do organise can achieve success. Even small efforts by a handful of people can alter redevelopment for the better.

References

Atkinson R (2015) Losing one's place: narratives of neighbourhood change, market injustice and symbolic displacement. Hous Theory Soc 32(4):373–388

Bagge H (2014) Protest group halts removal of state-owned house. New Zealand Herald, 17 Oct 2014. https://www.nzherald.co.nz/nz/protest-group-halts-removal-of-state-owned-house/ L7ASIZSWDJ4DKD3XF6TDZFNHCQ/. Accessed 27 Oct 2022

Bradford S (2015) Hikoi for homes—time for action on housing. https://www.nzherald.co.nz/nz/ sue-bradford-hikoi-for-homes-time-for-action-on-housing/KFK7XUOWKR2WSVGJ5GSYB 2TEHA/. Accessed 27 Oct 2022

Burawoy M (1998) The extended case method. Sociol Theory 16(1):4–33

Cole V (2015) 'We shall not be moved': community displacement and dissensus in Glen Innes, Tamaki Makaurau. Dissertation, University of Auckland

Collins S (2013) State house tenants heckle Smith. The New Zealand Herald, 19 June 2013. http:// www.nzherald.co.nz. Accessed 27 Oct 2022

Collins S (2014) State houses sitting on goldmine, The New Zealand Herald, 15 Nov 2014. http:// www.nzherald.co.nz. Accessed 27 Oct 2022

Davidson M (2009) Displacement, space and dwelling: placing gentrification debate. Ethics, Place Environ 12(2):219–234

Gihousing (2017) Press release: sit-in occupation to stop Niki's eviction. https://gihousing.wordpr ess.com/2017/01/22/press-release-sit-in-occupation-to-stop-nikis-eviction/. Accessed 27 Oct 2022

Goossens C, Oosterlynck S, Bradt L (2020) Livable streets? green gentrification and the displacement of longtime residents in Ghent, Belgium. Urban Geogr 41(4):550–572

Gordon R (2015) State-led gentrification and impacts on residents and community in Glen Innes, Auckland. Dissertation, University of Auckland

Hackworth J (2002) Postrecession gentrification in New York City. Urban Aff Rev 37(6):815–843

Hartman C, Keating D, LeGates R (1982) Displacement: how to fight it. National Housing Law Project, Washington

Lees L, Slater T, Wyly EK (eds) (2010) The gentrification reader, vol 1. Routledge, London

Lefebvre H (1991) The production of space (trans: Nicholson-Smith D), original work published 1974. Blackwell, Oxford

Marcuse P (1986) Abandonment, gentrification and displacement: the linkages in New York City. In: Smith N, Williams P (eds) Gentrification of the city. Unwin Hyman, London, pp 153–177

Morrison PS (1995) The geography of rental housing and the restructuring of housing assistance in New Zealand. Hous Stud 10(1):39–56

Murphy L (2004) To the market and back: housing policy and state housing in New Zealand. GeoJournal 59(2):119–126

New Zealand Herald (2013) The Glen Innes social experiment. The New Zealand Herald, 23 Nov 2013. http://www.nzherald.co.nz. Accessed 27 Oct 2022

New Zealand Herald (2017) Beneficiary's fight not to be evicted from state home of 21 years. The New Zealand Herald, 24 Jan 2017. http://www.nzherald.co.nz. Accessed 27 Oct 2022

Online News Team (2015) Tāmaki Housing Group to protest against housing regeneration plan. https://www.teaomaori.news/tamaki-housing-group-protest-against-housing-regene ration-plan. Accessed 27 Oct 2022

Chapter 8
Spatial Justice and Planning: Bridging the Gap

Abstract The book has addressed the epistemological and ontological value of critical spatial thinking and spatial justice, its perceived, conceived, and lived domains, and their interaction in the context of social housing redevelopment. The complex layering of spatial–temporal landscapes resulting from dynamic spatial processes has been explored as the basis for community characterisation and assessment of social housing redevelopment. The research findings contribute to understanding the issues and challenges facing planning for quality community life for all. The research is also expected to advance theories of urban morphology and embodiment research by extending their use in planning for justice. The integration of spatial justice strategy into the established planning system is essential for achieving just outcomes from urban change, particularly urban and building design schemes, development plans, and urban policy statements at both national and local levels.

Keywords Spatial justice · Social housing redevelopment · Planning · Urban design

8.1 Reflections on Spatial Justice Theory and Practice

Improving the situation of socially and economically deprived communities is a complex process that involves a dynamic interaction between planning, built forms, and local residents (Bloom et al. 2015). As such, the study of urban regeneration warrants a spatial justice perspective in which processes and outcomes are both dialectically dependent on and reproductive of space (Ferrari 2012; Merrifield and Swyngedouw 1997). The conceptual framework of spatial justice based on Thirdspace theory offers a new perspective on changes arising from the process of social housing redevelopment, and thereby helps to identify development problems in this process.

This book is primarily concerned with the question of perspective. It has explored in what way and to what extent spatial justice can be applied to understanding and improving community regeneration, especially the delivery of medium-density and mixed tenure in state-housing areas. A spatial theory of justice emphasises both the outcomes of unjust processes and the processes that lead to unjust situations. The 'space' in spatial justice is not only a good or resource that is expected to be (re)distributed justly, but also closely related to the ideas and values underlying the practices of placemaking professionals and experts, as well as to space users' needs and desires. Spatial justice is achieved through negotiation between the built environment, policies and plan making, and users' agency and struggles. Soja's ontological trialectics of Sociality (social/societal)—Historicity (temporal/ historical)—Spatiality (spatial/geographical), along with his trialectics of Firstspace (perceived)—Secondspace (conceived)—Thirdspace (lived) support the extended study of spatial justice. They shed light on the distribution and redistribution of physical space, how institutions, policies, and practices are involved in formulating the organisation of space, and how this dynamic process shapes human interactions. Further, these trialectics contribute to the exploration of the production of (in)justice in this process.

Although the focus of spatial justice on both the outcome and process of space production and reproduction has the potential to assist cities to achieve just geographies and deal with developmental challenges, its practical use is limited. Spatial justice is more aspirational than operational. This book has thus explored in what way and to what extent this conception can be applied in an empirical study of social housing redevelopment, and how it can be integrated into the established planning system. A new conceptual framework has been developed for spatial justice to strengthen its intellectual basis and its use in urban planning.

8.2 Key Research Findings

8.2.1 Town-Plan Analysis and Spatial Differentiation: Reducing Spatial Segregation or Producing New Segregation

Developed over the last century, the morphological method, primarily investigated by urban morphologists, provides a valuable tool for distinguishing and characterising the structure of the urban landscape according to its development history. Just as spatial justice is far more than physical planning, morphological research provides a source of evidence relating to processes. A morphological investigation of historical planning and design in Glen Innes revealed the political-economic ideas that characterise different periods of development. The pattern of streets, the structure of street blocks, the pattern of plots, the building materials, and even how rental costs are calculated are deeply embedded within broad ideological commitments.

Over the past 70 years, Glen Innes has experienced three morphological periods: early post-war development (1950–1969), repletion and consolidation (1970–1999), and transformation and regeneration (post–2000). Developed as the largest state-housing area in New Zealand, Glen Innes is representative of varying government policies and actions towards the distribution of public goods. In the early post-war development period, when the government was trying to build a welfare state, standalone state houses on big sections gave effect to the 'Kiwi dream'. In the transformation and regeneration period (post-2000), the pursuit of land-use efficiency and land value has contributed to the transformation of the built environment, turning Glen Innes into a medium-density suburb. The spatial characteristics of developments in the post-2000 period can be described as follows: (1) major plot changes as a result of the regeneration programmes (the plot changes can be characterised as orthomorphic, hypometamorphic, and metamorphic); (2) diversified building types; and (3) new patterns in the distribution of housing ownership.

Six plan units were identified: (1) post-war residential area, which can be further divided into traditional plot series with post-war houses; (2) late twentieth-century area; (3) new residential area developed in the 2000s; (4) regenerated residential area developed in the 2010s; (5) town-centre unit; and (6) green space unit. The resulting map of plan units provides an informed understanding of the structure of the urban landscape to support the formulation of process strategies for achieving valued spatial–temporal and representational outcomes.

8.2.2 Policies and Planning That Define and Contextualise Glen Innes

As in Australia and Canada, New Zealand has a tradition of discussing justice issues in relation to indigenous residents, immigrants, and people from different income backgrounds. New Zealand has implemented some of the world's most progressive, sustained, and successful policies. The image of New Zealand as a classless utopia defined by egalitarianism has contributed to formulating a mainstream cultural identity and national character (Belich and Weaver 2008). A core aspect of egalitarianism is access to housing (Saville-Smith and Saville-Smith 2018).

The building and transformation of social housing reflect changing government attitudes and actions towards equity and justice, which have been significantly influenced and shaped by prevailing political and social ideologies in different periods. As an important reflection of Keynesian economic policy at the time, the government became involved in housing provision and Glen Innes was among other suburbs developed as state-housing areas in the 1950s. The concept of egalitarian distributive justice served as the main driver for building a welfare state to justly allocate public goods, such as housing, education, and health. After 1984, neoliberal political and economic reforms, including welfare reform, resulted in the financialisation and deregulation of the housing market. The government stepped back from state-housing provision, turning its focus to community redevelopment and opening up the provision of social and affordable housing to investment from the private and third sectors, as reflected in the mixed-tenure and medium-density regeneration occurring in Glen Innes.

In this process, the discourse portraying Glen Innes has changed from a workers' utopia with gardens, to a run-down suburb blighted by poverty and crime, to one of the affordable choices for Auckland first-home buyers. The justification for the current redevelopment policies and plans is enhancing land values and the effectiveness of land use by building medium-density, mixed-tenure housing in response to the need for growth. While enhancing land values and the effectiveness of land use are not necessarily unjust, these are among the primary aims of neoliberal policies. As David Harvey (2006) says: 'the fundamental mission of the neoliberal state is to create a 'good business climate' and therefore to optimise conditions for capital accumulation no matter what the consequences for employment or social well-being… [It] looks to further the cause of and to facilitate and stimulate (by tax breaks and other concessions as well as the infrastructural provision at state expense if necessary) all business interests, arguing that this will foster growth and innovation and that this is the only way to eradicate poverty and to deliver, in the long run, higher standards to the mass of the population' (p. 25).

By this definition, Glen Innes redevelopment programmes have followed the principles and logic of neoliberalism. As a result, the operation of state-housing delivery has been significantly altered through different redevelopment programmes. The general trends identified across 20 years of redevelopment are: (1) seeking to build mixed-tenure housing and achieve medium density in Glen Innes through zoning changes implemented by Auckland Council; and (2) the formation of multi-sector partnerships. Although the central government and Auckland Council formerly played an active and important role in social housing provision, the existing social housing redevelopment programmes have been undertaken 'within neoliberal parameters', with the state working as a partner with third-sector housing developers (Craig and Cotterell 2007).

The rationales for regeneration activities in Glen Innes have varied across projects, ranging from social inclusion and strong sustainable communities, liveability and diversity of activities, to healthier and safer communities, to cultural diversity, community cohesion, and inclusive neighbourhoods. The wider political-economic context is the most fundamental factor in the direction of housing policy and plan making, and for determining the structure and process of decision-making. Seeking to reconstruct the image and recover the reputation of Glen Innes, these rationales serve the goals of capital interests. The final outcome of these projects remains focused on how to maximise the land value and investment income.

8.2.3   Embodied Experience

Previous publications discussing the relationship between space and justice pay little attention to what constitutes well-being and thus lack normativity (Olson and Sayer 2009). Just as most social phenomena are complex and linked to multiple bodies of knowledge, a multi-disciplinary approach offers a rich understanding of the relationship between (in)justice and spatiality (Israel and Frenkel 2017). Different bodies of knowledge are woven into the dialogue presented here, drawing upon theoretical conceptualisation, a geographical morphological analysis, housing policy and plan analysis and embodied research. This dialogue reveals the processes that influence the physical, social, political, and economic conditions determining the outcomes of justice in space at both the individual and group levels in the community.

The importance of embodied knowledge in planning is attracting research attention. Traditional ideas of 'people' focus on 'human', the abstract body as an organism, as opposed to lived individuals' experience, emotion, affect, subjectivity, identity, and agency. Focusing on the tension between the body as a medium for socio-cultural relations and animate existence bearing pain, pleasure, anxiety, fear, and other emotions (Johnston 2009), embodiment research provides a tool to articulate the dynamic interactions between places, people, and policy. As Sandercock (2004) argues, 'what has been missing from most of the collaborative planning/communicative action literature is this recognition of the need for a language and a process of emotional involvement, of embodiment' (p. 26). She believes that exploring embodiment helps present the 'whole person' in negotiations and deliberations and deal with the emotions within many planning issues.

The social-spatial transformation generated by the Tāmaki Regeneration Programme has great significance for long-time state tenants, private owners, and newcomers. From the perspective of embodied research, Chap. 6 examined residents' lived perceptions and experience of regeneration processes, to understand the diverse voices in Tāmaki. This perspective helps to identify the processes and the outcomes of the making and implementation of urban design, planning, and policies by exploring the body of power, the experiencing body, and the embodied encounter.

In relation to the body of power defining and contextualising individuals, direct and indirect displacement occurred in the neighbourhoods of Tāmaki residents. Residents witnessed visible changes to the physical environment as well as dramatically changing social relations due to the regeneration and redevelopment taking place. This process resulted in a sense of loss of place and significant uncertainty. Residents' voices have been mostly ignored in the process of regeneration, and the resulting misunderstandings between the decision-makers and residents have raised further criticisms around gentrification.

The research found that: (1) the experiencing body, the residents, complained about social problems, such as illegal drugs, unhealthy food, alcohol abuse, and safety issues, as well as the poor condition of the old social housing, and the associated physical and mental health problems due to damp, cold, and overcrowding. They expressed a strong desire for the old houses to be upgraded; (2) former state tenants who moved into new houses in Glen Innes experienced improvements in housing quality, but claimed the regeneration programme had disrupted their lives and privileged the wealthy newcomers; (3) local residents expressed a desire for more changes because they thought these changes would bring greater hope to their community; and (4) local residents actively expressed their agency in activities against regeneration activities, such as establishing the Tāmaki Housing Group, which launched protests against the gentrification and demanded to be involved in the decision-making process.

Through the lens of the embodied encounter, the social contact and interaction between former residents and new residents is another social outcome of the redevelopment activities. The Tāmaki regeneration programme aimed to create a mixed housing area by building different housing types and introducing new homeowners. However, putting together people with different home tenure and from different economic backgrounds does not automatically lead to social interaction and social inclusion. Although some long-time residents believed that introducing newcomers would have a positive impact through exposure to different life habits, most participants admitted they had limited interaction with other groups.

The findings show that the requirements for successful redevelopment and sustainable communities are similar: both need to attend simultaneously to economic, social, and environmental development. Social housing redevelopment presents challenges requiring careful attention to design, services, management, and safety. At the same time, the challenges of social exclusion and poverty need to be addressed. Building community empowerment, cohesiveness, and problem-solving capacity requires ongoing investment beyond the initial efforts. It is acknowledged, however, that the housing authorities in Glen Innes are also attempting other changes, such as generating employment initiatives to counter the stereotypes of unemployment, crime, and violence.

The dominant planning system excludes participation by local residents in urban management, with residents appearing to be at the end of decision-making processes. The empowerment that is essential to planning practice appears to be limited in social housing redevelopment. However, this research offers a rich and multidimensional understanding of power in its many and varied manifestations, including the articulation and workings of power at the level of the individual body.

8.3 Implications for Planning Practice and Research

Soja's theory of spatial justice allows us to conceive new spaces, or new uses of space that we can project into the future or use to imagine either some ultimate demise or regeneration of urban space in terms of the way we look at it. Social science researchers and geographers tend to explore the allocation of resources, while planners and architects are interested in utilising allocated resources and thus focus on methods of planning (Alfasi and Fenster 2014). Practising architects tend to focus on the design of the built environment as generating terms of justice, while planners and geographers take into account the provision of social services and the allocation of resources. Although this does not mean that planners are not interested in justice or that geographers do not evaluate good planning, the divide is apparent in practice. Spatial justice is expected to bridge the gap by strengthening processes (practical reasoning) for achieving valued results (outcomes) in social housing redevelopment.

Urban design and placemaking are largely physical or tactile processes involving mapping, shaping, and connecting landscapes; the morphological approach to the spatial structuring of landscape forms is, therefore, essential to plan-based development coordination and control. In considering the historical context of Glen Innes and spatial justice, this research shows that redevelopment involves both continuities and changes in the specificities of physical change, as well as in the more abstract ideologies, and social, economic, and political practices. Politico-economic processes always produce spatial unevenness. The newly built forms encouraged by the Auckland Unitary Plan can be seen as introducing new adaptations and types, regulated and guided by the needs of contemporary society. However, to gain wide community consensus, the development of urban landscapes and their resulting typological manifestations should be considered in the preparation of new regulations and rules, to ensure continuity in the evolutionary process of the valued urban landscape as well as socio-cultural development.

Although social housing policies, or housing provision policies, are made by the central government, local authorities such as Auckland Council nevertheless influence community-based regeneration activities. The key functions and responsibilities of local government enacted through planning determine the physical landscape, economy, society, and culture of the city. In the case of Glen Innes social housing redevelopment, Auckland Council has responded to central government redevelopment activities, such as the Northern Glen Innes redevelopment project, and to the demand for land by managing development controls and design criteria for land use and housing construction. It has also contributed to building facilities and allocating resources such as funding.

Planners and decision-makers working within the political and economic system are responsible for their public sector organisations, consulting firms, and non-profit organisations; however, they have limited power to make and implement a policy regarding the values they hold. Nevertheless, acting as an 'expert' in plan-making processes, including land-use planning, Resource Management Act (RMA) planning, Growth Management or Urban Development Strategies, and spatial planning, they are expected to incorporate their expertise, including regarding spatial justice, into urban projects.

Social housing redevelopment in Glen Innes is not only about the distribution and redistribution of social housing, but also the interplay between the (re)production of the spatial characteristics of neighbourhood, housing and planning policy concerning regeneration, and the formation of new communities. Spatial justice provides a lens for understanding and interpreting how policy and other factors influence the social-spatial changes in community regeneration, and the outcomes of these changes. In conjunction with spatial justice studies in other parts of the world, this project not only makes a timely contribution to the search for solutions to the acute planning problems in social housing development in New Zealand, but also adds a stronger New Zealand dimension to international efforts to promote justice in urban change.

8.4   Prospects for Future Research

This book has attempted to build a new framework to understand and interpret social housing redevelopment in Glen Innes. It has also contributed to a more holistic and deeper understanding of the process of urban regeneration in the New Zealand context in relation to how housing policies and plans have promoted this process, what this process means for the physical and social environment in low-income suburbs, and what it means for disadvantaged groups.

However, a number of research limitations are acknowledged. First, in relation to the data collection, most of the 17 local residents interviewed were long-time social housing tenants, with only a few newcomers. Further, the personal voices of long-time private owners are missing. Information on their experiences of social housing redevelopment is mostly from secondary sources, especially articles in *The New Zealand Herald* and the *East and Bays Courier*. However, they may have provided a significantly different perspective in person.

Secondly, Glen Innes is historically a special area in Auckland due to the high proportion of Māori and Pacific people who have traditionally lived there. The authors were successful in obtaining ethics approval to interview Māori and Pacific Islanders, and half of the participants belonged to one of these two groups. However, when discussing individual lived experiences, the authors tried to be consistent in asking the same questions of different groups, and ethnicity has not been considered in the interpretation of the data.

Social justice is a thriving field of enquiry involving researchers from a wide diversity of disciplinary, linguistic, and cultural backgrounds. This book presents complex and potentially significant research that has necessitated careful reading and study, significant effort, and careful time management to achieve the research objectives. While it records recent progress and outcomes of development, social housing redevelopment is ongoing in Glen Innes under the Tāmaki Regeneration Programme and so understanding of physical and social outcomes may change with further development.

This research and its results have implications for how we understand the process of urban regeneration in the New Zealand context, how housing policies and plans have promoted this process, what this process means to the physical and social environment within low-income suburbs, and what it means to disadvantaged groups. It is expected this research will inspire different approaches to planning and policymaking in the future.

Based on the research findings and achievements, three areas are suggested for further work. First, the plan unit as a geographical scale has the potential for application to explore the mechanics of space production and lived experience. A plan unit stands out from its surroundings in terms of morphologically different streets, plots, and buildings. Moreover, it is understood as a geographical scope with homogeneous characteristics in Firstspace, which actively interacts with policies and people. Discussing the spatial characteristics of each plan unit, the physical changes within it, and the factors that led to the changes helps to create a deeper understanding of the production of space and the negotiation between the actors involved by systemically analysing the concrete and physical differences. Secondly, there are diverse people with different body abilities and capabilities living in the original houses built in different suburbs. With the development of urban regeneration, their voices and life experience should be a focus of attention in wider regeneration agendas, such as education, employment, and social well-being, as well as social housing redevelopment. Thirdly, more work is needed to further develop the connection between Thirdspace theory and spatial justice to make spatial justice theory more practical for application in planning practice.

Spatial justice is a burgeoning field of research inquiry with researchers from a wide range of disciplines contributing to its development. While this diversity has been fundamental to understanding the complexity of spatial justice, controversy has also arisen over the various theoretical explorations by researchers from different academic and professional backgrounds. One cannot escape the feeling that (in)justice, as defined for example by Young, is quite intuitive (Israel and Frenkel 2017). Research into and the practice of spatial justice are still in a state of flux. Nevertheless, it provides principles and operational values for urban development activities. This study of spatial justice endeavours to advance its theory and practice.

References

Alfasi N, Fenster T (2014) Between socio-spatial and urban justice: Rawls' principles of justice in the 2011 Israeli protest movement. Plan Theory 13(4):407–427

Belich J, Weaver L (2008) Understanding New Zealand cultural identity (discussion paper). Stout Research Centre for New Zealand Studies. https://www.wgtn.ac.nz/stout-centre/research/public ations/Understanding-NZ-Cultural-Identities-2008.pdf. Accessed 27 October 2022

Bloom ND, Umbach F, Vale LJ (2015) Public housing myths: perception, reality, and social policy. Cornell University Press, Ithaca, USA

Craig D, Cotterell G (2007) Periodising neoliberalism? Policy Polit 35(3):497–514

Ferrari E (2012) Competing ideas of social justice and space: locating critiques of housing renewal in theory and in practice. Int J Hous Policy 12(3):263–280

Harvey D (2006) Neo-liberalism as creative destruction. Geogr Ann Ser B Hum Geogr 88(2):145–158

Israel E, Frenkel A (2017) Social justice and spatial inequality: toward a conceptual framework. Prog Hum Geogr 42(5):647–665

Johnston L (2009) Body. In: Kitchin R, Thrift N (eds) International encyclopaedia of human geography. Elsevier, Amsterdam, Netherlands, pp 326–331

Merrifield A, Swyngedouw E (1997) The urbanization of injustice. New York University Press, New York

Olson E, Sayer A (2009) Radical geography and its critical standpoints: embracing the normative. Antipode 41(1):180–198

Sandercock L (2004) Towards a planning imagination for the 21st century. J Am Plann Assoc 70(2):133–141

Saville-Smith N, Saville-Smith K (2018, June) Declining egalitarianism and the battle for affordable housing in New Zealand. Paper presented to European Network of Housing Researchers Conference, Uppsala, Sweden

Index

Printed by Printforce, United Kingdom